The Baptist Revival Fellowship (1938–1972)
A Study in Baptist Conservative Evangelicalism

Philip Douglas Hill, BA, MPhil.

WIPF & STOCK · Eugene, Oregon

Wipf and Stock Publishers
199 W 8th Ave, Suite 3
Eugene, OR 97401

The Baptist Revival Fellowship
By Hill, Phillip Douglas
Copyright©2018 Apostolos
ISBN 13: 978-1-5326-6944-6
Publication date 9/23/2018
Previously published by Apostolos, 2018

More Books from Apostolos:

The Emergence of Pentecostalism in Wales

New Exodus in Hebrews

Reading Scripture in the Fellowship of the Spirit

A Comprehensive Reference Dictionary of Linguistics

For details of all our publications visit www.apostolos-publishing.com

ABSTRACT

This book explores the history of the Baptist Revival Fellowship (or BRF), from its foundation in 1938 as a movement to promote spiritual renewal in the Baptist Union of Great Britain (or BU) until it withdrew from its affiliation in 1972. Drawing upon denominational records, press reports, some writings of its leaders and the archive of the BRF, it aims to redress the comparative neglect by Baptist scholars of this significant movement. The BRF is placed within its historical context in relation both to the BU and to evangelical life in England between 1900 and 1972, paying special attention to Baptist life. The role of its founders is considered, Theo Bamber (1891–1970) and Geoffrey King (1908–1986), who sought to promote among Baptists conservative evangelical beliefs and Keswick-style 'Higher Life' teaching. The movement is shown to have three phases of development, to each of which a chapter is devoted. The first is its early development between 1938 and 1960 when it mainly emphasized personal spiritual renewal and prayer for revival but in the late fifties moved into more fundamentalist territory. The second phase consists of a period between 1960 and 1966 when the older emphases were diminished by the influence of early charismatic renewal and Reformed theology, resulting in renewed impetus and serious engagement with contemporary Baptist debates. The final phase was between 1966 and 1971 when the BRF adopted a policy of secession from the BU. The significant influence is shown from the late fifties onwards of the prominent Free Church evangelical D. Martyn Lloyd-Jones (1899–1981). The final two chapters deal with the process by which the BRF finally seceded from the BU in reaction to a Christological controversy in the BU between 1971 and 1972. These chapters provide the first comprehensive analysis of this significant controversy.

CONTENTS

ABSTRACT 3

CHAPTER ONE
INTRODUCTION 11
Focus and Method 11
Relation to Existing Scholarship 12
Terminology 13
Denominational Background to the Founding of the BRF 15
Conclusions 21

CHAPTER TWO
THE EARLY DEVELOPMENT OF BRF VISION AND STRATEGY (1938–1960) 22
The Origin and Early Development of the BRF 22
Post-war Evangelicalism 29
The Free Churches and the New Conservativism 32
The BRF and Post-war Baptist Life 34
The Carey Hall Dispute 43
Conclusions 46

CHAPTER THREE
THE PROBLEM OF PAYNE: BRF RESPONSES TO A NEW BAPTIST AGENDA (1960–1966) 47
The BRF and Liberalism 47
The BRF and Ecumenism 49
The BRF and Denominational Centralization 53
'Liberty in the Lord' 55
An Evangelical Alternative to Ecumenism 62
The BRF and Denominational Loyalty 66
The BRF and Charismatic Renewal 70
Conclusions 73

CHAPTER FOUR
THE ROAD TO SECESSION (1966–1970) 76
The 1966 Evangelical Alliance Assembly 76

    The Impact of Lloyd-Jones' Message on the BRF 80

    The Marginalization of Denominational Loyalists in the BRF 81

    Hesters Way Baptist Church, Cheltenham 85

    The BRF and 'Baptists at the Crossroads' 87

    The 'Baptists and Unity' Debate 91

    The 1969 BU Assembly 93

    The 1969 BRF Conference and the Adoption of Secession as a Definite Policy 95

    Denominational Approaches to the BRF 98

    BU Consideration of a New Confession of Faith 104

    Conclusions 106

CHAPTER FIVE

'HOW MUCH OF A MAN WAS JESUS?': THE CHRISTOLOGICAL CONTROVERSY OF 1971 107

    The 1971 Assembly and the Beginning of the Controversy 107

    The Development of a Denominational Policy 112

    The Emergence of Protest Among Baptist Loyalists 113

    Tension Begins to Mount as Moderates Reconsider their Loyalties 117

    The BRF Strategy 117

    Peter Masters and the Metropolitan Tabernacle 123

    The First Official Attempt to End the Controversy 128

    The Loyalist Campaign for Orthodoxy 130

    The Second Attempt to End the Controversy 133

    Conclusions 134

CHAPTER SIX

'WE CANNOT IN CONSCIENCE REMAIN': THE SECESSION OF THE BAPTIST REVIVAL FELLOWSHIP AND THE RESOLUTION OF THE CHRISTOLOGICAL CONTROVERSY 136

    The November Council and Its Aftermath 136

    The November BRF Conference and the Decision to Secede 141

    Sir Cyril Black's Campaign Against Russell's Policy 143

    The March Council and the 1972 Baptist Assembly 151

Conclusions 154

CHAPTER SEVEN

CONCLUSIONS 157

   Reaction to Wider Trends in British Church Life.. 157

   BRF Reactions to Trends within Evangelicalism 160

   The BRF as Keepers of a Baptist Heritage.. 161

   The BRF and Exclusivity 162

   The Failure of the BRF 164

Bibliography 165

   Primary Sources... 165

APPENDIX ONE 180

THE ORIGINAL DOCTRINAL BASIS OF THE INTER-VARSITY FELLOWSHIP (IVF) 180

APPENDIX TWO.. 181

THE CONSTITUTION OF THE BAPTIST REVIVAL FELLOWSHIP ADOPTED AT THE BRF ANNUAL CONFERENCE, 1964........................ 181

APPENDIX THREE 184

LETTER FROM THEO BAMBER TO BT, FEBRUARY 29, 1940: 'A CLARION CALL.' 184

APPENDIX FOUR 185

CHRISTIAN UNITY – A PAPER BY THEO BAMBER............................... 185

   UNITY URGENTLY NEEDED 185

   WHAT BAPTISTS REQUIRE... 186

   THE PRELIMINARIES 187

   THAT THEY ALL MAY BE ONE 187

   THE TRINITY 188

   SOME CONCLUSIONS... 189

APPENDIX FIVE 191

STATEMENT APPROVED BY THE DENOMINATIONAL CONFERENCE HELD AT SWANWICK, MAY 23–26, 1961 191

APPENDIX SIX 193

OPEN LETTER OF 1964 FROM THEO BAMBER TO ERNEST PAYNE REGARDING RE-UNION AND ISSUES CONCERNING DENOMINATIONAL CENTRALIZATION, FOLLOWED BY PAYNE'S REPLY 193

APPENDIX SEVEN 197

STATEMENT OF THE BAPTIST REVIVAL FELLOWSHIP REGARDING THE ECUMENICAL MOVEMENT AGREED AT THE BRF CONFERENCE OF 1967.................... 197

APPENDIX EIGHT.................... 200

'HOW MUCH OF A MAN WAS JESUS?' 200

APPENDIX NINE 210

THE RESOLUTION AND ADDENDUM AS AGREED BY THE BAPTIST UNION COUNCIL OF NOVEMBER 1971 FOR PRESENTATION TO THE BAPTIST ASSEMBLY OF 1972.................... 210

APPENDIX TEN 212

THE RESOLUTION OF THE BRF CONFERENCE OF NOVEMBER 1971 CONCERNING WITHDRAWAL FROM THE BAPTIST UNION 212

APPENDIX ELEVEN 213

BRF LETTER TO DAVID RUSSELL: THE FINAL PLAN FOR A NEW BAPTIST BODY 213

APPENDIX TWELVE.................... 215

'THE CHRISTOLOGICAL CONTROVERSY IN THE BAPTIST UNION' 215

APPENDIX THIRTEEN 220

THE 1972 ASSEMBLY RESOLUTION ON 'THE ASSEMBLY ADDRESS' 220

APPENDIX FOURTEEN.................... 223

MARTYN LLOYD-JONES' PREACHING ENGAGEMENTS IN BAPTIST CHURCHES BETWEEN 1950 AND 1973.................... 223

APPENDIX FIFTEEN 235

BRF BOOKLETS AND PAMPHLETS 235

APPENDIX SIXTEEN 236

BRF CONFERENCE THEMES AND SPEAKERS 236

APPENDIX SEVENTEEN.................... 238

BRF OFFICERS AND COMMITTEE MEMBERS FROM 1938–1972.................... 238

CHAPTER ONE

INTRODUCTION

Focus and Method

The Baptist Revival Fellowship (or BRF) was a movement founded in 1938 to work for spiritual renewal and biblical fidelity within the Baptist Union of Great Britain and Northern Ireland (or BU). This book examines the history, policy, and doctrinal beliefs of the BRF up to the time that it withdrew from its denominational commitment in 1972. The final year of the BRF's existence will be covered in detail, in view of the interaction between the BRF and the BU over a Christological controversy which began at the 1971 Baptist Assembly. A detailed analysis will be provided of conservative evangelical reactions to the controversy in general and of the BRF in particular.

The purpose of this research is to chart the course of a significant but neglected Baptist movement, to review its place within the wider evangelical scene, to evaluate its influence on Baptist life and to consider its relationship with what was possibly the most difficult crisis the Baptist denomination in Britain has faced since its inception. It will be argued that the BRF began as an attempt by a prominent London minister, Theo M. Bamber (1891–1970) to preserve the pietist spirituality and biblicism that dominated conservative evangelicals in the first decades of the modern BU, emphases especially championed by the internationally famous Baptist minister F. B. Meyer (1847–1929). Alongside these commitments, Bamber developed a fundamentalist tendency in the 1950s in reaction to the growth of ecumenism and his perception of the increasing influence within the denomination of centralizing policies and liberal theology. In the 1960s the BRF became dominated by a younger generation of leaders whose inspiration was the Calvinistic and anti-denominational, the most prominent of whom was minister of Westminster Chapel, London, D. Martyn Lloyd-Jones (1899–1981). Jones's openness to the early charismatic movement was accepted by many BRF members. His secessionist message became its official policy in the late sixties, leading eventually to the resignation from the BU of a significant number of ministers after the Christological Controversy of 1971. It will be argued that the BRF provided a much-valued rallying point for conservative evangelicals in the Baptist Union and preserved important aspects of Baptist identity, but nevertheless failed in its original vision to influence the denomination.

The Baptist Revival Fellowship

Relation to Existing Scholarship

The BRF has received little attention from Baptist historians. American Baptist historians have produced a number of world surveys of Baptist life and thought,[1] including a professedly comprehensive survey of Baptist movements in the *Historical Dictionary of the Baptists*, but this does not even mention the BRF.[2] Only one of the American works which I have been able to consult mentions the BRF, where it is referred to simply as a 'strongly evangelical' voice of opposition to liberalism in a discussion of the 'Christological controversy that began at the British Baptist Assembly of 1971.'[3] Nor has the BRF been covered by most European scholars. Ernest Payne does not mention it at all in *The Baptist Union: A Short History*,[4] and no articles have been published specifically about the BRF in the *Baptist Quarterly* (hereafter *BQ*). In 2009 a survey was published of European Baptist life as *A Dictionary of European Baptist Life and Thought*.[5] Although several conservative evangelical movements are included in it, the BRF is overlooked. The BRF has received notice from three British Baptist scholars, however. David Bebbington refers to it in his *Evangelicalism in Modern Britain*.[6] He notes the BRF as an early supporter of charismatic renewal,[7] as an example in Baptist life of conservative evangelicalism,[8] and as an opponent of ecumenism.[9] Brian Stanley, in his historical survey of the Baptist Missionary Society (or BMS) acknowledged the role of the BRF in British Baptist debates about re-baptism in the Ceylon scheme for a united church, reflecting widespread suspicion among Baptists of the ecumenical movement,[10] while Ian Randall has paid more systematic attention to it, both in his *English Baptists of the Twentieth Century* and in some other writings.[11]

---

[1] Especially in recent decades by H. Leon McBeth, W. H. Brackney and J. L. Garrett (for which see Bibliography).
[2] William H. Brackney, *Historical Dictionary of the Baptists* (Lanham, MA: Scarecrow Press, 1999).
[3] James Leo Garrett, *Baptist Theology: A Four Century Study* (Macon, GA: Mercer University Press, 2009), 570–574.
[4] Ernest Payne, *The Baptist Union: A Short History* (London: Carey Kingsgate Press, 1958).
[5] John H. Y. Briggs (ed.), *A Dictionary of European Baptist Life and Thought* (Milton Keynes: Paternoster Press, 2009).
[6] David Bebbington, *Evangelicalism in Modern Britain: A History from the 1730s to the 1980s* (London: Unwin Hyman, 1989).
[7] Ibid., 230.
[8] Ibid., 251.
[9] Ibid., 267.
[10] Brian Stanley, *The History of the Baptist Missionary Society 1792–1992* (Edinburgh: T&T Clark, 1992), 417.
[11] Ian Randall, 'Look To Jesus Christ': English Baptists and Evangelical Spirituality'; *American Baptist Quarterly*, Vol. 25 No. 1, Spring 2006, 8–26; *Evangelical Experiences: A Study of the Spirituality of English Evangelicalism 1918–1939* (Carlisle: Paternoster Press, 1999); *The English Baptists of the Twentieth Century* (Didcot: The Baptist Historical Society, 2005).

Introduction

Randall noted particularly its significance in calling for spiritual renewal and in the defense of traditional Baptist values in the 1960s (when it had in membership a quarter all the BU accredited ministers), and its development into a platform for conservative evangelicals wishing to secede from the Baptist Union in the late sixties. I have built on this material by investigating mainly four primary sources: The Minutes of the Baptist Union, the Archive of the BRF, some published writings and sermons of its two leading figures, Theo Bamber and Geoffrey King (1908–1986), and reports concerning the BRF in the religious press, especially in the *Baptist Times* (or *BT*). Alongside this, I evaluate the BRF within the wider context of evangelical thought and practice.

Terminology

In this book, the so-called 'Bebbington quadrilateral' will be followed in regarding evangelicalism as having four key indicators: conversionism, activism, Biblicism, and crucicentrism.[12] Although Bebbington's thesis has recently been challenged, especially his view that the origins of evangelicalism lay in the Enlightenment,[13] the quadrilateral remains widely accepted with regard to the movement as a whole. Bebbington will also be followed in his identification of four main strands within evangelicalism during the mid-century: liberal (characterized as 'eager to welcome fresh light from modern thought and other Christian traditions'); centrist (those who 'tried to minimize the divide that had opened in the 1920s between liberals and conservatives'); conservative (a grouping which 'inherited its moderate conservatism from the inter-war debates' especially over the authority of Scripture); and fundamentalist (typically characterized by upholding the inerrancy of Scripture together with rejecting the theory of evolution, and denouncing those who disagreed with fundamentalism).[14] In order to avoid needless repetition, the term 'evangelical' will not normally be added when referring to the four sub-groups.

Use will be made of the term 'pietist' to refer to the early message of the Keswick Convention, founded in 1875 to promote the 'higher life' of receiving the fullness of the Holy Spirit in response to total consecration to God, entailing a stress on high moral standards—usually referred to as holiness teaching—but also a typical rejection of involvement with 'the

---

[12] Bebbington, *Evangelicalism in Modern Britain*, 2.
[13] See especially Michael A. G. Haykin: 'Evangelicalism and the Enlightenment: A Reassessment' in Michael A. G. Haykin & Kenneth Stewart (eds.), *The Emergence of Evangelicalism: Exploring Historical Continuities* (Nottingham: Apollos, 2008), 37ff.
[14] Bebbington, *Evangelicalism in Modern Britain*, 251–2.

world' of high culture and politics[15] and frequently of denominational involvement.[16]

Finally, the term 'secessionist' will be used to delineate rather than denounce the policy, or those who held the policy, of renouncing an existing denominational affiliation as an act of protest.

This introductory chapter will set out some essential background concerning Baptist Union life prior to the founding of the BRF in 1938. Chapter Two will explore the period 1938–60: from the founding of the BRF as a movement for spiritual renewal along well-established pietist lines to its forming more fundamentalist views in opposition to increasing liberal influence in Baptist thought and practice. In the third chapter, the period from 1960–1966 will be covered as a distinct phase marked at the beginning by the ascendancy of a different evangelical ethos influenced both by Reformed theology and by early charismatic renewal, and at the end by calls for evangelicals to leave the BU in favour of a more uniformly conservative Baptist structure. In between those two turning points lay a brief but important period of engagement with denominational debates about liberal trends, greater centralization of structures, and involvement with the ecumenical movement. Chapter Four will consider how secession became adopted by the BRF as a public policy, a controversial move which resulted in some of the founding members and leading figures leaving in protest. In the fifth chapter, the course will be traced of the Christological controversy of 1971 from its beginnings at the BU Assembly until the summer months of that year, when a circle of Baptist denominational leaders attempted unsuccessfully to defuse the confrontation. In Chapter Six, the final denouement of the BRF as a denominational society will be traced through its own failure to address the denomination effectively, largely because the BRF had already committed itself to secession rather than reform and so had lost its credibility within the BU. The BRF began as a vehicle for renewing Baptist life but ended as one for leaving it. These two chapters provide the first comprehensive analysis to be written of the Christological controversy.

---

[15] However, one of its leading exponents was the Baptist minister and evangelist F. B. Meyer (1847–1929), whose ministry embraced both Keswick spirituality and social engagement, as shown by Ian M. Randall in *Spirituality and Social Change: The Contribution of F. B. Meyer (1847–1929)* (Carlisle: Paternoster Press, 2003) 107ff.
[16] Bebbington, *Evangelicalism in Modern Britain*, 179.

Introduction

Denominational Background to the Founding of the BRF

The modern BU was founded in 1891 by an amalgamation of the General and Particular Baptist bodies as an evangelical denomination tolerant of moderate theological variety. In 1904 a succinct but theologically distinctive 'Declaration of Principle' was drawn up to express this identity. Its first article, as amended in 1906 to make explicit reference to the deity of Christ, stated:

> That the Lord Jesus Christ our God and Saviour is the sole and absolute authority in all matters pertaining to faith and practice, as revealed in the Holy Scriptures, and that each church has liberty to interpret and administer His laws.[17]

Perhaps the most distinctive aspect of the BU Declaration of Principle was its Christological focus, whereby the nature of authority for Baptists was traced to Christ himself, with the Scriptures providing a subordinate yet authoritative witness to him. Stephen Holmes has remarked that, 'When compared to other Evangelical statements of a Scripture principle, this is strikingly Christological; the Bible is a mode of transmission of the authority of Christ.'[18] The evangelical ethos of the Baptist Union was thereby given a more existential basis than the traditional Protestant assertion of the final authority of the Bible, while at the same time maintaining a high view of Scripture. This expressed the evangelicalism not only of less doctrinally precise Baptists but also of the two leading Baptist conservatives in the generation that gave birth to the modern BU: F. B. Meyer and C. H. Spurgeon (1834–1892). Ian Randall summarizes F. B. Meyer's theological outlook with a quote from Myer himself, who said that Christianity was, 'not a creed but a life; not a theology or a ritual, but the possession of the spirit of man by the Eternal Spirit of the Living Christ.'[19] Likewise, Spurgeon's spirituality has been analyzed in great detail by Peter Morden, who concludes that, for Spurgeon, the Christian life was 'a journey with Christ and to Christ'[20] because of which, as a contemporary who knew him well observed, he had '"two loves", Christ and his church.'[21]

The Declaration of Principle combined popular Baptist reverence for Scripture and evangelical experientialism with cautious openness to new

---

[17] *Baptist Union Handbook 1907* (London: Baptist Union, published annually), 10.
[18] Stephen Holmes, 'Baptists and the Bible' in *Baptist Quarterly* Vol. 43 (July 2010), 418.
[19] Quoted by Randall from Meyer's 1894 publication, *From Calvary to Pentecost* (in Randall, *Spirituality and Social Change*, 34).
[20] Peter Morden, *'Communion with Christ and his People': The Spirituality of C. H. Spurgeon* (Oxford: Centre for Baptist History and Heritage, Regent's Park College, 2010), 28.
[21] Ibid., 295.

trends in theology and biblical studies. Furthermore, the liberty given to local churches provided for differing views to be expressed corporately.[22] From the outset, therefore, the Union understood itself to be evangelical in ethos, but open to differences of opinion about matters such as the precise nature of biblical inspiration and authority. The Baptist scholar Leonard G. Champion (1907–1997) provided an insight into how this was understood at a popular level in a survey of Baptist life in the twentieth century delivered to the Baptist Historical Society in 1982. He considered that Baptist faith in his Edwardian era childhood was based on two pillars: the inner authority of Christ and the external authority of the Bible. He regarded these as constants in Baptist life throughout its history:

> The structures of Baptist church life built up during the seventeenth century were based on a firm and definite theological foundation. The inner Lordship of Christ and the external authority of Scripture constituted the basis on which were formulated patterns of worship in which the ministry of the Word was pre-eminent, an understanding of baptism was developed as the personal commitment of faith involving specific forms of personal behaviour, and an emphasis was made upon the obligation of membership in a gathered community of believers. Here was coherence of belief and practice.[23]

However, the existence of the Declaration of Principle did not prevent the occurrence of considerable debate in the early decades of the last century. Four areas of debate and discussion should be noted. Two of them constituted enduring paradoxes about Baptist Union life, and two reflected changing patterns of church life as the twentieth century progressed.

With regard to Baptist life, the first paradox concerned its evangelical identity. The affirmation of Christ's real and absolute authority located the BU firmly within the evangelical tradition, yet no extended set of beliefs was required of members. This created a number of theological disputes about core evangelical convictions, especially between the two world wars. A small but vocal fundamentalist element accused the Union of tolerating loose views of Scripture and mounted campaigns against those who were judged guilty, notably the BMS missionary and Serampore College Principal,

---

[22] In view of the controversies that would arise in Baptist life it is interesting to note that this identified the Baptist tradition of liberty as an ecclesial rather than a personal right. In matters theological, this would become a principle maintained more in the breach than the observance of it.
[23] L. G. Champion, 'Baptist Church Life,' in K. W. Clements (ed.), *Baptists in the Twentieth Century* (London: Baptist Historical Society, 1983,) 11–12.

Introduction

George Howell (1871–1955) because of his rejection of biblical infallibility.[24] In 1930, the Cambridge classicist and leading Baptist layman, T. R. Glover (1869–1943) caused major controversy by ridiculing traditional evangelical opinions, especially the doctrine of the substitutionary atonement, in a BU study booklet.[25] A third major problem arose in 1933 about the description of Jesus as 'our God and Saviour' when E. J. Roberts, an accredited Baptist minister and sometime tutor at the Midlands Baptist College, resigned his personal membership of the BU to protest against having to accept in the Declaration of Principle the phrase 'Jesus Christ our God' because of his rejection of the deity of Christ as traditionally understood. As his ministerial accreditation also required acceptance of the Declaration, his position was referred to the Ministerial Recognition Committee and Legal Committee. The matter eventually entered the public domain when these committees advised the BU Council to withdraw his accreditation. Although he consequently withdrew his objections, his case stirred a debate through which the Declaration of Principle was altered in 1933 to speak of Christ somewhat more elastically as 'God manifest in the flesh.'[26]

The second paradox regarding Union identity concerned the tension between independence and denominational structures. The BU affirmed that 'each church has liberty to interpret and administer the laws of Christ' but at the same time created a complex system of committees and procedures. This led inevitably to disputes when local church independence seemed threatened. The same issue, together with a concern to maintain a witness to credo-baptism, underlay controversy about reunion and the place of Baptists in early ecumenical life. The most notable example occurred when J. H.

---

[24] Ian Randall, *English Baptists of the Twentieth Century* (Didcot: Baptist Historical Society, 2005), 125.
[25] Ibid., 171ff.
[26] The first *Baptist Handbook* to include the change was that of 1939 (London: Baptist Union, published annually), 13. It has been disputed by Douglas Sparkes in *The Constitutions of the Baptist Union of Great Britain* (Didcot: Baptist Historical Society, 1996), 37ff. that the change was related to the investigation of E. J. Roberts. It is beyond the scope of this study to discuss the matter in detail, but such a conclusion neglects the role of George Howell, himself a previous subject of attack by the fundamentalist Bible League over his rejection of the infallibility of Scripture while serving with the BMS in India. He was on the committee that investigated Roberts' refusal to accept the phrase in the Declaration of Principle 'Jesus Christ our God and Saviour' and within a fortnight of the first committee discussion indicated to M. E. Aubrey, the BU General Secretary, that he would propose a change to it. He subsequently remained in such close personal contact with Roberts that when various proposals were put to the Council regarding Roberts, he advocated a form of words which he openly acknowledged took Roberts' approval. Evidence of this can be found from a comparison of the relevant Minutes of the Ministerial Recognition Committee, of the committee which considered and proposed the change, and of the BU Council sessions at which the case of Roberts and the proposal for change were debated.

Shakespeare (1857–1928), General Secretary of the Baptist Union from 1898 to 1924, advocated ecclesiastical re-union based on episcopacy in his 1918 book, *The Churches at the Crossroads*. Shakespeare envisioned what he called 'a United Evangelical Church of the Empire' that would 'end the divisions created in 1662.'[27] He was effectively censured at the 1919 Baptist Assembly when T. R. Glover, seconded by the venerable Baptist leader John Clifford (1836–1923), achieved unanimous support for a motion calling on the BU to reject 'any basis of union which implies the irregularity of its ministry long blessed by God, or is inconsistent with the priesthood of believers.' Peter Shepherd, in his study of Shakespeare's role in Baptist life, believed that after 1918 'the mood among the churches, including the Baptists, swung increasingly against him, and his lack of realism was increasingly evident as the issues were explored in greater depth.'[28] The Baptist minister and eventual President[29] of Bristol Baptist College, W. M. S. West, believed it also created a decade-long backlash against ecumenical engagement by the Baptist denomination, resulting in the BU declining to send a deputation to the first Conference on Faith and Order in 1927.[30]

Michael Walker noted the two changes in church life during the period under review in his survey of Baptist worship in the twentieth century. The first was the decline of the great preaching centre churches. Walker described the nineteenth century as 'a golden age of preaching, in which Baptists shared to the full.' It declined 'not because the men necessary for it were no longer to be found. It was the congregations that died, not the preachers.'[31] The second change to which Walker drew attention was a greater interest in liturgy. He identified as significant M. E. Aubrey's *Minister's Manual*, produced in 1927 and Taite Patterson's *Call to Worship*, first produced in 1930. An older Baptist view was, he said, that 'there could be no dissembling between catholics and nonconformists.'[32]

In the two years prior to World War Two, an unfortunate but remarkable confluence of all the above issues occurred in the Baptist Union. In 1937, the BU approved an official delegation to the Second Faith and Order

---

[27] J. H. Shakespeare, *The Churches at the Crossroads: A Study in Church Unity* (London: Williams and Norgate, 1918), 199.

[28] Peter Shepherd, *The Making of a Modern Denomination: John Howard Shakespeare and the English Baptists 1898–1924* (Carlisle: Paternoster Press, 2001), 113.

[29] The traditional title at Bristol Baptist College was 'President' until 2000 when the new post-holder adopted 'Principal' (cf. *The Baptist Union Directory 1999–2000*, 24 and *The Baptist Union Directory, 2000–2001–2002*, 28).

[30] Randall, *English Baptists of the Twentieth Century*, 56.

[31] Michael Walker, 'Baptist Worship in the Twentieth Century,' in K. W. Clements (ed.), *Baptists in the Twentieth Century* (London: SPCK, 1988), 22.

[32] Ibid.

Introduction

Conference whereas ten years earlier Baptists had declined to participate. The same year, a 'Baptist Polity Committee' advocated 'some kind of connexional organisation for the payment of ministers from a common fund.'[33] In 1938, an *Outline of a Reunion Scheme between the Church of England and the Evangelical Free Churches of England* was published which appeared to have (though he denied it subsequently) the backing of the General Secretary, M. E. Aubrey (1885–1957).[34] The same year, the BU altered the Declaration of Principle as noted above. And alongside that change there was a concerted attempt to create a joint headquarters for the BU and BMS, suggesting a new phase of denominational centralization.[35] Though the BU as a body responded negatively to reunion, the central payment of ministers, and the idea of a joint headquarters, the proposals indicated how some leading voices in the denomination saw the future. Opposition to this vision was widespread and strong. For many Baptists, the Congregational nature of the church and the survival of the credo-baptist tradition were at stake. Nor was Baptist energy limited to conducting internal debates about identity and structures. There were significant programmes for social engagement, discipleship, and evangelism, as well as great interest in revival during the early 1920s. However, it is undeniable that the two decades after the end of the Great War witnessed enervating disagreements.

Meanwhile, church attendance was known to have been in continuous decline since the end of the Great War.[36] Some Baptists believed that a United Free Church was the rational answer to a shrinking constituency over-provided with local churches which shared the same fundamental ethos across their denominational boundaries. On the more conservative wing of the Union, however, another analysis existed, identifying the fundamental problem as spiritual decline within Baptist life.[37] A leading speaker representing the conservatives was Theo Bamber, pastor of Rye Lane Baptist Church, Peckham. When he began his ministry there in 1926 the church already boasted 793 members and in the intervening twelve years it had grown to 1137, making it the third largest Baptist church in London.[38] Bamber's stature was early recognized by Spurgeon's College, where he had

---

[33] Minutes of the Baptist Polity Committee, December 8, 1937.
[34] Randall, English Baptists of the Twentieth Century, 175.
[35] Roger Hayden, *English Baptist History and Heritage*, 2nd Edition (Didcot: Baptist Union of Great Britain, 2005), 187.
[36] Kenneth Hylson-Smith has demonstrated that this was true for all the Protestant denominations, especially from 1901–1945: *The Churches in England from Elizabeth I to Elizabeth II: Volume III, 1833–1998* (London SCM, 1998), 143–159.
[37] See, for example, Henry T. Wigley, 'The Free Churches Today' in *The Baptist Quarterly*, Vol. 13, (1949–50), 100.
[38] According to *The Baptist Handbook* for 1938, The Metropolitan Tabernacle was largest, with 1650 members, followed by West Ham Central Mission, which had 1157.

trained. He was the student speaker at the 1917 College conference, and only nine years after his ordination he was chosen to represent former students as 'a speaker at Principal McCaig's farewell from Spurgeon's College in 1926.'[39] At the beginning of 1938 he expressed his concerns about re-union schemes in a letter to the *Baptist Times* [or *BT*], roundly declaring:

> our supreme need at this critical moment is not what are the conditions upon which we may unite ecclesiastically but what are the conditions in which God the Holy Spirit will visit us again in a mighty revival.[40]

Bamber was articulating the standard Keswick message. Bebbington has noted that the Keswick experience of receiving 'entire sanctification' by faith provided also a new spiritual power.[41] Ministers who underwent such an experience testified commonly to having a new spiritual authority in their preaching. Bebbington gives an example he regards as typical. A Mr. Grane of Shanklin attended the 'Oxford Conference' that led to the annual Keswick Convention. He testified that 'I came here because I felt a great want in my ministry. Crowds came and went, and yet with small result. I could not believe that all was right, and I came to see what was the secret of spiritual power which some of my brethren possess.'[42]

Yet Bamber was not likely to be branded an obscurantist or troublemaker for providing such an analysis. F. B. Meyer has been previously noted as a leading Baptist figure of his time famous for his advocacy of the Keswick message. He had made similar judgements himself about Baptist life. He founded a 'Baptist Ministers and Missionaries Prayer Union' as early as 1887 to meet the very need which Bamber identified.[43] Randall states that 'Meyer was determined to bring Keswick's spirituality into Baptist life.'[44] The Prayer Union initiated regional structures, an annual three-day conference and fringe meetings at the Baptist Assembly, a pattern that Bamber repeated in the BRF. Within ten years of starting, the Prayer Union had a membership of 770 out of the 2000 ministers in the Union. It was entirely an authentic Baptist note struck by Bamber when he raised the same question of spiritual empowerment on the same terms as Meyer had a generation before and only months later initiated a renewal movement using the same strategy. [45] In fact,

---

[39] David Bebbington: 'Baptists and Fundamentalism,' in Keith Robbins (ed.), *Protestant Evangelicalism: Britain, Ireland, Germany and America c.1750–c.1950*, (Oxford: Basil Blackwell, 1990), 325.
[40] *BT*, February 24, 1938, 4.
[41] David Bebbington, *Evangelicalism in Modern Britain*, 151.
[42] Ibid., 152, quoting from the written testimony of Mr. Grane.
[43] Randall, *Spirituality and Social Change*, 63.
[44] Ibid.
[45] Ibid., 64.

Meyer had died only ten years before Bamber began the BRF and it is probable that Bamber was influenced by hearing Meyer speak and perhaps by a more personal acquaintance with him.

Conclusions

The Baptist Union belonged firmly within the evangelical tradition of Britain. It was founded on a balance of authority between the living Christ and the written Word of God in which life was ordered by a spiritual relationship with Christ whose Lordship was expressed in both the teachings of the Bible and personal guidance from His Spirit. As a denomination, therefore, it was at the evangelical centre, but it had a large conservative presence to the right, as well as a small liberal one to the left. As members of a new denominational grouping, dating from 1891, the first generation of BU leaders faced occasional controversies while the boundaries of acceptable belief and practice were established. From this process, the denomination emerged as evangelical in spirit and defensive of its independent ecclesiology, whilst at the same time remaining within the mainstream of British theological and ecclesiastical life.

However, the mainstream churches began visibly to decline after the 1914–18 War, so that as well as having to refine its identity as a denomination, another kind of uncertainty grew about the effectiveness of the Baptist denomination in mission. It responded to this especially by producing literature and various schemes for evangelism and discipleship, and by exploring closer relations with sister denominations, as much for theological reasons as practical ones like rationalizing resources. A different answer to decline was proposed by Theo Bamber, who saw the need for 'a divine visitation'; a call which struck a chord in his generation as it had fifty years before among the more conservative evangelical members of the Union.

CHAPTER TWO

THE EARLY DEVELOPMENT OF BRF VISION AND STRATEGY (1938–1960)

In this chapter, the early vision and strategy of the BRF will be considered and related both to the wider evangelical scene and to Baptist Union life. The purpose of this is to establish first what kind of evangelicalism it represented and how that evolved; and second, how it perceived itself and was perceived by others in the denomination. The end of this first phase is marked by a change of theological and spiritual emphasis in BRF life from pietism towards Calvinism, a change to which the next chapter will be dedicated.

The Origin and Early Development of the BRF

Ian Randall describes the beginnings of the BRF thus, quoting a phrase from its constitution:

> Meetings between some London ministers concerned about 'the low level of spiritual life in the churches' led to Theo Bamber, Geoffrey King, minister of East London Tabernacle, Angus McMillan, minister of Lewin Road Baptist Church, Streatham[1], and others, forming the Baptist Revival Fellowship (BRF) in 1938.[2]

The leading figures were ministers in churches noted for their continued numerical strength despite a general decline in large churches at the time. The 1938 edition of *The Baptist Handbook* lists Bamber's membership at Rye Lane, Peckham as 1137, Lewin Road as 469 and East London Tabernacle as 409. East London Tabernacle nevertheless was one of those large churches already in decline, having had a membership of over 1200 before the First World War.[3] Geoffrey King had the especially difficult challenge of maintaining its strength despite its East End location, an area renowned not only for social deprivation but for a higher than average decline in church attendance. Indeed, King (as did other East End ministers) frequently used *BT* to appeal for funds for his church's demanding ministry in a deprived

---

[1] McMillan was in fact the minister at Lewin Road, Streatham, from 1942. In 1938 he was at Madeira Street, Leith (1936–42), while Stephen Madden, another minister close to Bamber, was the minister at Lewin Road (1932–42).
[2] Randall, *English Baptists of the Twentieth Century*, 230.
[3] According to the Baptist Handbooks, in 1917 the membership had fallen to 680 and by 1927 stood at 412. When King left the church in 1954 the membership was 387.

The Early Development of BRF Vision and Strategy (1938-1960)

area as well as using sales of work and jumble sales despite the condemnation of them common among conservative evangelicals.[4]

Bamber and King shared much in common. Both of them were products of Spurgeon's College and both were appointed to significant London pastorates early in their ministries (Bamber after one pastorate and King upon his ordination), eventually becoming leading personalities in London Baptist life and members of the BU Council. Both of them were gifted writers used regularly by *BT* in the early years of the BRF (as occasionally were other BRF members).[5] Both of them became widely respected speakers whose published sermons were well-received in evangelical circles. Their pietism and premillennialism were characteristic of the conservative evangelical movement of the time and their ministries were sufficiently well-known to bring both of them invitations to speak at the Keswick Convention[6] (though King more regularly). However, they were opposites in their temperaments. Bamber was a controversialist while King was a conciliator. Bamber, who had the authority of a strong personality, attracted followers, and his London church grew significantly. King was a gentler spirit whose ministry sustained his two churches but did not increase their memberships.[7] Bamber would frequently use the emotive language of crisis and prophetic declamation while King's preference was for carefully constructed sermons[8] delivered more with the heart of a pastor than a prophet. The difference between them is well illustrated by their respective treatments of the Second Coming. Bamber was explicit in his interpretation of the premillennial scheme, and was prepared to dogmatize on the divisive subject (among premillennialists) of the exact nature of the 'Rapture':

> There are some who think that Christians who are not looking for his coming will not take part in the rapture in the air. But the Church is one, and its unity is in the faith in the precious blood of the Lord Jesus. Those looking for His coming will rejoice to have their faith

---

[4] In a conversation on August 1, 2010 with Geoffrey Fewkes, a Baptist minister and close friend of King during his latter years, I was informed that King decried evangelical sensibilities about raising funds only through direct giving, because of his experience of doing otherwise at his East End Church (Fewkes worked with King through the Bible and Advent Testimony League in the 1970s).

[5] Bamber, for example, wrote 'The Quiet Hour' on November 3, 10 and 17, 1938 while Larwood wrote it for December 12; and Rudman on February 2, 1939.

[6] *BT* noticed his first visit with pleasure in a report of the 1938 Keswick Convention (*BT*, August 21, 1938, 575).

[7] As previously noted, East London Tabernacle stood at just over 412 members when he went there and at 387 when he left 26 years later; West Croydon Tabernacle had a membership of 569 at the commencement of his ministry and 568 ten years later at its close.

[8] I interviewed several people who heard him preach who all recounted the originality of his sermon structures.

> confirmed. The others will be something like Thomas in the post resurrection days of doubt and uncertainty, and there will be a humbling joy at His feet as they rebuke themselves for their unbelief.[9]

Bamber was willing to specify exactly the future of the Jews: 'Israel will return to the land in unbelief ... they will welcome Antichrist as false Messiah. The ancient worship will be restored and the temple, as prophesied by Ezekiel, will be re-built.'[10] King's approach was far more pacific, as demonstrated in a sermon published in 1957:

> I shall delight to declare unto you, in the whole counsel of God, the second advent of the Lord. You may disagree with some of the points of this doctrine, but I think we all find common ground in this, that God's climax for the ages is in the return of Jesus Christ.... It is the conviction of my own mind and heart that the Lord Jesus Christ is coming back to this earth in person, in bodily form, to establish a material Kingdom. There is a growing school of thought among Evangelicals that the material kingdom of our Lord is not to be found in the Scriptures, but that all is to be taken spiritually. I do not agree. If you do, then we must be true to our beliefs, and agree to differ.[11]

The temperamental difference between them can also be observed in their respective roles within the BRF. Although they were both regarded as the founding fathers of the BRF, Bamber was always the Chairman: the leader, spokesman and driving force. King took the role of Prayer Secretary and would never have wanted anything more.

Two documents indicate the early spirit of the BRF. The first is its constitution.[12] Although it was adopted only in 1964, it stated the origins of the BRF when the founding members were still present to provide information. The BRF began through informal meetings of a group of London Baptist ministers who were burdened by the low level of spiritual life in the churches. As they prayed and studied the Scriptures together they saw clearly their own spiritual weakness and personal need of renewal by the Lord and also the need for Revival in the Church.[13]

The second document is a letter from Bamber, published in *BT* on February 29, 1940. This latter document, though not officially sent in the name of the

---

[9] Bamber, *His Glorious Appearing*, 29.
[10] Ibid., 39.
[11] Geoffrey King, *Truth For Our Times* (London: Lutterworth Press, 1957), 23.
[12] See Appendix Two for the full text.
[13] Baptist Revival Fellowship Constitution and Rules, adopted at the Annual Conference of 1964.

The Early Development of BRF Vision and Strategy (1938-1960)

BRF, nevertheless reveals Bamber's influential thinking.[14] It is a classic exposition of personal holiness as the basis for revival. His concern was 'for the Christians of this country to come back to God in humble repentance.' Bamber sought to stimulate this by calling a 'public assembly' for confession of sin and repentance before God. He specified a number of things he had in mind. Firstly, he alluded to several personal spiritual issues, such as 'secret sins' and 'lack of love.' Next, Bamber mentioned issues concerned with personal salvation and sanctification, and finally 'our failure to proclaim the end of the age in the personal return of the Lord Jesus Christ.' Bamber's letter provides the essential manifesto that the BRF went on to pursue under his leadership – personal dedication, faithfulness to Scripture, the need for revival, and the expectation of Christ's personal return (interpreted according to the pre-millennial scheme).

The meaning attached to 'revival' was not the American one of 'an evangelistic mission,' but rather the British experience of spiritual renewal among believers resulting in evangelistic success, such as the Welsh Revival of 1904, and the Suffolk Revival of the early 1920s, both of which were warmly received and well-remembered by Baptists at that time.[15] It should further be distinguished from the emphasis of D. Martyn Lloyd-Jones (1899–1981), assistant minister and then minister of Westminster Chapel from 1939–1968.[16] After the war, his became a leading voice on the subject of revival, calling for renewed interest in the eighteenth-century evangelical revivals, in contrast to the less Calvinistic and rather pietistic emphases of early twentieth century evangelicalism in Britain.[17] Lloyd-Jones participated in at least one of the BRF London Rallies for revival during the war,[18] but his early influence was not as great as that of the movement's own Baptist leaders. When Billy Graham held his London Crusades in the early fifties, for

---

[14] The full text appears in Appendix Three.
[15] For example, Spurgeon's College students recounted remarkable 'outpourings of the Spirit' during the 1904–5 revival (see Randall, *English Baptists of the Twentieth Century*, 34), and similar scenes were reported in East Anglia in 1921 (ibid., 149ff).
[16] Lloyd-Jones eventually set out his view of revival in a series of sermons preached during 1959 at Westminster Chapel, London. These have been published as *Revival: Can We Make It Happen?* (Basingstoke: Pickering & Inglis, 1986).
[17] John Brencher, in his study of Lloyd-Jones, makes only passing references to Lloyd-Jones' emphasis on revival, mainly to note a link between that and his interest in the early charismatic movement. *Martyn Lloyd-Jones (1899–1981) and Twentieth Century Evangelicalism* (Milton Keynes: Paternoster, 2002), 200–205. Iain Murray's biography of Lloyd-Jones devotes a chapter to its importance as a major aspect of Lloyd-Jones' thinking: *D. Martyn Lloyd-Jones: The First Forty Years* (Edinburgh, Banner of Truth, 1982)], 203ff.
[18] Records are incomplete and therefore no more definite information is available.

example, the BRF resisted Lloyd-Jones's opposition to taking part in them, even when that opposition was voiced by some of its own members.[19]

The early activities of the BRF bear witness to its pietistic outlook. Its first publication, produced in 1939 while not only the secular but the religious press was preoccupied with Nazism and the threat of war, was a booklet on 'soul-winning' written by Geoffrey King entitled *By All Means Save Some*.[20] In 1940 the BRF began regular large-scale prayer meetings, some of which were all-night events, but at these meetings the calls were largely for personal revival in keeping with the Keswick message as if there were no war at all. The first of these was held at Rye Lane Chapel but as they developed more central London venues were used, notably Bloomsbury Baptist Church and the Metropolitan Tabernacle.[21] This emphasis was, however, a message for the denomination and not a general appeal to the Christian public. Even during the war years when organizations tended to reduce their programmes, the BRF began an annual rally during the Baptist Assembly in 1942. It was reported in *The Christian* by F. Cawley, a fellow Baptist, that Ronald Park (minister at Plumstead) chaired it while B. T. J. Pritchard, Geoffrey King and Theo Bamber spoke. Cawley called it 'a youthful "Spurgeonic platform"' which 'packed the building.'[22] This indicates a denominational strategy that was at once loyal and critical: loyal in that the strategy was clearly thought of as something from *within* rather than *outside* the Baptist constituency, but critical in that it was self-evidently seeking to provide a somewhat different emphasis from that which might be heard on the Assembly platform. Bamber was already critical both of ecumenical and liberal trends in the BU. As early as 1927 he had cast doubt on the ecumenical movement, probably in response to the first Faith and Order Conference taking place that year. He contrasted it with the hope of Christ's return as the proper inspiration of the church.[23] His scorn for liberalism was hinted at in his 1940 letter to *BT* advertising a 'service of repentance.' There he made only an oblique reference to it as 'our sin in giving the world our own opinions instead of proclaiming what God has revealed in His word.'[24] In his own church he was less restrained. In his 1939 sermon series *His Personal Return*, Bamber took the Methodist preacher Leslie

---

[19] Cf. *BRF Bulletin* No. 46, July/September 1955, 1.
[20] In a private letter to me dated January 12, 2009, Joseph Murray (a former BRF member) noted that the copy he owned had been stamped as circulated by the Irish Auxiliary of the BRF from 54 Dublin Road, Belfast, adding that 'these premises were vacated shortly before or after the war began in September 1939.'
[21] Bamber wrote a letter to *BT* advertising the event (*BT*, February 29, 1940, 132).
[22] Taken from a photocopy of an un-numbered page dated April 30, 1942, found in the BRF Archive, File 63/84.
[23] Bamber, *His Glorious Appearing*, 20.
[24] Ibid.

The Early Development of BRF Vision and Strategy (1938-1960)

Weatherhead to task for rejecting the literal interpretation of Christ's Second Coming, and noted also that there were some Baptists with the same viewpoint:

> I remember a speaker at a meeting of the London Baptist Association declaring that the present trouble in the world gave satisfaction to nobody except to the Second Adventists. It caused a ripple of laughter, but it was a jibe at the expense of truth. In any event the outlook is gloomy – wars, rumours of wars, strife and bloodshed. Our Lord said it was for the world, for when these things begin to come to pass the child of God was "to look up." Modern Christendom is so anxious to identify itself with the world that of course it is compelled to share its outlook. That is part of the divine punishment![25]

Bamber proceeded to an extensive analysis of 'modernist' preaching.[26] First, 'the modernist acts as if the things of earth were everything.' Secondly, the modernist 'is always taking people's minds back to Jesus 1900 years ago … yet they miss the most glorious fact of the New Testament, "In Him dwelleth all the fullness of the Godhead in bodily fashion".' Third, 'the modern preacher … has little interest in the beyond save of a traditional heaven in which, no doubt, all people working for good ends will assuredly be warmly welcomed.' Next, whereas the 'Second Adventist' calls the believer to personal and practical 'soul-winning,' the Modernist speaks about politics, of which Bamber says: 'Sermons on the League of Nations will never save a soul, nor make a man conscious of His condition before God as a sinner.'[27] This indicates that Bamber was close to the fundamentalist mentality in his open antagonism towards theological opponents. However, in the early phase of the BRF he refrained from making such attacks in the name of the BRF.

The BRF was nevertheless sufficiently credible as a Baptist movement for King and Bamber to be included in a 1944 Baptist Union working-party on the spiritual welfare of the churches alongside such leading figures as Arthur Dakin, President of Bristol Baptist College, Ingli James, then East Midlands Area Superintendent, R. Rowntree Clifford, minister of the West Ham Central Mission, and BU General Secretary M. E. Aubrey. The BU subsequently published their report, entitled *Speak – That They May Go Forward*.[28] On the other hand, as early as 1943 a long letter appeared in *BT* which expressed trenchant criticism of the new movement, written by 'A

---

[25] Theo Bamber, *His Personal Return*, (London: Rye Lane Chapel, 1939), 12–16.
[26] Ibid., 14.
[27] Ibid.
[28] Randall, *English Baptists of the Twentieth Century*, 239.

The Baptist Revival Fellowship

Minister's Wife.'[29] She asserted that the BRF was 'entirely superfluous,' because their emphasis 'has been the basis of work for thousands of Baptist ministers who have given, or are giving, their life to the Baptist cause.' She then outlined the hard work and long hours performed by her husband in 'his OWN CHURCH' (sic). She affirmed that such a minister 'values the fellowship and inspiration of meeting with those like-minded with himself, and so he supports wholeheartedly the Baptist Union and Baptist Missionary Society' or 'the LBA, his own Group,[30] and the Minister's Fraternal.' She evidently believed that involvement in the BRF entailed an implicit criticism of the regular programme and vision of Baptist life. She went on to speak a little sarcastically of the kind of minister who chose rather to:

> spend an hour on the platform at a special meeting outside his home church rather than to spend that hour talking with a family about church membership; or explaining our Baptist position to the parents of a young fellow who wishes to be baptized. [31]

As an accusation of the BRF leaders this was unfair. Both Bamber and King were greatly respected in their own churches and were more active than most in Baptist denominational life, including election to various positions of leadership. However, the writer correctly identified a danger inherent in claiming to live 'the higher life,' of assuming spiritual superiority over even conscientious Christians who did not identify with Keswick teaching. Bebbington goes so far as to describe the Keswick movement as having 'all the standard criteria of a sect,' noting that one of its early leaders actually commended it as 'a spiritual freemasonry which the outer world cannot comprehend.'[32]

The BRF began as a means of giving fresh voice to the Keswick-style pietism whose great champion had been lost ten years earlier with the death of F. B. Meyer. The founding of the BRF took place at a time when there was a confluence of international crisis, denominational conflict and religious decline in public life, a scenario that had the drama of an apocalyptic sign to those who believed the Second Coming was imminent. Bamber gave fresh impetus to an old message by speaking constantly in terms of international, national and denominational crises that required divine intervention which began in the life of individual believers. This explains several factors in the early development of the BRF, such as capturing the attention of younger conservative ministers who bemoaned the low spiritual state of the churches, establishing successful prayer gatherings during the war, and attracting

---

[29] *BT*, October 14, 1943, 4.
[30] The London Baptist Association (LBA) had established area groups across the metropolis.
[32] Randall, *English Baptists of the Twentieth Century*, 179–180.

crowds to the early annual rallies during the Baptist Assembly. Bamber's criticism of the BU was essentially that it fiddled while Rome burned, a message that met with approval among many conservatives but criticism of the kind referred to above from 'loyal Baptists' who could sense, if not clearly identify, the difference between what the denomination leaders and the BRF represented. The BRF was, from the outset, a body that was critical of official Baptist life on the grounds of what they perceived as its spiritual and theological failure.

Post-war Evangelicalism

The new mood of post-war conservative evangelical life may fairly be called 'new conservatism' on account of certain key differences from what went before that began to emerge over a period of some years. It was shaped less by the Romantic outlook to which Keswick pietism belonged and more by a cultural modernism that brought it closer to contemporary society. Displacing some of the Romantic elements in evangelicalism such as its emphases on poetic insight and subjective feeling, this culturally modernist approach conceived the road to faith as through the mind to the heart rather than the heart to the mind, and poetic insight was typically displaced by academic learning, especially in the sciences. Bebbington has noted that a key factor in this development was the influence of the Inter-Varsity Fellowship (or IVF), a conservative evangelical student movement founded in 1928 in reaction to liberal trends in the Student Christian Movement (or SCM). Hylson-Smith concurs, judging that the IVF 'enjoyed quite phenomenal success in the post-war decades.'[33] The key IVF leaders were not usually theologians but scientists or medical professionals.[34] This reflected in the first place, a certain reluctance among conservative evangelicals to study theology or The Arts at university;[35] and secondly, the IVF policy of maintaining student rather than staff leadership of the local Christian Unions. The result was that the IVF tended to produce future leaders with a scientific background, often with higher degrees. As a consequence, the new speaking style, even for clergy, became less 'a sermon' and more 'an address,'

---

[33] Hylson-Smith, *Vol. III*, 219.
[34] Bebbington emphasizes the role in this of several IVF groups: The Graduates Fellowship, the Christian Medical Fellowship, founded in 1949, and the Research Scientists Christian Fellowship, founded in 1944. Bebbington, *Evangelicalism in Modern Britain*, 260.
[35] Academic theology presented difficulties for conservatives who sought to defend traditional views as necessary orthodoxies With regard to the Arts, I recall discussions about this while on the staff of the IVF (later UCCF) from 1973–77. Much attention had been given by then to encouraging students in the Arts, which had long been avoided as 'unsound' or 'worldly.' It is indicative of the IVF's concern to further the agenda for evangelicalism first established after World War 2.

though maintaining the pietist suspicion of theological expertise. Theological writings nevertheless began to emerge from within conservative circles, especially in biblical studies, but they usually defended traditional views against more recent judgments of such matters as authorship and date, which led Baptist writers of note publicly to doubt that the IVF mentality was capable of sufficient open-mindedness to produce genuine theological scholarship.[36]

With regard to the newer style of evangelicalism exemplified by the IVF, it is instructive to compare the BRF with two other Revival Fellowships that were formed after the Second World War, the Methodist Revival Fellowship and the Congregational Evangelical Revival Fellowship.[37] The Methodist writer Martin Wellings links all three together as examples of post-war optimism about the prospect of revival, suggesting that the BRF can be understood as anticipating that mood.[38] However, the Congregational and Methodist Revival Fellowships were strongly influenced by the new evangelical conservatism, whereas the BRF had no connection with it in its first decade. They were in the vanguard of the new approach while the BRF was at the tail end of the older one. Wellings himself notes that the founder of the Methodist Revival Fellowship, John H. L. Barker (1903–76), had been a Travelling Secretary with the Inter-Varsity Fellowship, and that the MRF was characterized by its adoption of the IVF Doctrinal Basis.[39] The 'Congregational Evangelical Revival Fellowship' was similarly influenced. Founded by two young ministers (one of them the emerging leader in British evangelical life, Gilbert Kirby [1914–2006]), it had a specific agenda to represent evangelical beliefs as well as to seek revival:

> two Congregational ministers, Harland Brine and Gilbert Kirby, concerned at the `spiritual decline of their denomination, felt led of God to begin a Congregational Evangelical Revival Fellowship (CERF). This Association, formed in 1947, was open to individual members of Congregational Churches and sought to witness to

---

[36] Book reviews from this period in the *BQ* of conservative evangelical publications were routinely critical. See, for example, H. H. Rowley's critique of B. B. Warfield's *The Nature and Inspiration of The Bible* in *BQ* Vol. 13 (1949–50), 133ff. and W. S. Davies' review of *The Christian and His Bible*, by Douglas Johnson in *BQ* Vol. 16 (1952–53), 92. Rowley was a particular critic of conservative defensiveness: see R. E. Clements' analysis of Rowley, 'The Biblical Scholarship of H. H. Rowley' in *BQ*, Vol. 38 (1999–2000), 70–82.

[37] A Church of England 'Fellowship of Prayer for Revival' was in existence in the early 1960s, chaired by Preb. Colin Kerr, a leading conservative evangelical of his day, but I was unable to trace any official records of it.

[38] Martin Wellings: 'The Methodist Revival Fellowship 1952–1986' in *Proceedings of the Wesley Historical Society*, October 2009, 91–98.

[39] Ibid., 94ff.

evangelical truth and to the need for Holy Spirit Revival in the Church.[40]

Oliver Barclay has no doubt about the renewed vitality of conservative evangelicalism in the post-war period, describing it in his survey of evangelical life in the last century under the chapter heading, 'New Beginnings.'[41] Rob Warner has argued to the contrary that this was the moment when conservative evangelicalism became inward-looking to the degree that it became an 'elaborated conservative hegemony of the mid-twentieth century that was predominantly anti-critical and calvinistic, with fundamentalising tendencies evident in a continuing rightward drift.'[42] This is a misrepresentation. In the first place, the new conservatism reversed the attitude of hostility to academic studies in theology, embraced variety on secondary issues, made much of communicating the gospel in a contemporary style and carefully distinguished itself from fundamentalist stances, as may be seen in the original IVF Doctrinal Basis, which became a standard for other new conservative statements of belief.[43] Secondly, the new conservative leaders were often from the urbane world of public schools or Oxbridge, such as Oliver Barclay (Eton and Cambridge), F. F. Bruce (Cambridge), Dick Lucas (Sherborne and Cambridge), James I. Packer (Oxford), John Stott (Rugby and Cambridge) and Donald Wiseman (Oxford). Far from being inward-looking, this generation of leaders related well to wider society and was more successful than the previous one in reaching it with evangelistic programmes. Thirdly, the Billy Graham missions in the fifties made traditional evangelicalism both a new force in the churches and once more a publicly-known movement in British life, but without the fundamentalist agenda Graham had espoused earlier in his ministry.[44] The post-war era produced not so much a rightward swing among conservative evangelicals as their renewed identity as a culturally relevant and

---

[40] The Evangelical Fellowship of Congregational Churches Website (http://www.efcc.karoo.net/history.html)
[41] Oliver Barclay, *Evangelicalism in Britain 1935–1995* (Leicester: IVP, 1997) 50ff.
[42] Rob Warner, *Reinventing English Evangelicalism 1966–2001* (Milton Keynes: Paternoster Press, 2007), 25.
[43] See Appendix One for the original doctrinal basis, enunciating the infallibility but not the inerrancy of Scripture, the personal return of Christ but neither the premillennial scheme nor the nature of hell, thus allowing for some form of annihilation.
[44] While in Britain, Graham learned to appreciate a wider circle than his fundamentalist origins, and became an object of attack by his one-time fundamentalist friends, leading him by 1955 to the conviction that 'If a man accepts the deity of Christ and is living for Christ to the best of his knowledge, I intend to have fellowship with him in Christ. If this extreme type of fundamentalism was of God, it would have brought revival long ago. Instead it has brought dissension, division, strife, and has produced dead and lifeless churches.' Billy Graham, *Just As I Am* (London: HarperCollins, 1997), 251.

theologically engaged movement,[45] especially in comparison with the failure to adapt of the liberal, centrist and fundamentalist wings of evangelicalism. In short, conservative evangelicalism became more educated, more middle-class and more in tune with modern life than in its pre-war manifestation had been.

The Free Churches and the New Conservativism

It is noticeable that Free Church representatives were not significant in the new evangelical conservatism. At that time relatively few of them shared the middle-class or upper-middle-class background that now became characteristic of the leading figures, and whereas it was possible to belong to opposing ecclesiastical parties in Anglicanism without denominational loyalties being questioned, the situation was different in the smaller environments of the Free Churches, where personal relationships developed across the theological spectrum and acted as a brake on overt partisanship, although informal 'ginger groups' did exist behind the scenes such as 'The Cassock Club' that gathered around E. A. Payne while he was a tutor at Regent's Park College.[46] The Free Churches were also united (in a way the Anglicans were not) in their distinctive ecclesiological identities, as well as in the consciousness of broadly sharing the same evangelical inheritance. A further consideration is the close relationship that existed between the Free Churches and the SCM. It is likely that Free Church loyalists were regarded with some hesitation because of these factors by the wider conservative evangelical movement, but it is certainly the case that there were almost no Free Church ministries (in England, at least) comparable with those produced by the Evangelical Anglicans. In addition, the 'sound' alternative to Evangelical Anglicanism within the new conservative movement was the Open Brethren, which was similar to Evangelical Anglicanism both in its middle-class affinities and its theological exclusivity. Both Bebbington[47] and

---

[45] An example may be found in W. C. G. Proctor of the moderation to be found among early post-war conservatives. Proctor, an Irish Anglican and theological tutor, wrote *Evangelical Thought and Practice* in 1944, which was published in 1946 by the widely trusted evangelical publishing house, James Clarke. Proctor recognized the resurgence of evangelicalism around him and was willing to describe it as 'a New Fundamentalism' which now accepted two principles on which intelligent evangelicals built their interpretation of Scripture: '1. Nothing in the Bible need be interpreted contrary to Truth as otherwise ascertained; and 2. The more knowledge we possess, the greater our ability for interpreting Scripture aright.' Regarding verbal inspiration he affirmed it in the sense that God 'granted to the prophet or evangelist *the right word* [his italics] to describe the meaning God intends to be conveyed by the passage as a whole' (23).

[46] See Don Black, 'The Cassock Club' in *BQ* Vol. 40 (2003–04), 436ff.

[47] Bebbington, *Evangelicalism in Modern Britain*, 259–263.

The Early Development of BRF Vision and Strategy (1938-1960)

Shuff[48] have noted the importance to the new conservatism of Open Brethren influence, in particular through Douglas Johnson, the long-serving General Secretary of the IVF, and the business magnate and generous benefactor, Sir John Laing.

There was one outstanding exception to this pattern, in the remarkable ministry of D. Martyn Lloyd-Jones (1899–1981). Lloyd-Jones will be noticed in more detail under a discussion of his influence in the 1960s, but it should be recognized here that he was a key leader of the new conservatism. Not only was he exceptional as a Free Church minister whose medical training and social connections gave him considerable status, but also he was already regarded as the outstanding conservative preacher in post-war Britain, able to communicate the evangelical faith to 'modern man' with great intellectual and spiritual authority.[49] He thus fitted the profile of the new conservatism twice over, despite having previously achieved national prominence a generation earlier as a hero-figure in the Romantic style when in 1928 he sacrificed his meteoric rise in medicine (his first appointment being assistant to the Royal Physician, Lord Horder) in order to become a preacher. By contrast, most Free Church conservatives were neither as contemporary in their application of the evangelical faith to modern life nor as 'clubbable' in their social connections with post-war conservative circles, even when like Bamber and King, they were leaders of conservative orthodoxy in their denominations.

Bamber's response to post-war conservatism was probably ambivalent. On the one hand, he was by then a middle-aged product of the older school of thought and there was always a streak of fundamentalism within him, as evidenced by the style of his attacks on ecumenism and liberal theology. On the other hand, he was neither a thorough-going fundamentalist nor unwilling to identify with new developments. This can be seen by his acceptance, in 1947, of a place on the board of London Bible College, founded in 1943 explicitly to promote high academic standards among conservative evangelicals.[50] The doctrinal basis of LBC avoided reference to biblical inerrancy, in contrast to fundamentalist organizations such as the Bible League.[51] Bamber was evidently perceived to be a suitable guardian of the less strident position. Furthermore, he was also used as an appropriate speaker not only for the students but at LBC events for his ministerial

---

[48] Roger Shuff, *Searching For The True Church: Brethren and Evangelicals in the Mid-Twentieth Century* (Milton Keynes: Paternoster Press, 2005), 74 *et passim*.
[49] Brencher provides a thorough analysis of how he addressed modern problems with authority in his book, *Martyn Lloyd-Jones and Twentieth Century Evangelicalism*, 40ff.
[50] Ian Randall, *Educating Evangelicalism* (Carlisle: Paternoster Press, 2000), 12ff.
[51] Ibid., 26–27.

colleagues.⁵² His choice as a representative leader is the more significant in view of the strong Baptist presence in LBC, not only in its student body but in staff members and visiting speakers.⁵³ It may therefore be said that Bamber identified with the new conservatism even though he and King were more at ease with the pietist world of thought. Their guarded approach may be seen over the early Billy Graham missions. Lloyd-Jones decided not to associate publicly with him, in part because of his emphasis on making 'appeals' at the close of each meeting, in part because Lloyd-Jones was doubtful about mass evangelism, and in part because Graham invited non-evangelicals on to his platform to gain credibility.⁵⁴ When the question was raised in BRF discussion, Bamber firmly supported Graham, saying:

> Hundreds of Christians find themselves in difficulty not knowing whether his message has anything to do with the manifest blessing of God or whether the blessing is in spite of his message. Those who have the problem must seek for the Divine answer, but for ourselves we think it is the message gathered up and expressed through the man that is a vital element in the extraordinary results that are being seen. Let those who can secure little response meditate carefully upon the phenomenon of this mid-century Crusade in which the Gospel of Moody and Sankey is found to be as powerful now as ever. It is surely instructive. ⁵⁵

The BRF and Post-war Baptist Life

Post-war life, according to Hylson-Smith, brought enormous challenges that were 'quite overwhelming' for British society, and notably for the churches.⁵⁶ While all the denominations would be affected, he regards the challenges as more acute for the Free Churches⁵⁷ and especially for the Baptist Union.⁵⁸ To understand his analysis it is necessary to provide some brief historical context.

It was only in the early twentieth century that the Free Churches had definitely gained public respectability and recognition. This was an unexpectedly brief experience for them, however. Adrian Hastings identifies

---

⁵² Ibid., 61, which recounts Bamber speaking at a minister's course in 1944 at LBC.
⁵³ Ibid., 75.
⁵⁴ However, Lloyd-Jones allowed one of his deacons to become a senior steward at Graham's Harringay Crusade, as noted in Brencher, *Martyn Lloyd-Jones and Twentieth-Century Evangelicalism*, 70.
⁵⁵ *BRF Bulletin* No. 42, April 1954, 3–4.
⁵⁶ Hylson-Smith *Vol. III*, 216.
⁵⁷ Ibid.
⁵⁸ Ibid., 256.

The Early Development of BRF Vision and Strategy (1938-1960)

a symbolic beginning and end to it. The beginning was the first time a reigning monarch officially attended a Free Church service, at their united post-Armistice Thanksgiving Service at the Royal Albert Hall in November 1918.[59] The end he associates with 'the last serious attempt to treat Nonconformity as a politically serious force' when Lloyd George sought its support for his 1935 campaign to resurrect his political fortunes through a *Call To Action*, a plan for countering unemployment and promoting international peace.[60] Lloyd-George based much of his hopes for success on Free Church support (although Aubrey, to the approval of Theo Bamber, would not give Baptist endorsement to it).[61] The Free Church Federal Council endorsed Lloyd-George but could not deliver a victory, demonstrating that they were no longer politically powerful. The full significance of this was not realized at the time, in part because their status seemed rather to undergo a remarkable improvement through the founding of the British Council of Churches in 1942, 'which brought Free Churchmen more into the mainstream of English church leadership.'[62] If anything, there was an anticipation that the end of the war would herald a new era of success for the Christian Church, as may be seen from the response to the Anglican report calling for a new national mission strategy, *Towards the Conversion of England*, which Hastings says 'received at the time considerable acclaim.'[63] It has previously been noted that the Baptist Union shared this optimism by producing its own report in 1944, entitled *Speak: That They May Go Forward.*

The above considerations explain Hylson-Smith's analysis of the Free Church situation after the war. The Baptist position will be considered in due course, but all the Nonconformist denominations now faced a crisis for which they were ill-prepared. That crisis came, Hylson-Smith suggests, almost at a stroke as post-war society turned sharply towards the secularism that had been growing in Britain since the end of the Great War,[64] a tangible expression of which was the Labour Party's unexpected landslide victory in the 1945 General Election. It was not the end of that Christian-centred culture which had given Britain a particular identity, but it was the certain portent of that end being close. Hugh McLeod has pointed out that a range of alternative options in this period increasingly drew people away from church-going.[65] Only twenty years after the war the demise of Britain's

---

[59] Adrian Hastings, *A History of English Christianity 1920–1990* (London: SCM, 1991), 100.
[60] Ibid., 266.
[61] Randall, *English Baptists of the 20th Century*, 195.
[62] Hastings, *English Christianity 1920–1990*, xxii.
[63] Ibid., 437.
[64] Hylson-Smith, *Vol. III*, 216ff.
[65] Hugh McLeod, *The Religious Crisis of the 1960s* (Oxford: Oxford University Press, 2007), 29 and 170.

The Baptist Revival Fellowship

Christian heritage was complete, as Callum Brown has persuasively argued in *The Death of Christian Britain*.[66]

Hylson-Smith's view of the situation for Baptists is that their denomination had even more to lose than the other main Free Churches because the BU, according to his analysis, had been an exceptional beneficiary of greater Free Church respectability during the earlier decades of the twentieth century, moving it towards a more churchly style than was to be found in its traditional identity and to 'a more sedate and restrained tone for which the ever-increasing number and proportion of middle-class members was largely responsible.'[67] Consequently, he argues, the drastic increase of secularization in post-war society produced numerical decline for Baptists after the war as exceptional as was its social gain before the war, describing the decline as 'well under way by 1945.'[68] Hastings confirms the situation at the end of the war in his own discussion of the Baptist denomination in the 1940s. He reports that their membership for 1906 stood at 434,741 but by 1946 it had fallen to 354,900.[69] Hylson-Smith provides no evidence for his claim that there was exceptional Baptist decline after the war, but they certainly shared the misplaced optimism of all the denominations and if he is right, to a dangerous degree. Into this situation of considerable confusion in the face of radical change came the BRF's message that divine intervention was available and that nothing less could meet the need. It struck a note of confidence yet also of realism about the challenge before the churches and as a result the BRF achieved a new degree of popularity.

The first indication of increasing strength came as early as 1945, when the *BRF Bulletin* began publication, issued quarterly and edited by Bamber.[70] At this stage the Fellowship was well-focused on Union life. It has been pointed out already that Bamber and King were members of the strategy group for post-war Baptist advance. The movement also took an interest in local church growth. Randall notes that 'the largest group of Baptist churches in 1946 ... had under 50 members, and the BRF, with its concern for revival within local churches, sought to reach out to these congregations.'[71]

Growth continued in the years that followed, such that in 1954 the BRF was able to found an Annual Conference. The speakers that year were Duncan Campbell, the Scottish evangelist who had led a local revival in the Western

---

[66] C. G. Brown, *The Death of Christian Britain* (Abingdon: Routledge, 2001). See 1 and 193.
[67] Hylson-Smith, *Vol. III*, 193.
[68] Ibid., 256.
[69] Hastings, English Christianity 1920–1990, 265.
[70] Unfortunately, there are no editions from the first ten years in the BRF archive or in the libraries of Spurgeons or Regents Park Baptist Colleges. I have failed to locate any other sources.
[71] Baptists of the Twentieth Century, 230.

The Early Development of BRF Vision and Strategy (1938-1960)

Isles of Scotland in 1949, and the Baptist minister Stanley Voke, then at the prominent north-country Baptist church, Bethesda, Sunderland, who was also deeply concerned about spiritual renewal. The *BRF Bulletin* reported the attendance as consisting of 46 ministers.[72] The conference would grow in popularity over the next ten years, but the BRF's public commitment to the pietist-premillennialist outlook already made it out of step with the new style of conservative evangelicalism.

At the same time, as conservative evangelicalism was evolving away from the traditional Free Churches, the Baptist Union was becoming increasingly open to more liberal and ecumenical influences, threatening to marginalize the BRF in denominational life. In 1948, when the World Council of Churches (or WCC) came into being, the BU was one of its founding members. Conservative evangelicals usually viewed the WCC with suspicion, according to Oliver Barclay,[73] and it has already been noted that Bamber shared this viewpoint. The suspicion was mutual. The evangelical apologist Francis Schaeffer (1912–1984) reported hearing in 1947 the future WCC leader Visser't Hooft speak at a Youth Conference in Oslo, where 'he challenged the young people to confront the Bible-believing Christians in their churches in order to "drive the greyheads out" to have more churches in the World Council.'[74] However, neither perspective was universally held. British Baptist engagement in ecumenism was certainly an exception. Percy Evans, Principal of Spurgeon's College from 1925 until 1951, had been active in ecumenical affairs for some years before the WCC was founded, and George Beasley-Murray (1916–2000), Principal from 1958 until 1973, would follow his example in his time. Nor was it the case that evangelicalism was as despised within ecumenical circles as Schaeffer concluded from hearing Visser't Hooft. A popular and widely-read book in favour of post-war ecumenical advance was *The Coming Great Church* by Otto Wedel, published in 1945.[75] Wedel was an American Episcopalian cleric who had renounced his evangelical upbringing to become a High Churchman, but part of his ecumenical journey had involved renewing his appreciation of his evangelical heritage. In his introductory chapter, Wedel affirmed that:

> It has taken many years, indeed, before I have come to recognize again the full value of the evangelical heritage with which my life in the Church began. I see that value now – and the rediscovery has led me to appreciate once more Reformation evangelicalism generally. I

---

[72] *BRF Bulletin* No.42, April 1954, 2.
[73] Barclay, *Evangelicalism in Britain*, 58.
[74] L. G. Parker, *Francis Schaeffer: The Man and his Message* (Eastbourne: Kingsway Publications, 1985), 59.
[75] Otto Wedel, *The Coming Great Church* (New York: MacMillan, 1945).

> hope the following pages will give some evidence of this appreciation. But my experience leads me to a criticism of Protestant Evangelical Church life also.[76]

Paradoxically, the title of his book became standard conservative rhetoric for denouncing the World Council of Churches.[77]

E. A. Payne (1902–1980), became General Secretary of the BU in 1951 (remaining in office until 1967) following the retirement of M. E. Aubrey. He would lead the denomination in a strongly pro-ecumenical direction as one of his greatest priorities and he promoted a higher view of denominational authority than his predecessor, encouraging Baptists to consider structural changes to achieve it. Payne was not only less sympathetic to conservative evangelicalism than Aubrey, but was 'somewhat naturally shy,'[78] more remote as a personality than his predecessor. Percy Evans had keenly supported Payne's appointment and was aware that Payne needed to develop better relations with the conservative wing of the denomination. His offer of help was a major factor in Payne's decision to accept the office of General Secretary. However, Evans died suddenly just as Payne was taking up his new role. Ian Randall judges that Payne was personally devastated by this loss.[79] And there was ample reason for his reaction. Evans had been able to retain the admiration of conservatives while earning much respect in wider Baptist circles. He was capable of confronting liberal trends in theology without rancour. In a study of the atonement published in 1950, for example, he stated of universalism that 'Our commission as preachers does not include "the larger hope" but it does include "the largest love", the divine love which will do the utmost that can be done for man's salvation.'[80] His intellectual interests were revealed in this book, in which he engaged with the theological opinions of writers as diverse as Vincent Taylor (p. 15) and Edward Irving (p. 25), with the political writings of Gladstone (p. 37), and with the historians Macaulay (p. 53) and Trevelyan, (p. 53). Evans' sudden death was a setback as much to the place of conservatives in the denomination as to the acceptance of Payne. Evans was perceived to have held firmly to traditional evangelical theology and spirituality despite engaging with a wider theological world than his own. Thus, in a 1944 publication, when Evans had already become involved in ecumenical affairs

---

[76] Ibid., 6.

[77] In the 1960s, I frequently heard the phrase, or the variation of it, 'the coming world Church,' in denunciations of ecumenism as the home of 'The Anti-Christ.'

[78] Morris West, 'The 1961 Denominational Report,' in *Baptists Together: Papers Published in Memory of W. M. S. West, JP, MA, DTheol, Hon. LLD, 1922–1999* (Didcot: Baptist Historical Society, 2000), 72.

[79] Randall, *English Baptists of the Twentieth Century*, 262.

[80] Percy Evans, *The Cross as a Tree* (London: Marshall, Morgan & Scott, 1950), 50.

The Early Development of BRF Vision and Strategy (1938-1960)

through the Faith and Order Conference, Geoffrey King spoke of him as 'my beloved Principal, Mr. Evans.'[81]

Yet another setback was the retirement, in 1956, of Townley Lord as editor of *BT* (Lord had been part-time editor while also serving as minister of Bloomsbury Baptist Church), and his replacement by Walter Bottoms (1908–1996) as full-time editor. Bottoms was much less sympathetic to conservative evangelicals and wrote outspoken articles expressing his views. This was done despite the significant number of conservatives in the BU. The changes of direction that took place in this period and in particular the diminution of public affirmation for conservative Baptists exacerbated the potential for a collision course between the more liberal and conservative wings of the denomination.[82]

The conservative voice in the denomination was thus less central and less publicized than a generation before, yet the BRF was well placed to voice opposition to the new trends. The BRF certainly continued to grow during the fifties. This was reflected by the launch, in 1954, of what became an Annual BRF Conference.[83] The conference consolidated a network for developing relationships between like-minded ministers and church leaders, growing from an initial attendance of 46 to filling the High Leigh Conference centre by the end of the decade.[84] In its earlier phase the conference primarily addressed the central BRF agenda of revival, such as the event in 1954 when Duncan Campbell spoke of his experience in the Lewis Revival.[85] But it also provided a platform to discuss denominational issues and gave some authority to the BRF Committee as a representative voice within the BU. Furthermore, the *BRF Bulletin*, commenced in 1945, provided the means of circulating BRF concerns to its members. The Bulletins were published quarterly, and their recurring themes were the need for revival through

---

[81] In George E. Page, *A. G. B.: The Story of the Life and Work of Archibald Geike Brown* (London: Carey Kingsgate Press, 1944), 27. *And Finally* is a postscript by Geoffrey King, then pastor of East London Tabernacle, the church where Brown exercised his most influential ministry.

[82] Baptist Union churches and ministers have tended to avoid organised expressions of theological differences, so that references herein to liberals and conservatives should be understood as shorthand for differences of emphasis within an evangelical spectrum rather than as clearly defined movements or organised parties. Indeed, one of the main reasons for disquiet about BRF was probably its willingness to adopt a strategy of public organisation.

[83] D. Kingdon & R. Luland, *Liberty in the Lord* (London: Baptist Revival Fellowship, 1964), information stated in an introduction to the work of the BRF on the inside back cover.

[84] *BRF Bulletin* No. 63, January/March 1960, 1 reported that High Leigh had been filled for the 1959 Conference and No. 64 (April–June 1960) 4, that for the 1960 conference 'applications indicate a record attendance.'

[85] *BRF Bulletin* No. 41, January 1954, 1.

personal repentance, spiritual renewal in the churches, a return to the Bible, and the proclamation of the Lord's imminent return.

At this stage, the BRF was not strident in opposing liberal or ecumenical trends. For example, at the 1955 Annual Rally George Beasley-Murray, at that time ministering at Zion Baptist Church in Cambridge while he pursued his post-graduate studies at the university, spoke on *Baptists and Baptism*, despite his already public approval of BU engagement with ecumenism and of more liberal opinions than conservatives generally held, such as his endorsement of a late date for Daniel.[86] He was commended thus: 'all may be sure of a penetrating, stimulating exegesis of a vital issue.'[87] The annual conferences indicate the same spirit. In 1957 Godfrey Robinson gave the main addresses, a minister with a particular interest in liturgical worship, alongside Ernest Kevan, the first Principal of London Bible College and a BU minister (originally a Strict Baptist) who strove to establish LBC as an acceptable route into the BU ministry. Revival was not neglected as a subject, however. Robert Rowland also spoke that year, having been the main speaker only two years previously in 1955. Rowland was a BU minister who was becoming a popular choice to address the subject of revival because of remarkable scenes at evangelistic missions he conducted in the 1950s.[88]

But there was another note sounded in 1957, indicating a new development in the BRF. Geoffrey King spoke that year on 'the possibility of closing the gap between those of differing biblical suppositions.' This is the first mention in the BRF of a different conservative mentality from pietist-premillennialism. The obvious explanation was the growing influence of D. Martyn Lloyd-Jones, as evidenced by his appearance as a speaker at the BRF Conference in 1956 and his increasing number of Baptist preaching engagements for the period.[89] Bamber and Lloyd-Jones did not see eye to eye on matters of theology or experience, and it is obvious from the editorial content of the *BRF Bulletin* that Bamber was an autocrat and a dogmatist who treated disagreement with him as a spiritual weakness if not a personal affront. It could not have been a happy experience to see his status in the BRF diminished by the growth within it of a different theological outlook under a 'rival' evangelical leader. That King rather than Bamber should address internal differences is suggestive of Bamber feeling that he was more

---

[86] See George Beasley-Murray, 'A conservative Thinks again about Daniel' in *BQ* Vol. 12, (1946–48), 367ff.
[87] Advertised in *BRF Bulletin* No. 42, April 1954, 3.
[88] I heard him speak about these at the Keswick-in-Wales Convention in the mid-sixties, mentioning especially a mission held in Hay-on-Wye.
[89] See Appendix Fourteen. In the 1950s, Lloyd-Jones developed a growing network of BU ministers for whom he preached.

The Early Development of BRF Vision and Strategy (1938-1960)

personally involved than King and there is circumstantial evidence to that effect.

The first indication is that there would seem to have been little personal warmth between Bamber and Lloyd-Jones. Lloyd-Jones preached for several leading BRF figures including King, but not, according to his preaching diaries, for Bamber at Rye Lane. This is all the more remarkable because their two churches shared a certain flagship status among Free Church conservative evangelicals in London, Westminster Chapel north of the Thames and Rye Lane Baptist Church south of it. Lloyd-Jones was noted for readily accepting invitations to preach and therefore it is very probable that Bamber declined to make Lloyd-Jones such an invitation. And in fairness, Bamber had built up the BRF ministerial membership to a similar size as the Westminster Fellowship within a single denomination, and had done so on a well-accepted foundation of Keswick teaching. Now he had to face being overshadowed not only by a man his own age but by one who had a quite different theological outlook. That Bamber did not altogether like this can be gleaned from the fact that, although he is known to have joined the Westminster Fellowship sometime in the later fifties or early sixties,[90] his poor attendance was noted, drawing comment from fellow Baptists and BRF supporters.[91] Bamber was watching his influence wane, to the point of having to raise the question in the conference programme of different mentalities in the BRF. A man of Bamber's temperament would find that hard to take.

The wider ecumenical scene also disturbed Bamber in 1957, probably as a result of an apparently successful agreement between the Anglican and main Presbyterian denominations of England and Scotland, in which 'bishops, consecrated by Anglicans, were to be appointed as permanent moderators of presbyteries in England and Scotland.'[92] Although the scheme was ultimately rejected, Bamber was convinced that an ecumenical conspiracy was secretly taking place in which the BU was itself involved. Writing in the *BRF Bulletin* for March/June 1957, for example, he appears convinced that ecumenical conversations had gone much further than their public manifestation, to such an extent that secret agreement was close about 'an interim accommodation' for those existing ministers who disapproved of Episcopal ordination, while every ordinand thereafter would be obliged to

---

[90] No records survive of the Westminster Fellowship prior to the 1980s to provide more definite information.
[91] I received this information in a personal conversation with Basil Howlett, an FIEC minister and the current secretary of the Westminster Fellowship, who has regularly attended since the 1960s when he was a BU minister. He recalled Bamber's infrequent attendance and hearing comments about it from fellow Baptists in view of his leadership of BU conservatives.
[92] Hastings, *English Christianity 1920–1990*, 469.

receive it. With unusual confidence for one who took no part in ecumenical discussions, he declared:

> It is useless to ignore the fact that Baptists are contemplating some scheme of this kind. Baptists know very well that Anglicans will not budge on episcopacy ... they know that we know that episcopacy must be in the united Church, which means that in actual fact the Free Churches are to be absorbed with a view to their ultimate elimination.[93]

Bamber came increasingly to the view that within Baptist life there was a growing tendency to desert what he saw as historical evangelicalism. For example, he attacked the BU Citizenship Department for 'urging churches to become members of the United Nations Organisation,' saying that through this call Baptists had actually been 'dragged down to be the appendage of a political organization, pagan, godless, and earthly.'[94] Similarly, when invited to contribute a response in 1958 to the BU report *The Meaning and Practice of Ordination Among Baptists*, Bamber somewhat perverted a reference to properly ordained ministers having a right to be recognized by secular authorities to mean that their spiritual authority depended on such recognition, earning an unusual printed rebuke from the Editorial Board of the *The Fraternal*, the Baptist ministers' magazine in which it was published.[95] By 1958 he was even using apocalyptic language, claiming to discern that God's answer to prayers for peace was imminent judgment rather than deliverance. He scornfully speculated that 'someone will probably want a public resolution passed at the Assembly concerning the awfulness of a nuclear war, but it is doubtful whether any reference will be made to the oncoming judgments of God.'[96] Bamber was despairing of the future for evangelicalism in the denomination. When the editor of *BT*, Walter Bottoms, accused traditional evangelicals of being incapable of social involvement, Bamber simply wished it were more the case, saying:

> we are not here to make good citizens; we are here that men and women, through faith in Christ, may be born again! There are good citizens who can do good work of a political and social nature, but nobody can open the eyes of the blind to the need of being born again except the believer himself brought out of darkness into light. We

---

[93] *BRF Bulletin* No. 53, March/June 1957, 1.
[94] *BRF Bulletin* No. 54, July/September 1957, 1.
[95] *The Fraternal*, No. 107, January 1958, 14–15.
[96] *BRF Bulletin* No. 56, January/March 1958, 1.

> may be certain that good Christians will be good citizens, but there are many good citizens who are not Christians.[97]

It may be that Bamber took matters personally to the point of losing his equilibrium. It is certainly the case that his fundamentalist instincts were drawn out by the growth of ecumenism and liberalism in the denomination and that he openly speculated that there was an anti-evangelical conspiracy within it. Bamber was moving not only into more fundamentalist territory but also into a darker personal space.

The Carey Hall Dispute

At this point Bamber found an issue which he was able to turn into a major dispute, and through it he moved the BRF publicly towards more fundamentalist attitudes. In 1958, the BRF Committee felt it had discerned liberal trends in the Baptist Missionary Society (or BMS), the independent missionary arm of the denomination founded in 1792.[98] The committee approached the BMS, asking that women candidates should have liberty to train elsewhere than Carey Hall, the official training centre for female Baptist missionary candidates. Carey Hall was perceived as too partial, biased in favour of liberal theological beliefs. It was reported in the *Bulletin* that the BRF Committee had attempted 'to secure an assurance from the officers of the BMS that this would be done' but without success. A letter was then written to *BT*, which was declined for publication. Bamber went on to state:

> that he has felt for many years that the colour bar in some parts of the world is matched by a doctrinal bar within our denomination. Send your money up and by return of post you have a delightful letter of thanks; make a plea for liberty of conscience and there are obstacles all along the road.[99]

Bamber's concluding paragraph shows his awareness that this might be perceived as a fundamentalist-style attack on the denomination:

> We are not schismatics, we harbour no rancour, we are not interested in personalities, we do not wish to score points in argument. So far as we know our own hearts, we are more than grateful for all the personal relationships we enjoy within the Denomination with those who differ from us, and it is in sincere Christian love that we make our appeal.'[100]

---

[97] *BRF Bulletin* No. 58, July/September 1958, 3.
[98] For the background in the BMS context see Stanley, *History of BMS*, 377–81.
[99] *BRF Bulletin* No. 59, October/December 1958, 2–3: 'Liberty of Conscience.'
[100] Ibid.

The Baptist Revival Fellowship

Perhaps it was the BRF membership that he was concerned to reassure, since he certainly would have been resisted if it was thought that he was a rancorous schismatic. The reason people joined the BRF was precisely that it existed as a BU movement. Moreover, King's attitude was very different from Bamber's. In his 1957 collection of published sermons *Truth For Our Time*, King gave the title *Apostolic Christianity* to an exposition of Acts 5:29–32. Far from labouring the case for biblicism over against liberal theology, the shortest of his four points concerned apostolic doctrine, and for King the heart of it was the conviction that 'the Jesus who was crucified is risen, is ascended, is reigning, is saving.'[101] Norman Moon, a more liberal minister than King, reviewed the book for *The Fraternal*, the quarterly magazine of the denomination-wide Baptist Ministers Fellowship. Moon described King's spirit well, saying that 'there is no carping criticism of those not agreeing with the preacher, nor of any scolding of the congregation. The purpose all through is to exalt the Glorified Lord and to bring men to his feet.'[102] King shows himself here to echo the Christ-centredness of Meyer and also of the Spurgeonic tradition, rather more than Bamber with his greater approval of fundamentalist emphases.

The public report in the *BRF Bulletin* of these two unanswered approaches prompted a reply from J. B. Middlebrook (1894–1977), Home Secretary for the BMS, which was reproduced, with his permission, in the *BRF Bulletin* No.60 (January/March 1959). Middlebrook repudiated the claim that candidates were sent to Carey Hall 'in order that their theological convictions may be undermined and changed.'[103] He enumerated several practical reasons for using Carey Hall exclusively and concluded, 'They are sent to be trained in understanding of, and respect for, theological convictions other than their own, whatever they may be.' However, Middlebrook then undermined his own case by adding, 'We can quote cases where candidates of the conservative school emerged from Carey Hall with their original convictions as strongly held as ever, but held with full and sympathetic understanding of and tolerance for the views of others.'[104] This provided Bamber with the opportunity to suggest not only that some candidates did not survive as happily, but that there was indeed a one-sided theological emphasis. He noted that no mention was made by Middlebrook of 'those with liberal ideas when they entered Carey Hall who have derived such benefits from its curriculum that they have emerged strong and zealous conservatives.'[105] The perception was that there was not an equal

---

[101] Geoffrey King, *Truth For Our Time* (London: Lutterworth Press, 1957), 84.
[102] *The Fraternal*, No. 108, April 1958, 39.
[103] *BRF Bulletin* No. 60, January/March 1959, 1.
[104] Ibid.
[105] Ibid., 2.

The Early Development of BRF Vision and Strategy (1938-1960)

presentation of different theological convictions, nor any intention to challenge more liberal ideas, and Middlebrook was taken to have admitted as much. Middlebrook eventually took Bamber's request for a choice of colleges to be available before the BMS General Committee, and provided a formal response on their behalf on January 21, 1960, which was published in the same manner as the others. The General Committee had instructed Middlebrook to affirm the existing policy but to promise that 'if a candidate expresses a conscientious scruple concerning theological training at any particular college, sympathetic consideration will be given to the possibility of alternative arrangements for such a candidate.'[106] Bamber's suspicions were not allayed. He interpreted this as a mere deceit, on the basis that 'the promise is not compliance but "consideration."' His judgement of the BMS was that '"conservative" Baptists are only tolerated in the Baptist Missionary Society. They are not wanted and the day will be welcomed when this awkward squad is entirely eliminated from the Churches.'[107] One cannot help suspecting that Bamber was universalizing here how he experienced the Union himself. There is no doubt that conservatives were being thrown on to the back foot as liberals generally came to the fore in British Church life, but not all conservatives in the denomination shared his experience or his dyspeptic outlook. There seems to have been a particular frustration over the BMS, perhaps exacerbated by Bamber's church being habitually generous to the organisation. There was a suspicion that conservative evangelicals were treated as valuable providers but not partners in policy-making. The sense of being a disempowered minority within the BU grew.

Bamber continued his more confrontational style in *Bulletin No. 61*, April/June 1959. He warned the Baptist Union against falling into the trap of exercising 'carnal ownership instead of faithful stewardship'[108] of the denomination and citing (without quite saying so or identifying individuals) what appear to be instances in which he judged that this had happened. In the following edition he criticized *BT* for devoting its front page to allowing the leaders of the political parties to state their policies in the run-up to a General Election.[109] Bamber complained that ordinary Baptists would never be given such an opportunity on behalf of their churches or organizations, in contrast with 'these people, non-Baptists, architects of carnal policy, exponents of political vanity.'[110] Bamber's anti-political pietism was evident

---

[106] *BRF Bulletin* No. 60, January/March 1960, 1.
[107] Ibid., 2.
[108] *BRF Bulletin* No. 61, April/June 1959, 1.
[109] *BRF Bulletin* No. 62, October 1959, 1.
[110] Ibid.

once again. He believed that to encourage young Christians towards political matters was 'a most dangerous leaning.'[111]

Conclusions

The BRF began as a movement firmly rooted in the pietist tradition. Although its insistence on the spiritual poverty of the BU may have offended some, the Keswick message essentially represented by the BRF was sufficiently respectable to be recognized as an authentic voice among Baptists. More than that, it gave expression to widely held concerns among conservative evangelical Baptists for the spiritual renewal of church life as well as their own personal lives. This provided the first impetus that contributed to the growth of the BRF. With the emergence of Anglican-led post-war conservatism, the BRF became somewhat marginalized in evangelical life. In parallel with that, with the post-war advance of liberalism and ecumenism in Baptist circles the BRF became somewhat marginalized in Baptist denominational life, despite attracting growing support at grass-roots level. During the 1950s, however, a second phase of growth began under the influence of post-war conservatism and sometimes of Lloyd-Jones himself. These new conservatives were more theologically literate and confident than their predecessors. Thus, the BRF began to show contradictory aspects, sometimes positive towards the Union and sometimes negative, sometimes open to 'other biblical suppositions' and sometimes defensively reiterating the premillennial message of Christ's 'soon return.' Bamber himself was less certainly the leading personality and perhaps this made him feel somewhat threatened and defensive. He began to move in a more fundamentalist direction while many in the younger generation were more interested in debating the issues, following their theological mentor, Lloyd-Jones.

---

[111] Ibid.

CHAPTER THREE

THE PROBLEM OF PAYNE: BRF RESPONSES TO A NEW BAPTIST AGENDA (1960–1966)

A distinct and important phase in the BRF will now be discussed, discernable between 1960 and 1966. During this period, it moved on from presenting only the need for spiritual renewal or resisting anti-evangelical trends. Instead, the BRF became proactive concerning three key elements of denominational life which Payne promoted as General Secretary: greater theological breadth, centralizing policies, and ecumenical engagement. The BRF saw these three issues as directly connected. Denominational centralization was the necessary prelude to participation in a united Church, and therefore was directly related to the ecumenical agenda. Reunion could only be achieved through theological convergence, which implied for the BRF the ascendancy of liberal Protestantism in ecumenism as the means of achieving a reductionist approach to denominational and evangelical convictions, together with a sacramentalist theology to which Protestants would also have to agree. The BRF saw signs both of liberal reductionism and of sacramentalist accretions in modern Baptist thinking.[1] Therefore, it was considered necessary for the BRF to present a simultaneous and integrated case against all three issues.

The BRF and Liberalism

In the 1960s, the older form of liberal theology was somewhat displaced by a more radical perspective which initially seemed capable of communicating powerfully with an increasingly unchurched population. It received wide attention through the publication in 1963 of *Honest To God*, a radical polemic in popular language written by J. A. T. Robinson, Bishop of Woolwich.[2] It was, comments Hylson-Smith:

> inspired by three German theologians: Rudolf Bultman, Dietrich Bonhoeffer and Paul Tillich. Bultmann, with his concern to "demythologize" the gospel, was a challenge to the "biblical" theologians. Bonhoeffer, with his vision of a "religionless" Christianity, was a challenge to Christian escapism and undue pietism. Tillich, with his philosophy based on faith as ultimate

---

[1] Paul Goodliff has indicated the greater sacramental emphasis in Baptist life after the war and Payne's important place in it, in Paul Goodliff, *Ministry, Sacrament and Representation* (Oxford: Centre for Baptist History and Heritage, Regent's Park College, 2010). See especially 147ff.
[2] John Robinson, *Honest To God*, (London: SCM, 1963).

concern" with the "ground of our being" was a reminder of the call of the church to embrace all mankind in its concern.[3]

The book caused a considerable stir, becoming a runaway best-seller after being reviewed by *The Observer* in March of that year, 'when readers were confronted with a special article ... entitled "Our Image Of God Must Go".'[4] Robinson confidently rejected traditional concepts of the supernatural, of morality, and of God himself, offering in their place a naturalistic interpretation of religious experience and an existential morality. His dismissive attitude towards traditional orthodoxies led to condemnation of his views both by the High Church theologian E. L. Mascall and the Evangelical Anglican theologian J. I. Packer, though the liberal evangelical Max Warren praised it.[5] B. G. Worrall, in his survey of modern British Christianity, claims that 'many who felt the attraction of a spiritual interpretation of life but could not accept orthodox Christianity as they understood it were happy to accept this approach.'[6]

Bamber did not attack Robinson by name, but accused such attacks on orthodoxy at the time as a hypocritically 'illiberal liberalism,' saying of such liberalism that 'false religion is always marked by despotic dogmatism.'[7] By contrast, he said of the truly spiritual person:

> It is inevitable therefore that as the believer moves onward experimentally in the life of the Spirit he must know with what subtlety evil things can present themselves as good. Satan himself is transformed into an angel of light. As the time draws near for the Lord's return, so deception will become more active and increase.[8]

Bamber had always regarded the liberal theological perspective as antithetical to biblical faithfulness, but in this passage he adopted a more fundamentalist tone. Liberal teachings are 'evil things' that 'present themselves as good,' the fulfilment of Paul's warning in 1 Corinthians that Satan can be apparently transformed into an angel of light, and an example of the activities of the Antichrist, the false Christ whose 'deception will become more active and increase' in the last days. His ultimate verdict on the divide between liberal and conservative theology was that 'vital fellowship between the spiritual and the carnal is an impossibility even if they belong to the same denomination.'[9] Bamber's comment at this point is extremely

---

[3] Hylson-Smith *Vol. III*, 231.
[4] Hastings, *English Christianity 1920–1990*, 536.
[5] Hylson-Smith *Vol. III*, 232–236.
[6] Worrall, *The Making of the Modern Church*, 284.
[7] *BRF Bulletin* No. 76, July/September 1963, 3.
[8] Ibid.
[9] *BRF Bulletin* No. 77, October/December 1963, 1.

significant, indicating the essential rejection of his previous commitment to the inclusive nature of the BU. For Bamber an impasse was reached in the early sixties. In 1961 he concluded, while considering the attendance of Baptists at the New Delhi Assembly of the WCC:

> we Baptists cannot find a common ground [between liberals and conservatives]. Whether our denomination is flirting at Delhi or really contemplating engagement with a view to marriage is a secret not divulged. The moderns are in a majority.[10]

The BRF and Ecumenism

As early as 1927, Bamber had published views critical of ecumerism, probably (as noted previously) in reaction to the first Faith and Order Conference taking place that year:

In religion, the note is unity. Every disciple of the Lord Jesus Christ must deplore the marks of division in the Church visible. Even so, we must always remember that the true Church of the redeemed, the church invisible, is not divided, it is the Body of Christ in unbroken unity, an organism not an organisation. True unity of the Spirit is realized through obedience to the Spirit-given Word of Holy Scripture.[11]

Bamber did not attack ecumenism in the name of the BRF until the late fifties, in part perhaps because Percy Evans, the long-serving Principal of Spurgeon's College, was a widely respected conservative and also an ecumenist. By the sixties, however, Evans had been dead for almost ten years and Bamber had become a member of the Westminster Fellowship founded by Lloyd-Jones, where anti-ecumenism was a definite policy. The ecumenical movement then came more clearly and regularly within his purview.[12] In 1960 Bamber compared 'The Desolate House' of the Jerusalem over which Jesus wept with the modern church scene in Britain, including Baptists: 'when the truth of God is rejected the house cannot stand. Do Baptists believe this?'[13] He went on to warn Baptists that the Anglican Church was more interested in closer relations with Rome than with the Free Churches[14] – a judgment that would prove true enough in time. Such a church, it was believed, posed a total and imminent threat to evangelicalism. For those who were Baptists, it posed an additional threat to their ecclesiological existence

---

[10] *BRF Bulletin* No. 67, January/March 1961, 1.
[11] Bamber, *His Glorious Appearing*, 20.
[12] Anti-ecumenical comments, especially of anti-Roman Catholic nature, frequently appear from 1961 onwards: e.g. Nos. 69, 70, 71, 72, 73, 74, and 75 covering 1961–1963.
[13] *BRF Bulletin* No. 69, July/September 1960, 2.
[14] Ibid., 3.

as 'gathered churches' delineated by credo-baptism and Independency. It was for reasons of this kind that the Baptist Union of Scotland in 1957 withdrew for some years from the World Council of Churches, and both the Baptist Union of Ireland and the Strict Baptist Assembly declined to join it at all. These were not the fears of a jaundiced few. Brian Stanley has judged that 'although the anti-ecumenical stance of the BRF received little support from denominational leaders, it appealed to the large number of British Baptists who viewed the ecumenical movement with suspicion, if not hostility.'[15] The BRF voiced a widely held opinion. Indeed, even the Baptist World Alliance judged it expedient to remain distant from Rome by declining representation at Vatican II, somewhat to the ire of Walter Bottoms in *BT*.[16]

In the 1960s, ecumenism developed as perhaps the single most important issue in British church life. The recently-elected Pope John XXIII created the Secretariat for Promoting Christian Unity in 1958 and in 1960 Geoffrey Fisher, Archbishop of Canterbury, made the first, albeit private, visit of an Anglican Primate to Rome since before the Reformation, the final stage after visits that included Jerusalem and Constantinople during an 'Ecumenical Pilgrimage' which Fisher had undertaken prior to his retirement.[17] In 1961 came the New Delhi Assembly of the World Council of Churches, at which the Orthodox Churches were first represented, with the Assembly calling for an inter-relationship between evangelism and ecumenical co-operation; and in 1962 the Second Vatican Council opened with its ground-breaking acknowledgement of the need for Christian unity. In 1964, the British Council of Churches held the 'Nottingham Conference' which called, rather hopefully, for full re-union by Easter, 1980.[18] Ecumenism would no longer be limited to an essentially Protestant project, but what was a stupendous advance to pro-ecumenists appeared to Bamber (and many other conservative evangelicals) to be an imminent threat to the gospel message recovered by the Reformation. Three concerns were commonly expressed, that a united Church would have an exclusively sacramentalist view of grace embodied in compulsory ritualism; that it would exercise oppressive control over member churches to the point of silencing evangelical preaching; and that it would become an inter-faith body without even a basic priority given to the Lordship of Christ. David Pawson was neither an extreme conservative nor a leader within the BRF but in an article for *The Fraternal* he expressed similar views. He enumerated as many as five concerns: 'a

---

[15] Stanley, *History of BMS*, 417.
[16] Bamber commented disparagingly in the *BRF Bulletin* on Bottoms' judgement in *BT* that the BWA decision was 'a blow to better relations.' *BRF Bulletin* No. 73, September/October 1962, 3.
[17] Hastings, *English Christianity 1920–1990*, 522.
[18] See Bernard Leeming, 'The Nottingham Conference, in *The Furrow*, Vol. 15, No. 11 (November 1964), 709–713, at www.jstor.org/stable/27658850

The Problem of Payne: BRF Responses to New Baptist Agenda (1938-66)

syncretist trend in membership' which failed 'to define a Christian brother in terms of being born again of the Spirit'; 'a latitudinarian trend in doctrine' which ignored New Testament warnings 'against doctrinal compromise'; 'a sacerdotal trend in ministry' which neglected 'those fundamental insights of the New Testament which were rediscovered at the time of the Reformation'; 'a connexional trend in policy' in favour of 'hierarchical personages and representative councils' that might 'make the decisions at national and international level'; and 'a totalitarian trend in authority' which 'could be used' in fulfillment of the biblically prophesied 'one world state with an established religion led by a man of Christ-like appearance' that 'will be of the devil, not God.'[19]

With regard to sacramentalism and ritualism, BRF members noted the strength of Anglo-Catholicism and feared that it would develop even further to reverse the Protestant identity of the Anglican Church and carry its ecumenical partners with it on a journey back to Rome. This is reflected in repeated moments of high anti-ritualist rhetoric in the *BRF Bulletin*. For example, in the last edition for 1961 Bamber declaimed, 'The world loves a priest; it hates and detests the prophet.... Ritualism, the poliomyelitis of the religious world, is already spreading its contagion, even in Baptist churches.'[20] Bamber called for prayer, Bible reading and vigilance, and then followed this with a peroration that began:

> Let us be sure this is the supreme need at this tragic hour in world history. The sands are running out! The extraordinary enthusiasm for linking up our Evangelical churches with the dead and discredited ecclesiastical systems of the world tolls the death knell of the departing day. It is probably true that we cannot avert it but at least we can stand true and steadfast. [21]

This edition of *BRF Bulletin* marks a turning point in the BRF's public attitude to the denomination, and indeed, in its own agenda. Previously, the repeated theme was the need for spiritual revival and the policy was to work faithfully within the BU structures as friends and colleagues, if critical ones at times. In this edition of *The Bulletin*, a new issue rose to the top of the agenda and would remain there through the sixties: anti-ecumenism mixed with express doubts about the feasibility of remaining within the Union.

Bamber's view that Rome presented a genuine threat to the evangelical tradition was by no means uncommon among Baptists. Even W. D. Jackson (1894–1980), the Area Superintendent for London, reiterated it in his

---

[19] David Pawson, '1980: Must They Include Us In?' in *The Fraternal*, No. 136, 9–13.
[20] *BRF Bulletin* No. 70, October/December 1961, 2.
[21] Ibid., 3.

Presidential Address at the 1962 Baptist Union Assembly. He spoke of implacable Baptist hostility to the 'Church of Rome' on the basis of its being 'an enemy of the truth.' Jackson nevertheless called Baptists to engage fully with the British and World Council of Churches.[22] Bamber commented on Jackson's speech in the *BRF Bulletin*.[23] He considered the two affirmations incompatible, stating that 'there can be no logical reason for the World Council of Churches if, in its desire for Christian unity, it does not envisage some association with Rome. Certainly the Anglicans think this way.'

The second concern expressed by Bamber regarding ecumenism was that it would lead to a united and controlling Church, which he saw as inevitably opposed to the Independency of Baptist ecclesiology. Payne admitted that the goal of the ecumenical movement was to achieve unity, but he believed completely that Baptists should be committed to it in order to bear testimony to their distinctive witness, for example writing in 1959:

> Baptist representation in the World Council increases. Those associated with it find new opportunities of bearing their distinctive witness and of sharing in united Christian enterprises. This becomes the more important as ecumenical discussion begins to turn to the subject of baptism and as "united churches" come into existence.[24]

Bamber, however, did not believe that it would be possible for traditional evangelicals to 'bear their distinctive witness.' He was in no doubt that a re-united Church would be dominated by 'the Roman and Anglican Communions to which one day may be added the Free Churches when they have been episcopally shaped and obscurantically dismembered.'[25] Some evangelicals perceived ecumenism as even an immediate threat to the Free Church tradition when the Methodist-Anglican talks on re-union began in 1963 and the validity of non-episcopal orders became central, yet only a year later the British Council of Churches Nottingham Conference called for full re-union by Easter Sunday, 1980. Bamber believed that the Methodist reunion scheme constituted a warning to the other Free Churches, predicting that:

> Before the end of this century Methodists as such will have ceased to exist. The Parish Church will have added a few to its local congregation. The Methodist buildings will be up for sale or used as Parish Halls for all those things that the Parish Church Council loves. All that Wesley stood for will be in oblivion .... Unless we see this

---

[22] Reported in *BT*, May 3, 1962, 8.
[23] *BRF Bulletin* No. 72, April/June 1962, 2.
[24] *BQ*, Vol. 18 (1959–60) 265.
[25] *BRF Bulletin* No. 75, April/June 1963, 1.

> clearly, and NOW, then by the end of the century at the latest, there will be no use for a baptistery, making Christians by sprinkling at the font will be the only baptism known, Baptist Churches built at great sacrifice in this century and before, will be sold and the proceeds passed over by Act of Parliament to this thing that is called the united Church.[25]

Bamber's third concern was his prognosis that a united Church would become an inter-faith body shorn of its Christian content. The ecumenical prospect was even worse than an unhappy union of theologically disparate Protestants, or even a return to Roman sacerdotalism. It was a church so corrupt that it would be anti-Christ in nature, an evil political superpower rather than a spiritual fellowship:

> Probably it will come; Baptists will find themselves the prodigal sons of a World Church of which the Pope is the titular head, ultimately embracing the great pagan religions of the East and so exercising sway over the political powers of the world. Today we may laugh at such a possibility. Tomorrow the little flock maintaining the truth will marvel at our blindness.

Bamber regarded ecumenism as entirely the wrong approach to the decline of church attendance, one reason that was indeed put forward in favour of uniting the churches. His criticism of modern church life was that it was spiritually moribund. In 1961 he stated his belief that 'our fraternals, association meetings and annual assemblies are bogged down in a religious politico-social rut. We are a valley of dry bones.'[27] The BRF existed to call the BU to seek revival. Two years later he was even less convinced that the churches of Britain would heed that call. Instead, 'our hope is now directed to the closer union of our ecclesiastical systems as if a cemetery wedded to a cemetery will bring forth life when in reality we are a consortium of death.'[28]

The BRF and Denominational Centralization

The BRF was strongly attached to the traditional Baptist ecclesiology of Independency. Payne was not, and encouraged debate both about its credentials in Baptist history and about its value in modern denominational and ecumenical life. As far as the BRF was concerned, centralization and ecumenism were linked by the fact that the Baptists could not become part of a united church unless they had adopted a hierarchy of some kind that could then be adapted to the wider structure, which according to Bamber's

---

[26] *BRF Bulletin* No. 75, April/June 1963, 2–3.
[27] *BRF Bulletin* No. 67, January/March 1961, 3.
[28] *BRF Bulletin* No. 77, October/December 1963, 3.

analysis, would be some form of episcopacy.[29] Payne initiated an informal debate about these issues early in his time as General Secretary. In May 1961, he assembled a 'Denominational Conference' (at The Hayes Conference Centre in Swanwick, Derbyshire) to identify a definite programme for change. A summary statement was issued proposing 'interdependency' of the churches, a stronger role for the Associations, greater control of ministerial settlement and removal, the grouping of churches, new initiatives to educate and disciple church members, the establishment of commissions to study the issues in more depth, and finally a complaint that Baptists frequently misunderstood world affairs and the ecumenical movement.[30] This last item might seem incongruous, but it was a tacit acknowledgment that a link existed between the denominational and ecumenical agenda. Structural change had within it the possibility of at least reducing the significant obstacle to reunion of Baptist Independency. Randall judges that the Denominational Conference proposed in effect 'a significant move towards seeing the Union as "an association of Associations",' rather than as a union of local churches.[31]

The first report that publicly followed the Conference, produced under the chairmanship of L. G. Champion, was on 'The Doctrine of the Ministry.' This had been in the pipeline for some time, having been presented already to the General Purposes and Finance (or GP&F) Committee in February of that year. In 1964 a Commission on Liturgy was created but did not produce a report while Payne was in office.[32] In 1966, at the request of the Youth Department, another report was prepared under the chairmanship of G. W. Rusling, entitled 'The Child and The Church.' However, the key document was the report of a Commission established in 1962 under the leadership of W. M. S. West to consider the nature and practice of Association life. This duly reported to the Union in March 1964.[33] It recommended, among other things, 'a re-thinking of the relationship of the Association to the Union;'[34] that the BU should be 'the Associations associating together;'[35] that the

---

[29] This was a conclusion consistently drawn by the BRF about plans for centralisation. For example, see their 'Report of the BRF Sub-Committee concerning the 1964 Report of the Commission on the Associations' in the *BRF Bulletin* No. 86, January/March 1966, 5–6; and an article by David Pawson in response to the call by Kenneth Dykes for Baptists to join in the plan for Congregationalists and Presbyterians to unite to create the United Reformed Church in No. 87, April/June 1966, 5–6.
[30] See the full statement in Appendix Five.
[31] Randall, English Baptists of the Twentieth Century, 329.
[32] Perhaps because it was involved in producing the ecumenical *Joint Liturgical Report* of 1965.
[33] The report is contained in British Baptist Statements 1948–67, (a bound collection held at the Angus Library, Regents Park Baptist College, Oxford).
[34] Report on Association, 1.
[35] Ibid., 1.

The Problem of Payne: BRF Responses to New Baptist Agenda (1938-66)

Declaration of Principle could be used as 'a basis of doctrine';[36] the abolition of personal membership of the Union;[37] and the strengthening of the BU Council as 'the basic legislative body with the Assembly remaining as an occasion for fellowship and inspiration.'[38] Essentially, the report argued for a stronger role for the Associations locally and also nationally through basing the BU Council more on their elected representatives, with a corresponding need to ensure 'best practice' in Association life. By implication, this would change the centre of gravity in Baptist life from the local church to something more like a Presbyterian structure.

'Liberty in the Lord'

The BRF responded to the recommendations of the Denominational Conference by creating, parallel with the BU Commission on Association life, its own group to study the issues. This group produced its report in 1964, published under the title *Liberty in the Lord*. Although the two statements, from the Union and the BRF, seem to have been produced without any formal dialogue (there was informal contact) between the two groups of contributors, those who were behind *Liberty in the Lord* did have available to them another statement advocating change in the Baptist denomination. This was the 1963 publication by four leading Baptist Union thinkers, *The Pattern of the Church*.[39] W. M. S. West used his contribution to advocate a higher doctrine of the Church than Baptists generally held, including a more sacramental view of baptism in which 'God is involved ... the Church is involved ... the individual is involved'[40] and suggesting that the Baptist Union should be understood as a 'Baptist Church' where it was 'the logical thing to ordain men to the ministry of Jesus Christ'[41] centrally rather than the traditional practice of ordination taking place in and to a local church. Neville Clark contributed a theological essay on the nature of the church. He believed the structure of the Church should be worked out 'at the point of eucharistic assembly; for it is exactly in Eucharistic fellowship that the Church is given form and shaping under the Gospel as body of Christ.'[42] Alec Gilmore addressed 'Baptist Churches Today and Tomorrow,' building his understanding on the church 'as a community of love' that will 'include service to all the members of the community.'[43] He called for greater focus

---

[36] Ibid., 2.
[37] Ibid., 3.
[38] Ibid., 3.
[39] A. Gilmore (ed.), *The Pattern of the Church* (London: Lutterworth Press, 1963).
[40] Ibid., 38.
[41] Ibid., 51.
[42] Ibid., 101.
[43] Ibid., 114.

on a 'liturgical pattern' for worship,[44] for the local church 'to be willing to have her freedom restricted and to listen to others,'[45] 'association synods' with power to limit Independency,[46] and 'one comprehensive system of training organized on a national basis.'[47] Reunion was not thought to be an easy path, but 'action now' was demanded to educate the churches and to 'initiate conversations with our separated brethren.'[48] These issues, already signalled by the Denominational Report of 1962, provided the agenda for *Liberty in the Lord*.[49]

Eight men were invited to prepare the BRF booklet designed to answer denominational trends. The group operated independently of the BRF Committee, though six members of the group were nevertheless from it.[50] Two contributed papers (David Kingdon, a minister in West Wales who would eventually become Principal of the Irish Baptist College, and Ron Luland, a Spurgeon's graduate ministering in Bedford), while the other members listed were A. Morgan Derham (who would become the General Secretary of the Evangelical Alliance in 1966), Ivor J. W. Oakley (who would eventually succeed David Kingdon as Principal of the Irish Baptist College), and two local ministers well-regarded for their interest in theology, Samuel Nash and Herbert Ward.[51] Luland was 'appointed leader by his colleagues' according to the *BRF Bulletin*.[52] Randall notes that this booklet has been judged an important publication for its recognition of increasing secularization in church life and its articulation 'of the views of many conservative evangelicals.'[53] Leonard Champion had read it by June and persuaded the BU Officers' Meeting of June 5 to take up one of its

---

[44] Ibid., 120.
[45] Ibid., 144.
[46] Ibid., 149.
[47] Ibid., 156.
[48] Ibid., 163.
[49] It should be noted that the BRF had more than a theological interest in challenging greater centralization. In 1963, correspondence began between a Baptist insurance broker and the BRF committee concerning the terms of the BU Ministerial Superannuation Scheme. Gordon Anscombe, an Insurance and Annuity Consultant, pointed out that the scheme had recently increased its premiums by 50%. He was concerned that ministers would have to pay uncompetitive rates of contribution, but even more that the scheme was so devised as to 'tie the employee to the "firm"' and thus prevent ministers from leaving the BU. Anscombe became a long-standing member of the BRF through this initial approach (see Anscombe to Steen, December 31, 1963, File: BRF62/64).
[50] The eight members of the group were listed on the introductory page of *Liberty in the Lord*.
[51] David Kingdon & Ronald Luland, *Liberty in the Lord* (London: Baptist Revival Fellowship, 1964), 3–4.
[52] *BRF Bulletin* No. 80, July/September 1964, 2.
[53] Randall, *English Baptists of the Twentieth Century*, 332, quoting A. D. Gilbert's assessment in *The Making of Post-Christian Britain* (London: Longman, 1980), 150.

recommendations – 'to institute discussions between groups within the denomination holding various view points on ecumenical affairs.'[54] This is a telling comment in that it acknowledges the main issue as ecumenism and not simply denominational integrity and efficiency. Both the BRF and the BU therefore regarded centralization as related to the potential for Baptists to participate in any schemes for re-union.

The two documents represented radically opposed concepts of Baptist life, despite reaching sometimes similar conclusions about Baptist history. The position of the BU Report was that, biblically and historically, the early Baptists believed that 'churches do not stand as units in isolation from each other, and that, as a result, there is a need for mutual prayer, mutual financial aid, mutual advice and mutual pastoral assistance.'[55] In support of this position, the writers quoted the judgement of Baptist historian W. L. Lumpkin that "Formal associationalism was primarily the result of a native Baptist connectional instinct (for Baptists were never independents, strictly speaking)".[56] By coincidence, *Liberty in the Lord* referred to the same quotation but only in order to refute it. In the first place, they noted that Associations were strictly confessional so that 'such co-operation and consultation took place within a clearly defined context of agreed doctrine. If the inter-communion of churches was sought it was on the basis of doctrine, not at the expense of it.'[57] Secondly, the decisions of an Association:

> were regarded as "declarative" rather than as "legislative" in force.... A church could reject the advice and counsel of an Association, but if it treated it as of no importance then it could no longer remain a member of the Association in communion with the other Associating churches.[58]

On the nature of early Association authority, the BU Report and *Liberty in the Lord* were actually agreed. The BU Report advocated the great Puritan theologian John Owen's distinction between 'magisterial' and 'ministerial' authority,[59] which they understood in a similar way to the distinction in *Liberty in the Lord* between 'legislative' and 'declarative.' The Report advocated 'ministerial' authority only for the Association, which it explained as authority with the aim 'not that the churches might become subservient but that through the Association local churches in their mission and all their

---

[54] Minutes of the Meeting of Officers, June 5, 1964 (BU Minute Book January 1964–December 1965), 121–122.
[55] Report of the Denominational Conference, 10.
[56] Ibid., 7.
[57] *Liberty in the Lord*, 19–20.
[58] ibid., 21.
[59] Report of the Denominational Conference, 17.

activities might be served.'⁶⁰ However, the authors recognized a dilemma at this point:

> We are aware that this requires of us a statement of the polity which would be based upon such a definition and this we have tried to do in all that follows. We know there are those who advocate an introduction into the denomination of a polity resembling that of the Methodists or Presbyterians where authority is viewed as delegated from the local church to wider groups and ultimately to a grouping at the centre of the denomination. This solution we cannot accept as it appears to cut across the Baptist definition of the motive for associating and our understanding of authority. We believe it right to go perhaps the more difficult way, based on mutual trust between church and church in Association, and between church and church, Association and Association in the Union.⁶¹

The Report seemed to repudiate clearly enough the idea of central control, though *The Pattern of the Church* perhaps justified the counter-claim made in *Liberty in the Lord* that within the BU many 'desire a more centralized body with a more unified policy.'⁶² What the BU Report did advocate was greater influence from the centre based on the moral authority of churches exercising 'mutual trust.' The key recommendations to achieve this were to give the Associations responsibility for the support of wider Baptist witness, the ministry, the strategy of church extension, church closures, and Grants administration.⁶³ With regard to the central structures of the Union, the Report recommended either that the Assembly should remain as it was while the Council became a gathering mainly of Association representatives (so becoming a kind of parliament of Association leaders), or that the authority of the Assembly should be replaced by an enlarged Council of 350 members, so becoming the final authority in the Union. The problem with this whole scheme was that, although the emphasis was clearly upon servant-leadership, there was no explanation offered of the practical difference between exercising 'ministerial' and 'magisterial' leadership. The obvious difference was that one was advisory and the other compulsory, but instead the Report sought a distinction of motive: ministerial leadership would be exercised 'that the churches might be served.' This meant that the possibility remained, despite the rhetoric, of actual central control. By contrast, *Liberty in the Lord* made a simple case for continued Independency, each church under Christ 'having liberty under the guidance of the Holy Spirit to

---

⁶⁰ Ibid., 17.
⁶¹ Ibid., 18.
⁶² *Liberty in the Lord*, 35.
⁶³ Report of the Denominational Conference, 1.

interpret and administer His laws' and 'sufficient under Christ for the ordering of its life in obedience to His will.'[64] Indeed, the authors rejected the hope:

> that an inter-dependency, construed in terms of connexional church polity, involving legislative and executive authority for Associations and National Assembly, will remedy the spiritual malaise of our churches. Further, we believe such a change would bring many new dangers which outweigh any administrative advantages.[65]

On the other hand, Independency should not equate with isolationism. In an important passage, important because it provides the context for the booklet's title, the authors state:

> Isolationism and its resulting anarchy are seen to be alien to the Gospel. There is an Old Testament illustration of this in the time of the Judges when "every man did that which was right in his own eyes" (Judges 21.25). The chaos that followed provoked the demand for a king whose "public image" would provide the rallying point for united action. But it was pointed out that they already had a king, even though He was invisible. If every man had done what was right in *His* eyes, they would have had all the integrated strength they needed. When democracy fails, as it must, the answer is neither autocracy, nor bureaucracy, but theocracy. Where the Spirit of the Lord is, there is liberty rather than legislation.[66]

Both the Report and *Liberty in the Lord* sought to outline concrete steps forward, the former in favour of greater 'interdependency' and the latter in favour of spiritual co-operation with the like-minded. The Report, however, had a clear strategy whereas *Liberty in the Lord* did not; it ended rather lamely with 'some immediate conclusions and suggestions.' There were twelve, eight of the former and four of the latter.[67] The suggestions began with an item which proposed that the Union should consult 'all the churches' and have 'the fullest open debate in Assembly' before any change was agreed; item ix preferred to answer the 'paucity of spiritual leadership' in the churches 'by the re-establishment of the Eldership'[68] in place either of 'one man at local church level' or of 'a representative synod or group at

---

[64] *Liberty in the Lord*, 46.
[65] Ibid., 46–47.
[66] Ibid., 16.
[67] Ibid., 46–48.
[68] This indicates that the BRF by this time was moving away from traditional Baptist ecclesiology, despite its claim to represent it. While there is some justification for citing early Baptist church life for this, the current emphasis on it came from elsewhere. Both in highly Reformed and in charismatic circles shared eldership was beginning to find favour.

The Baptist Revival Fellowship

Association level'; item x proposed uniting in one congregation small village churches adjacent to one another rather than creating circuits of churches; item xi asked that 'the Baptist Union officers immediately initiate discussions between those whose viewpoint is represented in this Report and those of the other theological viewpoints in the denomination'; and item xii repudiated 'isolationism as contrary to the spirit and practice of the New Testament,' suggesting instead 'fellowship with one another on a wider scale, seeking always an adequate basis of doctrine and experience for such fellowship and provided always that its purpose is not legislative, but for mutual consultation and edification.'

The fundamental weakness of the Commission Report on Association, which represented the thinking within the wider BU leadership, was that it did not actually have a mechanism to prevent magisterial authority. The weakness of *Liberty in the Lord* was that it did not have one to prevent isolationism. Neither of the groups behind the publications was quite so keen as they professed on early Baptist practice. The Report had no appetite for strict confessionalism while *Liberty in the Lord* had none for qualified Independency.

A particularly important section of *Liberty in the Lord* revealed the understanding of the BRF writers of the theological tensions in the Baptist Union. The writers believed that evangelicalism (which they identified with conservatism in theology) was changing 'towards greater doctrinal definition and general growth of concern for doctrine.'[69] Evidence was seen for this in the revival of evangelical scholarship, the renaissance of Reformed theology, fresh evangelical currents of thought such as charismatic renewal and 'growing awareness of the "mixed condition" of denominations ... so that the question of what is the basis for true co-operation is acutely raised.'[70] Other trends among evangelicals were stated to be 'closer outward and visible fellowship' with like-minded people from other denominations, concern for revival, 'considerable reservations' about ecumenism,[71] and 'a rediscovery and return to New Testament simplicity.'[72] An analysis was then given of liberal trends in the denomination (defined in the booklet as 'those who hold "liberal" views, in varying degrees, of the inspiration and authority of the Scriptures').[73] In theology, it was thought that those views were leading to a degree of accommodation with 'paedo-baptist practice, openness to reunion without doctrinal foundations, centralization of the

---

[69] *Liberty in the Lord*, 33.
[70] Ibid., 33.
[71] Ibid., 34.
[72] Ibid.
[73] Ibid., 32.

denomination, and an over-emphasis on the sacraments.'[74] Of this agenda, *The Pattern of Ministry* was explicitly mentioned as presenting 'with great competence an integrated position.'[75] *Liberty in the Lord* identified confrontations within the Union as a result.[76] These were over: (a) theology, especially the final authority of Scripture, the nature of the church and the status of the Ministry; (b) the value and priority of ecumenism; (c) administrative centralization and control; and (d) the degree to which liturgy is important in worship. It is evident that the BRF considered the denomination to be under threat, and it conflated two causes of the problem: theological liberalism and a higher view of the Church. This was not a fair representation. Stephen Winward, for example, a leading advocate of a higher Baptist churchmanship, was strongly evangelical. It was perhaps more broadly the case that the tensions, which certainly existed, ran more roughly along the fault-lines identified by *Liberty in the Lord*.

That *Liberty in the Lord* should have made the impact it did is noteworthy. It was a serious attempt by the BRF to produce Baptist thinking that engaged with the denomination outside its own circle. It was, moreover, a position that resonated with many Baptists who were not as theologically definite as BRF members themselves, and had some potential to attract the attention of critics of Payne and of an inner circle around him. The influence of this circle was not universally approved even among senior Baptist figures. One such critic was Neville Clark, then minister of Amersham-on-the-Hill in Buckinghamshire and already established as a major theological scholar in the BU. He reviewed very favourably *Liberty in the Lord* in the *Baptist Quarterly*. While berating conservative evangelicals in the denomination for having avoided dialogue and for 'betraying most of the symptoms of theological illiteracy,' he considered that 'the significance of this booklet is that it suggests this realization is dawning.'[77] He then lauded the concern shown by the booklet about centralizing tendencies in the Union and for presenting an alternative 'coherent case' although he thought it was 'at least a decade late. Let us hope it is not too late.'[78] His fundamental verdict, despite some criticisms here and there, was that:

---

[74] Ibid., 34–36.
[75] Ibid., 38.
[76] Ibid., 37–45.
[77] *BQ*, Vol. 20 (1963–64), 326.
[78] Ibid., 327.

There are many important things wisely said. "The Baptist Union already contains an embryonic bureaucracy which is in a position to assume greater power if the movement towards centralization gains strength in the denomination at large." Too true.[79]

An Evangelical Alternative to Ecumenism

The scepticism about ecumenism common among conservative evangelicals was not entirely a negative force. Conservative evangelicals answered the appeal of ecumenism by asserting the spiritual unity of the invisible church propounded by Martin Luther at the Reformation. This had become a fundamental tenet of evangelicalism since the early nineteenth century at least and was expressed powerfully in the motto of the Keswick Convention: 'All One In Christ Jesus.' However, the attraction of mutual support grew when conservatives were obviously addressing the same questions and challenges apart from each other while ecumenists were doing so together. The result was to reinforce interdenominational co-operation where there was no question of having to abandon denominational convictions but where theological and spiritual like-mindedness could be more fully exploited, especially in reply to the challenge of ecumenism. In the early sixties, it led to a remarkable flowering of inter-denominational co-operation, in three ways in particular.

In the first place, many evangelicals interested in Reformed theology joined an informal network around the country, the hub of which was the Westminster Fellowship,[80] under the chairmanship of Lloyd-Jones. It was well-supported by Baptists, and it has previously been noted that even Bamber joined at some point in the fifties or early sixties.[81] John Brencher, in his study of Lloyd-Jones, states that 'in the 1950s Lloyd-Jones reached the peak of his power,'[82] and one aspect of this was that he developed a strong interdenominational network at local levels through travelling around the country to preach at special midweek services. It is noticeable that Baptist Union churches figured increasingly prominently as venues. In 1958, for example, out of thirty such engagements twelve were in BU churches while the next largest group was five Congregational causes.[83] The Westminster Fellowship provided a monthly meeting where an issue would be presented, usually by Lloyd-Jones, in the morning session followed by an open debate

---

[79] Ibid., 328.
[80] The Puritan Conference did something similar at a more academic level.
[81] Randall, *Educating Evangelicals*, 105.
[82] Brencher, Martyn Lloyd-Jones and Twentieth-Century Evangelicalism, 25
[83] See Appendix Fourteen for the list of Lloyd-Jones' preaching engagements between 1945 and 1973.

in the afternoon. For Lloyd-Jones, this kind of informal network was the only ecumenism that was safe. Regarding the official movement he warned evangelicals against 'all authoritarian tendencies and all tendencies to ecclesiasticism and the hierarchical principle in the life and activities of churches, or groups or councils of churches,' making reference explicitly to the new openness to Rome in ecumenical circles.[84] Bamber began to echo Lloyd-Jones' virulent anti-denominationalism and anti-ecumenism, as well as his pessimism about the future of the mainline Free Churches.[85] Like Lloyd-Jones, he reached this point after a pilgrimage from doubt to definite opposition during the fifties. His earlier position was expressed in the November/December issue of the *BRF Bulletin* for 1956. There, Bamber posed the question 'What is an Evangelical?' He believed that in the 'church re-union movement' the ascription was too loosely applied to Baptist ministers who 'use the term "Word of God" in varying meanings' and who sought an accommodation with paedo-baptists for the sake of ecumenical unity. At that point, he was not committed to extreme negativity, opining rather that 'a clear definition of these terms, an honest facing up to our differences, are essential if we are to have the blessing of God.'[86]

A second alternative to formal ecumenism was found in the Evangelical Alliance, which had been rescued from some decline by the appointment as General Secretary in 1956 of Gilbert Kirby, noted previously as one of the founders of the CERF.[87] The EA positioned itself within the 'new conservative' movement without adopting stances divisive of wider conservative support and became a significant point of contact between evangelicals from different church traditions. One notable example was that in 1966, Martyn Lloyd-Jones and John Stott appeared together at the opening of the EA Assembly (though not with happy consequences, as will be discussed below). Stott was the Rector of the prominent Evangelical Anglican church in London, All Soul's, Langham Place, and was the leader of the Evangelical constituency within the Church of England.[88]

---

[84] Quoted by Brencher, *Lloyd-Jones and Twentieth Century Evangelicalism*, 85, from the published edition of Lloyd-Jones' address '*1662–1962*' (London: Evangelical Library, 1962).
[85] Lloyd-Jones' views are thoroughly explored by Brencher, *Lloyd-Jones and Twentieth Century Evangelicalism*, Chapter 4: Incipient Romanising, 83ff). Bamber wrote very similarly in the *BRF Bulletin*.
[86] *BRF Bulletin* No. 61, November/December 1957, 1.
[87] For Kirby and the Evangelical Alliance see I. Randall and D. Hilborn, *One Body in Christ: The History and Significance of the Evangelical Alliance* (Carlisle: Paternoster, 2001), chapters 9, 10 and 11.
[88] Cf. the two-volume biography of Stott by Timothy Dudley-Smith, *John Stott: The Making Of The Man* (Leicester: IVP, 1999), *John Stott: A Global Ministry*, (Leicester: IVP, 2001).

The Baptist Revival Fellowship

A third indication of evangelical co-operation of this type was the increasingly friendly relationship between the revival fellowships in each denomination. The Congregational and Methodist Revival Fellowships have already been noted alongside the BRF. At some point another society was formed on similar lines in the Church of England: the Anglican Fellowship for Prayer and Revival (sometimes referred to at the time as the Anglican Revival Fellowship), chaired by Prebendary Colin Kerr, and having as one of its vice-presidents the well-known evangelical cleric and convention speaker A. W. (Bertie) Rainsbury. The four fellowships began to hold occasional consultations, and joint meetings such as one advertised in the *BRF Bulletin* at St. Paul's, Portman Square on September 16, 1960, at which the speakers were Kerr and Lloyd-Jones.[89] The BRF organized a similar event for 1962 when the speakers were Bertie Rainsbury and Martyn Lloyd-Jones.[90]

The omnipresence of Lloyd-Jones in interdenominational conservative evangelical co-operation is significant. When he first arrived in London he was well within the traditional Free Church constituency. The editor of *The Baptist Times* reported his ministry under the heading 'New Voice in the London Pulpit,' remarking that 'the preacher has a distinct message and tells it with conviction and enthusiasm. The presence of Dr. Lloyd-Jones adds strength to the evangelical forces in London.'[91] By the 1960s Lloyd-Jones was less interested in being a traditional Free Churchman and more in developing a radical response to ecumenism, leading him at first to encourage greater solidarity between evangelicals and then to call for them to leave theologically more inclusive denominations.[92] Roger Shuff finds in this a distinctly 'independent Brethren' influence, which he traces to Lloyd-Jones's ex-Brethren son-in-law, Sir Fred Catherwood.[93] Shuff observes:

> It was the ecclesiology of independent Brethren as an informal network of autonomous and untainted evangelical fellowships that gained Lloyd-Jones's most positive attention as a potential solution to the pressing problem of liberalism and ecumenism in the mainline denominations.[94]

Although Shuff is convincing about Lloyd-Jones' interest in the Brethren as being solidly evangelical without the need for a hierarchical structure, it

---

[89] *BRF Bulletin* No. 65, July/September 1960, 4.
[90] Letter from the BRF to the other revival fellowships dated February 6, 1962, advertising a joint meeting at Westminster Chapel Tuesday, April 10, 1962 (BRF File 62/64).
[91] *BT*, October 6, 1938, 750.
[92] A more detailed survey of his life and thought is available in Brencher, *Martyn Lloyd-Jones and Twentieth Century Evangelicalism*.
[93] Shuff, *Searching For The True Church*, 212.
[94] Ibid., 211.

should be recalled that he already had a model ecclesiology in the Independency shared by Congregationalists and Baptists, and his largest single circle of contacts consisted of *the Baptists who supported him*, a phenomenon which has not generally been recognized.

Evangelical inter-denominationalism achieved something of a golden age, or at least a golden opportunity, in the early sixties. It seemed to offer a genuine alternative to the ecumenical movement, where the Keswick vision of 'All One In Christ Jesus' might translate into more than occasional moments of warmth at an annual convention meeting. Lloyd-Jones, although opposed to annual conventions for spiritual renewal, was in the vanguard of a new pan-evangelical impetus that drew strength from a Reformed vision. As early as 1950, he co-operated with and supported J. I. Packer, then a younger and emerging Evangelical Anglican leader, in founding the Puritan Conference, an event designed to generate renewed interest across Protestant church life in the Reformed tradition. It was a partnership and friendship that would turn sour through the controversial activities of both of them in the second half of the sixties. Packer would seriously jeopardize his evangelical credentials by co-operating with Anglo-Catholics to oppose the Anglican-Methodist re-union scheme.[95] Lloyd-Jones in his turn would antagonize denominational loyalists when in 1966 he accused them of sinful guilt for failing to separate from denominations in which there was theological breadth.[96] The 'golden age' of interdenominational co-operation ran out of gold all too quickly.

The various forms of inter-denominational co-operation between conservatives were welcomed in the BRF. Their participation in such events, noted above, increased their importance within and outside the Baptist constituency and embraced both the older and newer voices of conservatism. For example, the Anglican cleric Bertie Rainsbury was a Keswick speaker but he preached alongside Lloyd-Jones in these events, as previously noted. The growing influence of Lloyd-Jones has been noted above in the BRF publication *Liberty in the Lord*. A new generation of members had emerged who took more seriously the study of Reformed theology and Baptist history and principles. Some of these leaders were academically gifted and highly competent. Notable examples were the Welsh minister Graham Harrison and his English contemporary Robert Horn, both of whom did first degrees at Cambridge before taking up theology and ministerial training at Regent's Park College, Oxford (where Horn was elected student president), and David Kingdon.

---

[95] Hylson-Smith, *Vol. III*, 264f.
[96] Brencher, 88ff.

The Baptist Revival Fellowship

The BRF and Denominational Loyalty

The Baptist Union was an increasingly uncomfortable place for traditionalists like Bamber by the 1960s. Not only were ecumenism, centralization and liberal theology gaining a greater hearing, but confidence in the older patterns of church life was breaking down. Michael Walker cites two significant changes in Baptist worship at that time. The first was a decline of confidence in the ministry in comparison with professions such as social work and teaching, and the second was the widespread introduction of the Family Service on Sunday mornings. This latter change marginalized preaching even more than the general decline of confidence in the ministry.[97] Of such changes, Leonard Champion remarked in 1982:

> The regular pattern of worship which obtained in the first half of this century afforded stability, security and peace. The experiments of recent decades have given to some a sense of relevance and meaning, have demonstrated the adaptability of the faith but have weakened a feeling of coherence in Baptist witness.[98]

Bamber was a thorough-going traditionalist and his essential answer was to call Baptists to return to that 'regular pattern of worship which obtained in the first half of this century.' He found a traditionalist ally in Lloyd-Jones, who resolutely adhered to the so-called 'hymn sandwich,' which typically consisted of four hymns interspersed with a Bible reading (from the Authorized Version), a 'pastoral prayer' (in Elizabethan English) and a sermon (usually of fifty minutes in Lloyd-Jones' case). But the 'old paths' he championed were new paths as well. Lloyd-Jones favoured the Puritans, the eighteenth-century revivalists and the nineteenth century Princeton Calvinists; but he was also anti-Keswick, anti-Arminian, anti-denominations, anti-ecumenism, anti-evangelistic appeals, anti-crusade evangelism, and anti-modernization to the slightest degree in worship. Bamber endorsed the message of Keswick, was broadly Arminian in his theology, was a denominationally accredited minister, and approved of Billy Graham and therefore of evangelistic appeals and mass evangelism. He must have been sometimes rather uncomfortable with Lloyd-Jones, but he nevertheless became one of many who began to question their denominational allegiance as well as ecumenism.[99] His editorials from the late fifties onward have been noted previously as leading clearly in that direction, but he was out of step not only with many long-established

---

[97] Randall, *Baptists in the Twentieth Century*, 26.
[98] L. G. Champion, 'Baptist Church Life' in Clements (ed.), *Baptists in the Twentieth Century*, 6.
[99] Randall, *Educating Evangelicals*, 149.

members of the BRF but curiously, also with Lloyd-Jones. Despite his disaffection with denominationalism, Lloyd-Jones was still encouraging at that point a policy of standing for conservative beliefs within the historic denominations. Lloyd-Jones agreed in principle with Bamber's attitude to the BU, facing a similar situation himself in relation to the Congregational Union. However, in practice he was more pragmatic. As early as 1947, Lloyd-Jones had proposed that Westminster Chapel should leave the Congregational Union. Meeting too much resistance among his members, he settled on a compromise by which the church remained in the Union formally on condition that it did not participate in any way in denominational affairs. This remained the case until 1966, when the church resigned rather than sacrifice its Independency when the Congregational Union became the Congregational Church preparatory to joining a new United Reformed Church.[100] Lloyd-Jones had long adopted a pragmatic approach in his own pastorate to the very issues confronting Baptists and the BRF chose to walk at Lloyd-Jones' pace rather than Bamber's. That this exceptionally close relationship did not lead the BRF to walk also in his path of total disengagement may perhaps be explained by Lloyd-Jones' awareness from his close relationship with many Baptist ministers that conservative evangelicalism was closer to the heart of Baptist life, and a much stronger presence in the BU than in the Congregational Union. Whatever the reason, Lloyd-Jones' pragmatism prevailed over Bamber's growing conviction in the early sixties that conservative evangelicals had reached the point of being compromised by remaining in the BU. In fact, Bamber's' status in the BRF was about to be dealt a severe blow.

In 1964 Bamber reached the age of seventy-five. He was still an active man, however (he had retired from his pastorate only three years previously), and he remained the chairman of the BRF. His influence was beginning to wane, nevertheless, as a younger generation of leaders emerged whose outlook was influenced deeply by Martyn Lloyd-Jones. With the support of the more traditional BRF members who disagreed fundamentally with Bamber's increasing hostility towards the BU, they had already taken the lead in mounting a serious and well-informed campaign of engagement with the denominational agenda, as *Liberty in the Lord* amply demonstrated. In 1964 they succeeded in moderating Bamber's rather exclusive authority as chairman through providing the BRF with a formal constitution. It not only created a more accountable structure for business, it articulated a doctrinal identity similar to that of the IVF, thus bringing the BRF formally into the

---

[100] Brencher, *Martyn Lloyd-Jones and Twentieth Century Evangelicalism*, 119ff.

new conservative sphere in which Lloyd-Jones was so prominent, though it thereby diminished the older Baptist view of 'the inner authority of Christ and the outer authority of Scripture,' as L. G. Champion put it. The 1964 statement of faith contained the more usual Protestant affirmation of the final authority of Scripture. Significantly, the constitution also committed the BRF to giving 'testimony in the Baptist Denomination.'[101] Not only did the constitution somewhat turn from Bamber's older kind of conservatism, it rejected his anti-Union stance. Yet there was more discomfort to come for Bamber.

The significance of the constitution and of the renewed influence of the denominational loyalists emerged clearly the following year. In 1964, Bamber had retired as editor of the *Bulletin* and after some temporary measures it was decided in 1965 to elect a permanent replacement for him. The new constitution was clearly the work of new conservatives but it required that the Annual Conference should now elect officers democratically. The more traditional BRF members made their presence felt. The outcome was not the appointment of someone from the Reformed group but of a long-standing committee member who was deeply committed to the BU, Leslie Larwood. He lost no time in changing the tone of the *Bulletin*. He stated in his tribute to Bamber that 'although there have been times when his approach has given concern to his closest friends who share his convictions, the BRF is deeply grateful to God for such a "Valiant For Truth."'[102] The new editor wanted the *Bulletin* to shake off Bamber's critical and defensive attitude to the BU. But he was also willing to resist the more Reformed members. How far he was prepared to go was revealed in the next two editions, in which he carried two articles on ecumenism that challenged the simple rejection of it by conservatives. This was indeed a different editorial line, different even from the policy of Lloyd-Jones. The two articles therefore deserve special notice.

In the first, he invited a pro-ecumenical minister to comment on the BRF as an outsider. W. F. Bacon had trained at Spurgeon's College, entering his first pastorate in 1949, and eventually serving in Bristol where he took an active part in denominational life. His perspective is interesting as someone who had studied at Spurgeon's in the latter years of Percy Evans. He confessed that even in the late forties a view circulated in the college that the BRF 'was more negative than positive – a protest group, rather enjoying, in fact, sniping at denominational and other leaders ... that it was divisive rather than unifying' treating ecumenical pleas for unity in a 'cavalier fashion,' and

---

[101] See in Appendix Two: The Constitution of the BRF, Clause 6.
[102] *BRF Bulletin* No. 83, April/June 1965, 1.

The Problem of Payne: BRF Responses to New Baptist Agenda (1938-66)

that 'it was too prone to encourage the cult of personalities.'[103] Nevertheless, Bacon believed the BRF met a need for a 'right-wing' pressure group in the Union to ensure that traditional evangelical views were represented 'within denominational organizations' and to take part in ecumenism in order to ensure it 'gives a proper place to the evangelical conviction that salvation ... is by faith and faith alone.' Bacon was aware that many ecumenists grounded co-operation on a common baptism rather than a common faith. Thirdly, Bacon wanted the BRF to be a unifying influence by embracing the ecumenical vision for one visible church, though he confessed to having no clear understanding of what that might involve.[104]

Larwood followed that article with one by a schoolteacher in membership with Durham Baptist Church, D. A. MacMurtrie, encouraging a more careful response than immediate opposition to ecumenism. MacMurtrie acknowledged frankly that Rome was becoming friendlier to ecumenism, but would insist that the 'ultimate object of ecumenism is to unite all Christians under the Vicar of Christ.'[105] Nevertheless, he considered that ecumenism was 'no ephemeral thing and evangelicals must reckon with it.' He suggested that evangelicals considered what aspects of ecclesiology were essential at any cost, what was 'the Biblical teaching about the Church' and about Christian unity, and finally depending on the answers to these questions, what action was needed by evangelicals in regard to ecumenism. No conclusions were offered by the author. Judging from the tone of the article they would have been too sympathetic to ecumenism for most of the BRF members. This indicates that there were now two rather different conservative mentalities in the BRF. The Reformed people might be described as conservatives who were in the Baptist Union and the more traditional members as Baptists who were conservative. Both were committed to conservative evangelicalism and wished it to become the mainstream of Baptist life and that was what drew them together, but it will be seen in due course that their coalition was soon to end in disastrous disagreements.

Meanwhile, active engagement by the BRF in denominational life grew further in the mid-sixties. The appointment in 1965 of a committee member, Hugh Butt, as an Area Superintendent suggests that even the BU establishment felt the Fellowship had left behind Bamber's negativity towards the denomination. That such was the case was evident in several ways. In July 1965, for example, a number of leading BRF members led by Stanley Voke met at Baptist Church House to agree a statement for presentation at a Day Conference organized by the London Baptist Association, the purpose of which was to respond to the Nottingham

---

[103] *BRF Bulletin* No. 84, July/September 1965, 4.
[104] Ibid. 5.
[105] *BRF Bulletin* No. 85, October/December 1965, 2.

statement calling for reunion.[106] The high point of this trend was reached in 1966. The *BRF Bulletin* drew attention to the fact that a number of BRF members were standing for the BU Council and needed prayerful and practical support. Furthermore, contributors were sought who could write for the BRF about denominational issues. The same edition published for the first time a list of representatives in each Association,[107] indicating that the BRF had ambitions to strengthen their presence and influence at regional and local levels as well as at the national one. The BRF was aiming to become a force within the Baptist establishment.

Geoffrey King requires particular notice at this point because he was as much a leading figure in the BRF as Bamber, but unlike his colleague he was fully in sympathy with these developments. Even before the publication of *Liberty in the Lord* and the new direction it signalled for the Fellowship, King displayed his loyalty to the Union by accepting, in 1962, the Presidency of the London Baptist Association. Moreover, he used his presidential address to proclaim the old revival call of the BRF, giving it the title, 'Rend The Heavens!'[108] In 1965, as the BRF campaigned for real influence in the denomination, he accepted nomination for the Vice-Presidency of the Baptist Union, though he was not in the event elected. His name was put forward for election by the traditionally conservative Home Counties Association supported by 25 'members of Assembly.'[109] This might not seem a ringing endorsement, but that year a college Principal (Henton Davies) and the minister of the famous West Ham Central Mission (Stanley Turl) were each proposed by only one association and another college Principal (J. Ithel Jones) by two.[110]

The BRF and Charismatic Renewal

Adrian Hastings, in his account of English Christianity in the last century, has stated of the charismatic movement that 'like so much else, it dates its English beginnings from around 1963.'[111] It has already been noted that the charismatic movement became an influence in the BRF at that very time, to the extent that *Liberty in the Lord* drew attention to it as one sign of a resurgent conservative evangelicalism.[112] Support for the charismatic experience of a

---

[106] Ibid., 3.
[107] *BRF Bulletin* No. 87, Apr/June 1966, 6–7 (see also Appendix Seventeen: List of BRF Officers)
[108] Geoffrey R. King: Rend The Heavens! The Presidential Address given at the Annual Assembly of the London Baptist Association, March 1962, (London: London Baptist Association), 1.
[109] BU Council Minutes, March 9–10, 1965 Item V: Nominations for the Vice Presidency 1965/6.
[110] Ibid.
[111] Hastings, *English Christianity 1920–1990*, 557.
[112] See above 64.

The Problem of Payne: BRF Responses to New Baptist Agenda (1938-66)

post –conversion 'baptism in the Holy Spirit,' surprisingly perhaps in view of his conservatism, can be traced first in Baptist circles to Martyn Lloyd-Jones' address at the 1956 BRF Conference. He urged Baptist Revival Fellowship ministers to be 'witnesses' to the truth of Spirit-baptism.[113] He spoke again on the subject at the 1960 Conference. David Pawson then gave it his endorsement at the BRF Conference of 1964.[114] The route by which Lloyd-Jones became increasingly influential has been previously noted. David Pawson's role in bringing charismatic renewal to the BRF began with his own experience that same year through attending the first renewal conference organized by the Anglican priest and charismatic pioneer Michael Harper, whose charismatic initiation was recent (and in which he had received encouragement from Lloyd-Jones).[115] Ian Randall has traced the rapid rise of Pawson as a Baptist pioneer of charismatic life to the suggestion of a Baptist minister and BRF member, Malcolm Piper. Earlier that year, Piper had been 'deeply affected' by hearing another early charismatic leader in the Anglican Church, George Forester of St. Paul's Beckenham.'[116] Piper then wrote to Alec Steen, the BRF Committee Secretary, to advocate finding a speaker for the Annual Conference 'who has personally experienced the baptism of the Holy Spirit recently.'[117] Leith Samuel had been booked to speak but withdrew at the last minute through illness, and commended David Pawson as having 'more to offer on the subject of revival than I have.'[118] The impact of his ministry was immediate and profound, including some present experiencing 'the baptism' for themselves. In this way, Pawson began a significant role in charismatic renewal among Baptists. In fact, the BRF Conference should be acknowledged as the original Baptist Union platform for charismatic renewal. The 1965 Conference focused exclusively on the Holy Spirit, and one of the speakers represented the charismatic viewpoint. This was Arthur Wallis (1922–1988) a Bible teacher from Brethren circles whose life and ministry radically changed through his charismatic experience.[119] However, most of the speakers took a different view and J. I.

---

[113] Murray, *The Fight of Faith*, 387.
[114] David Pawson had trained at Wesley Methodist College, Cambridge but left the Methodist ministry for a Baptist Union pastorate in 1961 (see David Pawson, *Not As Bad As The Truth: Memoirs of an Unorthodox Evangelical* (London: Hodder & Stoughton, 2006), 61ff.
[115] Ibid., 90ff.
[116] Ian Randall, 'Baptist Revival and Renewal in the 1960s' in *Studies in Church History, Vol. 44: Revival and Resurgence in Christian History* (Woodbridge: Ecclesiastical History Society; Boydell Press, 2008), 341ff.
[117] Ibid., 344. Quoted by Randall from a letter from Malcolm Piper to Alec Steen, April 9, 1964 (original in the BRF Archive). See also Peter Hocken, *Streams of Renewal: The Origins and Early Development of the Charismatic Movement in Great Britain*, rev. ed. (Carlisle: Paternoster, 1997), 133–5.
[118] Ibid., 348.
[119] Arthur Wallis, *The Radical Caristian* (Eastbourne: Kingsway, 1981), 10f.

Packer spoke with his customary caution about evangelical experientialism in an address entitled 'The Quest For Fullness.'[120]

Nonetheless, charismatic emphases were warmly welcomed by some, including Stanley Voke. In an article for the *BRF Bulletin*, Voke surveyed various trends that he regarded as 'Movements of Revival in Our Denomination.' One of these was charismatic renewal. Voke averred that 'there is no denying the experience many have had, nor the events that have occurred'[121] (a reference to charismatic manifestations). In the following *Bulletin*, Geoffrey King wrote a more cautious statement, neither rejecting nor welcoming charismatic gifts but recognizing the need for spiritual authority in the life and ministry of the church.[122] Harold Owen, on the other hand, testified to being baptized in the Spirit at the 1964 Annual Conference,[123] and subsequently renewal became an accepted aspect of BRF evangelicalism, as indicated by the fact that Owen would be chosen to succeed Bamber as chairman of the BRF. It is noteworthy that some ministers, like Owen himself, maintained both a Reformed theology and openness to charismatic renewal, with the approval of Lloyd-Jones. However, Randall has noted that Lloyd-Jones' public espousal in 1966 of ecclesiastical Restorationism as well his advocacy of 'baptism in the Spirit' led to a consequence he had not anticipated. A number of BRF supporters 'saw charismatic experience as needing to be embodied in new "Restorationist" churches – "restoring" the New Testament model – under the authority of apostles.'[124] [125] This led to tensions in the Revival Fellowship, tensions which remained secondary when attention was concentrated on separation from the BU in the late sixties. It will be noted in due course that differing agenda would undermine the vision of an all-embracing alternative to the BU: a number of BRF leaders would turn to new charismatic networks rather than to the proposed new Baptist alternative.

---

[120] *BRF Bulletin* No. 83, April/June 1965, 4.
[121] Ibid., 3.
[122] *BRF Bulletin* No. 84, Jul/Sep 1965, 1–3.
[123] Randall, *English Baptists of the Twentieth Century*, 326.
[124] Ibid.
[125] Owen is an example of this. He remained committed to Reformed theology but moved away from Lloyd-Jones' vision of church life. When he became chairman of the BRF in 1971 he revealed how far he had moved. In an article on revival for the *BRF Bulletin* he stated, 'The old wineskin of Victorian church services will never contain the new wine of revived Christianity. Much of our present institutionalism will have to go. Such reorganization will be difficult and extremely unpopular in many cases.' (*BRF Bulletin* No. 106, April/June 1971, 1).

The Problem of Payne: BRF Responses to New Baptist Agenda (1938-65)

Conclusions

The BRF at this point in its life was reaching towards a genuinely radical vision that embraced several significant aspects in openness to charismatic renewal combined with a new appreciation of scholarship, a more modern style of conservatism, and greater engagement in Baptist Union life to defend traditional Baptist ecclesiology and evangelical identity against the encroachments of centralization and liberal trends. The growth of ecumenism raised the same basic issues for conservative evangelicals in all the historic denominations. That fact drew them together in the early sixties, and a new phase began of inter-denominational co-operation. The Revival Fellowships were formal networks sharing similar goals within their various denominations and they began to reach out to each other, enabling them to share their concerns, especially about ecumenism and the need for spiritual renewal. The Evangelical Alliance provided a structure for developing that beyond their various denominational agenda and became again a major voice for conservative evangelicals under the leadership of Gilbert Kirby. However, the great influence on conservatives, in the Free Churches especially, was Lloyd-Jones. In the early sixties, he encouraged denominational renewal movements and even early charismatic life, in keeping with his belief that the only answer to Britain's moral degeneration and spiritual decline was a supernatural revival of biblically authentic Christianity. His hold over the BRF became so strong that it followed his each and every turn in the period under review. If the BRF was born as Bamber's baby, in the 1960s it became Lloyd-Jones' child, despite the fact that the Baptist loyalists were wary of both men having too much personal influence. Lloyd-Jones' influence took several forms.

First of all, he impacted the BRF by his leading role within the new conservatism, not only in his advocacy of its doctrinal but its inter-denominational ethos and its suspicion of ecumenism. Regarding doctrine, the BRF adopted a new conservative statement of faith that led it away from the older BRF message of pietist-premillennialism. Regarding inter-denominationalism, the new conservatism provided the BRF with a more contemporary alternative to the Keswick movement favoured by its older generation, not only by individuals attending the Westminster Fellowship or meetings of the Evangelical Alliance but also by official joint meetings with the other Revival Fellowships to reinforce their respective commitments to denominational renewal. Regarding anti-ecumenism, this wider circle enabled the BRF membership to move beyond exploring between themselves the perceived threat of the ecumenical movement to Baptist life and to identifying with a growing conservative evangelical consensus that it threatened the evangelical faith itself. Ecumenism was now perceived to be the common enemy of all 'true evangelicals' and had to be resisted for the sake, it was thought, of ensuring the very survival of the gospel message. Bamber had been saying as much for some years but his apocalyptic gloom offered no strategy for action. This was different. The confidence of the new conservatism answered the pessimism of premillennialism and inspired the BRF to attempt new inroads into Baptist life.

Secondly, Lloyd-Jones' advocacy of Reformed theology influenced a younger generation, especially in the Baptist denomination, to greater theological confidence and expertise. The inter-denominational rallying point was the Westminster Fellowship. The Baptists among them found a denominational one in the BRF, where they made a great impact. They were no more intimidated by denominational leaders than they were impressed by their ecumenical ambitions. Consequently, the BRF prepared a serious report offering a more traditional vision of Baptist life than Payne was prepared to accept. It defended the traditional Baptist ecclesiology and presented conservative evangelicalism as a renewed and well-informed movement in BU life. The BRF found new momentum as a result and increased to the largest membership in its history. It was aiming to influence the denomination by active involvement at every level and it seemed poised to do so by 1966.

Thirdly, Lloyd-Jones' advocacy of 'Spirit-baptism' and the early charismatic renewal movement led to it becoming an important element of BRF life and through the BRF it was first promoted among Baptists. Whatever verdict may be passed on the legitimacy of charismatic renewal or indeed of the Keswick teaching about 'the fullness of the Spirit,' they embodied much the same quest for empowerment by the Spirit. Charismatic renewal did so in a more contemporary style, but there was not as great an experiential distance as the charismatic emphasis on 'the gifts of the Spirit' implied and the BRF had been thoroughly committed to the Keswick version of it. Had the newer expression of spiritual empowerment become more central to the BRF's vision, the BRF would have found fresh relevance as a spiritual renewal movement. However, in 1966 the Fellowship would turn in a different direction, by following yet again the lead of Martyn Lloyd-Jones, as will be seen in the next chapter.

Finally, Bamber's influence in the BRF was diminished by that of Lloyd-Jones in two surprising ways in the mid-sixties. To begin with, Bamber had publicly questioned the place of conservatives in BU life by the end of the fifties while Lloyd-Jones continued to support making a stand within the mainstream denominations. The ability of Lloyd-Jones' followers to win the support of more traditional Baptist loyalists in the BRF took the Fellowship in his direction rather than Bamber's. There was a double irony about that.

The Problem of Payne: BRF Responses to New Baptist Agenda (1938-56)

Not only would Lloyd-Jones come to adopt the policy that had caused Bamber such discomfort, but so would the BRF.

The second example of Bamber's diminishing authority was a consequence rather than an expression of Lloyd-Jones' influence because it arose from the renewed importance of the Baptist loyalists as supporters of denominational engagement. When that led to the appointment of the denominationally committed Leslie Larwood, it was something of a come-uppance for Bamber. While he was editor he had ignored the pro-Union stance that was really more representative of the traditional BRF members than his own. It was also, however, an indication that the coalition between the loyalists and the Reformed group did not mean that people like Larwood were willing to exchange one dominant figure for another in Lloyd-Jones. Larwood did a rather clever thing to make the point. By providing space to an evangelical ecumenist as practically his first editorial decision, he contradicted not only Bamber, but Lloyd-Jones.

In the space of five or so years, then, the BRF returned from the margins of Union life as a force to be reckoned with, mounted its most effective campaign for traditional Baptist values, committed itself constitutionally to working within the BU, garnered ever-growing support in the denomination, and began to implement a strategy of engagement at every level of BU life. As will be shown in the next chapter, however, it would then proceed 'to snatch defeat from the jaws of victory' by polarizing completely between those whose vision was to stay, and those whose vision was to leave, the Baptist Union.

CHAPTER FOUR

THE ROAD TO SECESSION (1966–1970)

In this chapter, a sea-change in the direction of the BRF will be explored. As shown above, by 1965 it had achieved notable success as a coherent representative not only of committed theological conservatives and anti-ecumenists, but of a wider constituency of Baptists who shared its misgivings about the apparent questioning within the denomination of traditional Baptist ecclesiology in the drive towards greater centralization.[1] Within two years, this success was sacrificed to a new mentality and policy. The new BRF mentality would be that the BU was irredeemably lost to traditional evangelicalism, and the new policy would be that there was only one consistent response: secession.

The 1966 Evangelical Alliance Assembly

The Evangelical Alliance (or EA) had used its 1966 'National Assembly of Evangelicals' to consider an EA report on ecumenism published in 1965. Evangelical concerns were summarized by the new General Secretary, Baptist minister and BRF supporter, A. Morgan Derham:

> The steady development of the ecumenical movement, intensified by the "1980" Resolution of the Nottingham Conference, has prompted Evangelical Christians to consider urgently the matter of their relationships among themselves and to the churches in general.[2]

The 1965 Evangelical Alliance 'Commission on Church Unity' provided the basis for a number of papers to be delivered at the 1966 Assembly, in addition to contributions from Martyn Lloyd-Jones and John Stott. Of the speaking panel itself, four were Anglican (Julian Charley, David Winter, Maurice Wood, and Harry Sutton), four were Baptist (John A. Caiger, J. David Pawson, Alan Redpath, and A. Morgan Derham), and one was from the Elim Pentecostal denomination (John Lancaster).

---

[1] Roger Hayden provides personal testimony to this from his own experience in his survey of Baptist history, noting that the BRF 'provided a focus in the 1960s for opposition within the Baptist Union to ecumenism and growing centralisation.' Hayden, *English Baptist History and Heritage*, 194.
[2] A. Morgan Derham (ed.), *Unity in Diversity: Evangelicals, The Church and The World*, Ten papers given at the National Assembly of Evangelicals at Westminster, London, in October 1966, (London: Evangelical Alliance, 1967), 5.

The Road to Secession (1966-70)

Gilbert Kirby, the predecessor of Derham as EA General Secretary, had in his final months invited the leaders of the Free Church Revival Fellowships to send representatives to a meeting with the Commission members on January 13, 1966. Kirby wrote to the BRF on January 6, intimating that one question which would certainly arise would be when Baptists would reach the point of withdrawing from the Union over ecumenism; and if so, whether the general feeling would be in favour of joining the FIEC or whether they would 'be more interested in the possibility of the setting up of a United Evangelical Church.'[3] This indicates something which is perhaps difficult to appreciate at a distance of nearly fifty years. There was a strong sense that the ecumenical vision was on the verge of becoming reality. Anti-ecumenical conservatives tended to view this with alarm, believing that a world church united under the papacy would achieve political power and then use it to oppose Christians who remained outside it, even to the point of persecution. Had conservatives been more involved in ecumenical dialogue they might have realized how unlikely their vision was, but having isolated themselves from it they were free to believe the rhetoric of the most extreme ecumenical enthusiasts almost more than the enthusiasts themselves. This was the context of Kirby's question.[4] How far it was Kirby's own idea is difficult to say. Lloyd-Jones was also interviewed by the Commission and expressed the same vision while stopping short of suggesting a definite ecclesial body.

Lloyd-Jones was invited to state his views publicly at the opening rally of the Assembly as a preamble to the Assembly debate.[5] Although the papers were published in due course, he refused to allow his address to be included, in view, he said, of it not being a carefully prepared paper but rather a popular statement of the issues.[6] However, a summary was provided[7] in which Lloyd-Jones was recorded as setting forth the view that evangelicals had neglected the issue of ecclesiology in favour of reacting against theological threats through 'alliances, movements, and societies.'[8] Lloyd-Jones felt that the ecumenical movement presented 'a pressing problem to us as evangelicals, especially since 1948.'[9] He believed that the consequences were considerable, and that 'many Evangelicals were muddled, and quite unaware of the speed with which developments were taking place. He was

---

[3] Gilbert Kirby to Alec Steen, January 6, 1966 (BRF Archive: File 1965/66).
[4] For example, I recall from my student days that ecumenical involvement was labelled by its critics 'ecumania.'
[5] Morgan Derham, *Unity in Diversity*, 5–6.
[6] Ibid., 7.
[7] Ibid., 7–13.
[8] Ibid., 9.
[9] Ibid.

quoted as expressing the fear that 'our position is a pathetic one. Indeed, to me it is a tragic one.'[10]

Lloyd-Jones put forward his own answer to ecumenism. This was that evangelicals should form some kind of exclusive association, rather than remaining as minorities where they were. The issue, as reported in the summary of his address, was:

> whether we try to modify the situation as best we can, or whether we start afresh and 'go back to the New Testament.' Are we prepared to discover what the New Testament Church is really meant to be? The ecumenical people put fellowship before doctrine; Evangelicals put doctrine before fellowship. What doctrine? 'Our view of Scripture as the infallible Word of God; of the Deity of the Lord Jesus Christ; His virgin birth, miraculous and supernatural; His atoning, sacrificial, substitutionary death; His literal, physical resurrection; the Person of the Holy Spirit and His work – doctrines which are essential to salvation.' These are the true marks of the Church, and a church is a gathering of people who are in covenant together because they believe these things. Moreover, they have an *experience* of them.... What is needed is a number of such churches 'all in fellowship together, working together for the same aims and objects.[11]

Lloyd-Jones did not clearly propose what Kirby called a 'United Evangelical Church.' He was, by inclination and principle, an unapologetic Independent regarding church government.[12] However, he was recorded as issuing a blunt and immediate call to action, these key phrases being directly quoted by the editor:

> What reasons have we for not coming together? Why is it that we are so anxious to hold on to our inherited positions...? Don't we feel the call to come together, not occasionally, but *always*...? I am a believer in ecumenicity, Evangelical ecumenicity. To me, the tragedy is that we are divided.... Let us listen to what I believe is the call of God.... If we have one objective only, namely the glory of the Lord and the success of His kingdom, I think we shall be led by the Spirit to the true answer to these varied and varying problems and who knows but that the ecumenical movement may be something for which in years to come we shall thank God, because it made us face our

---

[10] Ibid.
[11] Ibid., 10–11.
[12] But see the discussion of this in Brencher, *Martyn Lloyd-Jones and Twentieth-Century Evangelicalism*, 98.

problems on the Church level, instead of on the level of movements, and really brought us together as a fellowship or association of Evangelical churches. May God speed the day![13]

Such was the force of his address that John Stott, the leading Evangelical Anglican and chairman of the meeting that evening, was moved to disagree publicly with Lloyd-Jones; furthermore, the persuasive power of Lloyd-Jones' oratory compelled him to issue a plea that 'no-one would take precipitate action as a result of what they had heard, and that the debate might be continued so that proper thought could be given to the subject.'[14] Warner describes this moment as 'a seismic fracture point' between Lloyd-Jones and Stott[15] although that is more accurate as a description of the different directions they took with regard to remaining in the mainstream of church life than of their personal regard for one another.[16] Conservative evangelical unity collapsed virtually overnight. Anglicans went on to a National Evangelical Anglican Congress at Keele in 1967, at which was affirmed renewed denominational commitment,[17] while the Free Church conservatives were left in disarray, having either to defy their hero or to follow him in order to 'start afresh' without knowing what that really meant.

Julian Charley, a younger Anglican leader, presented the first proper paper of the Assembly by way of reply to what he already knew to be Lloyd-Jones' stance. Although he utilized the nineteenth-century American Presbyterian theologian, Charles Hodge, his argument was essentially to justify a territorial and national church.[18] No speaker was asked to give a similarly sustained justification of any Free Church ecclesiology, an omission that was perhaps in deference to Lloyd-Jones, or it might be indicative of widespread uncertainty at the time about the future of the Free Church tradition The consequence was that a definite alternative to Lloyd-Jones was offered only to Evangelical Anglicans. The approved choices may have seemed then that Anglicans had theological grounds for remaining loyal to their denomination while Free Church members did not. That leaving their denominations was an idea already in circulation among Free Church evangelicals was indicated in the Commission's report a year previously. Derham recalled that the report recognized how some clergy in membership with the Alliance 'are in serious difficulties, and it was agreed that steps

---

[13] A. Morgan Derham, *Unity in Diversity*, 11–13.
[14] Ibid., 13.
[15] Warner, *Reinventing English Evangelicalism 1966–2001*, 39.
[16] Brencher recounts that, even after their public disagreement, Lloyd-Jones seriously invited Stott to consider the pastorate of Westminster Chapel in succession to him. *Martyn Lloyd-Jones and Twentieth-Century Evangelicalism*, 190.
[17] Hylson-Smith, *Vol. III*, 238–9.
[18] A. Morgan Derham, *Unity in Diversity*, 20ff.

should be taken to help them.'[19] Such a portrayal of the Free Church scene is misleading, however. The fact is that Lloyd-Jones did not speak for the many denominational loyalists, especially in the BU, who maintained a strongly evangelical position. Two examples representative of nearly forty years leadership in evangelical life were Ernest Kevan and Gilbert Kirby himself, one a BU minister and the other a Congregationalist, and both long-serving Principals of London Bible College.[20]

The Impact of Lloyd-Jones' Message on the BRF

The ecumenical issue thus reached a critical turning-point among BRF members. Lloyd-Jones' call to secede in favour of creating some kind of definitely conservative evangelical fellowship was taken very seriously by many of them. It was not thought that it required the rejection of Baptist Independency in the way that the ecumenical vision was perceived to do, though a more united ecclesiological expression of evangelicalism surely implied making baptism a secondary issue. Even this, however, was not completely alien to Baptist tradition, which since John Bunyan's lifetime in the seventeenth century had included followers of his view that Christians should not divide over the proper mode of baptism. As late as the twentieth century his convictions were reflected in the creation of 'union churches' where paedo- and credo-baptism existed side by side. It may nevertheless be argued that the BRF became institutionally disloyal because it displayed a marked sympathy with Lloyd-Jones' critical attacks on 'mixed denominations,' as he termed the mainstream church structures. The issue painfully divided all evangelicals after the Evangelical Alliance Assembly of 1966, and Lloyd-Jones added to the pain by allowing, if not engineering, the reconstruction of the Westminster Fellowship at the end of that year to exclude any members who did not accept his separatist stance at least in principle. In 1967 he went further by accusing – in an address to the British Evangelical Council – those who remained in theologically broad denominations of 'guilt by association':

> if you are content to function in the same church with such people, you are virtually saying that though you think you are right, they also may be right.... That, I assert, is a denial of the Evangelical, the only true faith.[21]

---

[19] Ibid., 6.
[20] Cf. Randall's comment about Kirby and Kevan when quoting Kirby's view in *Educating Evangelicalism*, 149.
[21] Quoted by Brencher, *Lloyd-Jones and Twentieth Century Evangelicalism*, 127.

The Road to Secession (1966-70)

As Brencher remarks, 'it carried all the marks of second degree separation'[22] (that is, not only withdrawing personally from 'mixed' denominations but also refusing fellowship with otherwise acceptable evangelicals who remained within them). His judgement is that 'in practical terms all it did was to marginalize Lloyd-Jones further'[23] than his 1966 address already had at the Evangelical Alliance Assembly. The effect upon Baptists of Lloyd-Jones' call for secession took several inter-related directions. These will be traced separately over a period of several years in order to highlight their development.

The Marginalization of Denominational Loyalists in the BRF

Membership of the BRF was at an all-time high of 1100 in 1966, including 440 of the 2000 or so accredited ministers.[24] However, behind that success lay serious differences of opinion about Lloyd-Jones' call for secession. Leslie Larwood, the pro-denominational editor of the *BRF Bulletin* made no bones about his own view of the situation. In an important paragraph, he commented on the decision to re-form the Westminster Fellowship as an anti-denominational body:

> The Westminster Fellowship: 'Many members of the BRF have been members of the Westminster Fellowship and have found much benefit and blessing in the Biblical studies and discussions under the leadership of Dr. Martyn Lloyd-Jones. They will regret, therefore, that at the meetings of the Fellowship on November 28th, Dr. Lloyd-Jones felt it right to announce the closure of the Fellowship. John Caiger writes: "He was moved to do this because he believed that the deep cleavage among us regarding the position of Evangelicals in their present denominations would lead to strife, and this must at all costs be avoided." The decision of a large number of the Fellowship at a subsequent meeting in the absence of Dr. Lloyd-Jones to (1) Endorse the appeal made by Dr. Lloyd-Jones at Westminster Central Hall, (2) Call a meeting to continue discussion, (3) Invite Dr. Lloyd-Jones to take the chair at this meeting, is likely to deepen the cleavage the Doctor was anxious to avoid, especially as the invitation to the meeting states, "All brethren are welcome excepting those who are convinced denominationalists." Many of us who sincerely believe that our place and witness is in our denomination are thus excluded from a fellowship of those who differ from us on this issue, yet between whom there has been no

---

[22] Ibid.
[23] Ibid., 131.
[24] Randall, *English Baptists of the Twentieth Century*, 326.

cleavage or strife. There would have been far less danger in continuing the Westminster Fellowship as it has existed so profitably for twenty-five years.[25]

The BRF Conference took place only weeks after the EA Assembly, and the tensions emerged at its AGM in several items of business. The most radical one was a proposal to open membership to churches as well as individuals, thus making the BRF an alternative ecclesial structure but within the BU. The Committee chose Douglas Jones, minister of Trinity Baptist Church in Gloucester, to voice its definite opposition. He was well-known as a Lloyd-Jones loyalist opposed to BU inclusiveness,[26] and therefore provided a steadying hand on the meeting, yet the discussion also provided an indication that the committee opposed the strategy of creating an evangelical association of churches without dealing with its relationship with the Union. Another sign of tension appeared over the committee elections. A proposal was tabled to make the chairman, secretary and treasurer subject to re-election rather than holding permanent ex-officio membership of the committee and it exactly divided the meeting, with 81 votes for and 81 against. Bamber exercised a casting vote from the chair against the motion.[27] The balance of power on the committee lay behind this, as can be seen in the elections to vacant seats that followed. The normal pattern had been for little or no contention to take place but this year there were more candidates than places and they were people with clear differences about the BU. Three denominational loyalists were elected (Glyn Morris, who had recently moved from Nottingham to Swansea) together with Leslie Larwood and Stanley Voke. Only one definite anti-denominationalist succeeded in winning a seat (Henry Tyler, minister then of Carey Baptist Church, Reading), leaving one of the most vocal anti-denominationalist candidates, George Stirrup, outside the committee. The BRF began to see a trickle of resignations, first from people who thought it was too supportive of the BU but soon from those who thought the opposite.

The BRF meanwhile continued its own debate about ecumenism. This would not prove to be a happy experience. In January 1967, the Committee invited Ronald Luland to draw up a statement about ecumenism to be offered for feedback before the next meeting.[28] The work was duly completed and approved for publication in the *BRF Bulletin*. It took a definite stance against

---

[25] *BRF Bulletin* No. 90, January–March 1967, 6.
[26] In 1968 Jones published an account of his pathway to secession in which he stated that he had been involved in discussions about it for some years before the event. The article appeared in his Church Magazine for November 1968, entitled 'They Were Not Of Us' (a copy of which is located in the BRF Archive, File: 1967/68).
[27] Minutes of the BRF Annual Meeting, November 22, 1966: Election of Officers.
[28] Minutes of the BRF Committee, 30/31 January 1967, Item 17: Ecumenical Movement.

ecumenical involvement by stating that evangelicals who supported it were 'grievously and seriously mistaken' in their judgement.[29] At the next committee meeting, on April 3, Leslie Larwood, the *BRF Bulletin* editor and a pro-denominationalist, advised postponement of the Statement. The committee decided to rebuff him and hinted that he had been deliberately tardy about publishing the *BRF Bulletin* in order to delay the statement.[30] Larwood was instructed to produce the next edition immediately. Then, without the committee's official approval and within days of the meeting, Henry Tyler gave a pre-publication copy of the statement to George Stirrup, who proceeded to write two articles about it, one for *The Christian and Christianity Today*[31] and the other for *The Life of Faith*.[32] Coverage then appeared also in *BT*. Stirrup presented the statement as representing a deliberate stand for truth by the BRF Committee, which took action after becoming frustrated because 'their attitude and desires have never been sought by the Baptist Union Officers or Council' and with the expectation that the Fellowship 'will no doubt lose some supporters'[33] as the price for adopting a definite stand. His presentation of events would ensure controversy, but far worse was the publication of the articles before the appearance of the *BRF Bulletin*. It seemed to the Union loyalists on the committee that an inner circle now existed who were prepared to ride roughshod over them. It appeared to the wider membership that the committee did not care anymore to consult its own members. Rather ironically, this was the very accusation Stirrup had laid in his article at the door of the BU leaders as proof of their ill-will.

The consequences were many and all of them severe. First, relations with the BU were badly damaged because Payne took great exception to the officers of the BU being (inaccurately) criticized in print without having first been approached privately.[34] Second, Leslie Larwood promptly resigned from the BRF committee and from the role of editor. He was understandably angry. Stirrup had undermined his editorial authority by acting like an official spokesman to the press, had usurped Larwood's editorial privilege by publishing ahead of him, and had snubbed him by failing even to forewarn him. In his letter of resignation, Larwood stated his belief that in his pro-

---

[29] Ecumenism: a statement of the Baptist Revival Fellowship Regarding the Ecumenical Movement, (Baptist Revival Fellowship, 1967).
[30] Minutes of the BRF Committee, April 3, 1967: letter from L. Larwood (he had presented his apologies).
[31] Published in *The Christian and Christianity Today*, April 14, 1967, 5.
[32] Published in *Life of Faith* April 13, 1967, 344.
[33] 'Baptist Revival Fellowship Condemns Ecumenism,' *The Christian and Christianity Today*, April 14, 1967, 5.
[34] E. Payne to A. Steen, April 17, 1967 (BRF Archive, File: 1967/68).

Union sympathies, he was 'now in a minority on the Committee.'[35] On June 6, he went further, asserting that 'there is not unanimity and I am one who is not in sympathy with some of the trends which seem to me to be changing the character and purpose of BRF and which are causing serious division in our membership.'[36] A third consequence was that other resignations from the committee swiftly followed from denominational loyalists. One of these was Ernest Rudman, minister of Victoria Road, Hove, and a revered and long-standing member of the BRF. Even more calamitous was the resignation of Hugh Butt, since 1965 the General Superintendent of the West Midlands Area. Butt was the only senior Baptist official in the BRF and had quietly helped the Committee with inside information about the Union from time to time, perhaps sometimes a little irregularly.[37] Now he was understandably infuriated at being associated not only with the statement but with the implied attack on him in the commentary supplied by Stirrup. In correspondence with Alec Steen, he expressed the view that 'this is obviously another attempt on the part of somebody in the same pressure group I mentioned before to get his own point of view across in Christian newspapers before even the BRF members have had the opportunity of considering it.'[38] Further dire consequences would follow. Such was the disquiet in the BRF and the Union, that Alec Steen was obliged to write to the periodicals asking them to publish a denial that Stirrup spoke in any official capacity for the BRF and claiming that he had in any case misrepresented the situation. None of them believed it and no-one would publish the denial. They evidently took the view that, as Stirrup obviously had privileged access to information that came from the BRF, such a denial was disingenuous. The BRF lost a great deal of credibility and the balance of power shifted to the secession party as the loyalists withdrew from leadership. This further eroded the credibility of the BRF as a denominational movement because it was far too public to be missed by those outside the BRF. W. H. Wragg commented on it in one of three articles about 'contemporary issues' in *The Fraternal* magazine, noting that some churches had withdrawn their membership from the BU and adding, 'Equally sad is

---

[35] L. Larwood to A. Steen, April 15, 1967 (BRF Archive, File:1965/1966).
[36] L. Larwood to A. Steen, June l 6, 1967, BRF Archive, File: 1965/66.
[37] See the Minutes of the BRF Committee, November 23, 1966, Item 15: Superannuation. Butt shared the contents of a letter from Payne to all Superintendents which dealt with controversies over Ministers leaving the fund prematurely, an issue that concerned a number of BRF members on account of following Lloyd-Jones' call to resign from broad denominations. Such Baptist Union ministers stood to lose substantial amounts of money by being disqualified from continuing in the Superannuation Scheme.
[38] Hugh Butt to Alec Steen, April 18, 1967 (BRF Archive, File:1967/68).

The Road to Secession (1966-70)

the urging of other churches by zealots – some of them not even Baptists! – to follow suit.'[39]

Hesters Way Baptist Church, Cheltenham

At this point, by a great misfortune of timing, a Baptist church's resignation from the BU not only brought the disintegrating relationship of the BRF with the denomination to a pitch but also heightened the BRF's own internal tensions. Hesters Way Baptist Church, Cheltenham sent in a letter of resignation to the BU in July 1967, just after the mayhem within the BRF committee. There were several reasons for the controversy it generated. In the first place, the Area Superintendent involved was none other than Hugh Butt. Added to that was the fact that Basil Howlett, the minister of the church, was close to his ministerial neighbour Douglas Jones, one of the secessionists who had caused controversy within the BRF committee. Furthermore, the Union had had little direct contact with the secessionists in the BRF, mainly using for communication BRF people who were loyalists recommended by George Beasley-Murray (who had formed an 'ad-hoc' group to encourage exchanges between such BRF members and leaders within the BU). Finally, the Union was seeking at that time to move away from exactly the kind of Independency that could declare itself free, as had Hesters Way. As the church was governed by a BU 'Model Trust,' the BU Corporation owned the premises and was in a position to reclaim them. As if anything more were needed to infuse this situation with conflict, the *Evangelical Times* (or *ET*) began publication that year as a voice for conservative evangelicalism of the kind represented by Lloyd-Jones, including the call to secede from the mainstream denominations. To compound matters even further, the founding editor was Peter Masters, a Baptist pro-secessionist himself. *ET* gave front page coverage to the case on several occasions as an example of Baptist Union intolerance of conservative dissent. The result was that Hesters Way became a very public test case in at least two ways.

First of all, the BU took a hard line over the church premises, in a conflict that would drag on for two years and would do little credit to the denomination, which allowed itself to appear as a Goliath battling a David. The church recognized from the outset that the buildings would present a problem because of their being held under a Model Trust Deed which tied the church to the BU. It offered to buy them at the market price but the BU Corporation refused and eventually decided to expel the congregation. Russell reported to the Officers the final outcome in 1969.[40] The seceding congregation was

---

[39] 'Baptists and Some Contemporary Issues,' in *The Fraternal*, No. 151, July 1969, 14.
[40] Minutes of the Officers Meeting, December 5, 1969, Item V: BRF Conference and Hesters Way.

evicted but a small remnant of members agreed to remain and continue the church; they later re-applied for BU membership.[41]

Secondly, it was a test case for Hugh Butt, as a BRF supporter who had only recently been appointed as an Area Superintendent. His reactions were not only under the scrutiny of his colleagues on the Superintendents' Board, but of David Russell, the new BU General Secretary, who knew people connected with the church.[42] Not only that, Butt had just been publicly humiliated by George Stirrup's articles because of their negativity towards the denominational loyalists in BRF of whom Butt was well known to be the most senior example. This led him to break his connection with the movement after decades of loyalty just as he began to deal with Hesters Way (a complication of which Howlett was at first unaware).[43] Butt came down hard. He effectively told Howlett he was under God's judgment, saying 'one day you and the Church will be accountable to God for the decisions you have made.'[44] Furthermore, he used his correspondence with Howlett to set out his own stall as a conservative evangelical working for the denomination:

> I cannot for one moment see how such a step [resignation] can either be to the glory of Christ or to the real advancement of His kingdom. The questions I would ask of you, and of others who have taken a similar step, would be, Did you leave as a first or a last resort? Did you leave reluctantly and sadly, or eagerly and gaily? To be driven out is one thing, to walk out is quite another, and I believe there is still a place within our Denomination for the seed of the Word of God to be sown, and I have faith enough to believe that one day it will bear fruit to the praise and glory of His Name.[45]

There was more. Butt had not only been a BRF supporter but had been in Lloyd-Jones' circle of admirers and he engaged in a more personal conversation with Basil Howlett. He told him that Lloyd-Jones had approved of his taking the Superintendency. This surprised Howlett so much that he

---

[41] It was reported to the BU Council in March 1970 that congregations were averaging 60 with 'a new and remarkable spirit of fellowship' (Minutes of the BU Council, March 17/18, 1969, Item XIII (j). The church had re-applied for membership, which was, perhaps unsurprisingly, accepted with some pleasure and brought before the 1970 Assembly Council meeting, despite the church stating in its application that it would not participate in ecumenical life, did not wish its Home Work Fund giving to be used for ecumenical work, and hoped for a waiver should it wish to call an unaccredited minister in the future. The BU Council was unusually accommodating, declining to dismiss such demands and instead agreeing that 'the points would be carefully considered' when the application was approved *nem.con.*

[42] Minutes of the Officers Meeting, December 5, 1969, Item V: BRF Conference and Hesters Way.
[43] Letter from Basil Howlett, July 29, 2010.
[44] Hugh Butt to Basil Howlett, July 12, 1967 (supplied to me by Basil Howlett).
[45] Ibid.

The Road to Secession (1966-70)

asked Lloyd-Jones to confirm it. 'The Doctor' recalled the conversation but insisted he had only said to do it 'if your conscience allows you to do such a thing, but I couldn't.'[46] The conservative voice in the denomination had become as thoroughly confused as the case of Hesters Way.

The BRF and 'Baptists at the Crossroads'

The BU kept open the lines of communication but seldom gave any ground to BRF concerns beyond meetings in order to talk about them. It certainly appeared that Russell's aim was not to affirm conservatism but to contain it. The BRF leadership meanwhile became more united by its commitment to secession. The anti-denominational stance was consolidated at its 1967 Annual Conference. The controversial statement on ecumenism was adopted as official policy, to the dismay of some members, but otherwise to widespread approval.

David Kingdon gave a paper at the conference on Baptist identity which was subsequently published by the BRF as *Baptists at the Crossroads*.[47] For Kingdon this was a crucial moment personally. He resigned from the BU list of accredited ministers the day before delivering his paper.[48] Only then did he feel free to speak his mind. He surmised that the current situation of the Baptist Union was 'at bottom doctrinal, and is, in particular, focused upon the issue of the purity of the Church.'[49] He therefore offered an historical analysis of Baptist attitudes to these issues in two doctrinal disputes, the first regarding Matthew Caffyn (1628–1714) in the seventeenth-century General Baptist denomination, and the second regarding the Downgrade Controversy in 1887–8.[50] It was Kingdon's purpose 'to consider how our forebears faced the issue of the purity of the church (or, as we shall see,

---

[46] Letter to me from Basil Howlett, July 29, 2010. It may seem unlikely that Martyn Lloyd-Jones would fail to condemn a conservative evangelical taking senior denominational office, given his secessionist statements at the time, but I recall from personal experience that Lloyd-Jones was often gentler in his pastoral advice than in his public statements.
[47] Kingdon must be credited with a deliberate reference here to Shakespeare's call for a united church.
[48] Mentioned (presumably accurately as it was published without editorial correction) in a letter requesting lay-membership of the BRF from Gordon Anscombe and John Bridger, Tunbridge Wells, in the *BRF Bulletin* No. 100, July/September 1969, 8.
[49] David P. Kingdon, *Baptists at the Crossroads* (London: Baptist Revival Fellowship, 1967), 3.
[50] The 'Downgrade' controversy occurred in the latter years of the 1880s, when Spurgeon, pastor of what became known as the Metropolitan Tabernacle from 1854 until his death in 1892, accused the Baptist Union of tolerating heterodoxy and withdrew himself and his church from the Baptist Union in consequence. A small number of other churches left under his influence, some of them joining the (then) denominationally unaffiliated Home Counties Baptist Association. Spurgeon's College also followed his lead and remained outside the Union until 1938. See Randall, *English Baptists of the Twentieth Century*, 224.

largely refused to face) the issue of the purity of the Church,' an issue which 'always concerns doctrine and discipline.'[51]

From Caffyn, Kingdon drew the conclusion that the General Baptists had failed to discipline him properly for his heterodox Christology and that biblical phraseology had been misused in an attempt to sound biblically faithful without affirming biblical truth. He then observed that:

> We see here two expedients which characterize the denomination today. We are told that it is sufficient to utter the Scriptural confession "Jesus is Lord", and all is well. But the whole question of the person of Christ is actually by-passed: is the Jesus we confess the Jesus of Chalcedon or Bultmann, of Gresham Machen or John Robinson, of B. B. Warfield or Paul van Buran? It is surely a misuse of Scripture to use the *terms* of Scripture to deny the plain *teaching* of Scripture, and it is high time we said so!

Then secondly, we see how the desire for the maintenance of denominational unity led to a refusal to face the denominational issue involved in the Arianism of Caffyn and his supporters. R. G. Torbet sees the issue as being "the thorny question of whether unity or orthodoxy was to be preferred."[52]

Kingdon noted the divided and unstable history of the General Baptists after these events, and the corresponding debate as to whether or not Baptists should subscribe to creeds and confessions in view of their emphasis on liberty of conscience. His conclusion was that the General Baptists were incapable of resolving their problems because they were unwilling to adopt and maintain a confessional standard, unlike the New Connexion a century later:

> If the New Connexion did not require a subscription to a confession of faith, how could it have dealt with the Arian members of the old General Assembly, especially when, as was the case, that body had never explicitly repudiated its original orthodox confession.[53]

Kingdon drew four conclusions: 'inaction in the face of heresy results in the loss of testimony'; 'the desire to maintain an outward unity at all costs is one of the chief obstacles to the disciplining of those who teach error'; 'failure … to define doctrine … and to take action against heresy, makes secession inevitable'; 'revival does not necessarily result in reformation.'[54]

---

[51] Baptists at the Crossroads, 3.
[52] Ibid., 4–5, quoting from R. G. Torbet, *A History of the Baptists*, rev. ed. (Pennsylvania: Judson Press, 1973), 65.
[53] Ibid., 7.
[54] Ibid.

The Road to Secession (1966-70)

Turning next to the Downgrade Controversy, Kingdon deprecated the change in the Baptist Union from its Calvinistic foundation in 1813 to its weak profession of 'the sentiments usually denominated Evangelical,' and then the abandonment even of the term 'evangelical' in 1873.[55] Having rehearsed C. H. Spurgeon's accusations against the Baptist denomination (summed up by the accusation that there was a theological 'downgrade'), which led to Spurgeon's resignation from the Union, Kingdon noted that the final attempt at reconciliation, through adopting a simple confessional statement by the Baptist Union, was a failure. It affirmed a doctrinal basis similar to that of the Evangelical Alliance, but Spurgeon rejected an explanatory footnote of 'historical fact' to the effect that some 'brethren … have not held the common interpretation' of eternal punishment.[56] Kingdon further noted that the confession of faith was printed only once in the Baptist Union Handbook, in 1888, and thereafter disappeared from view so that the Baptist historian Lumpkin was right to point out that 'no confession of faith was asked for or given by either group' when the New Connexion General Baptists united with the Union in 1891.[57] Kingdon went on to expound Spurgeon's view as being based on two basic convictions: that 'there was one Gospel, the same in every age, *the* faith once for all delivered to the saints;' and that 'any union of churches must be based on an explicit statement of and practical adherence to the doctrine of grace' and not simply 'believer's baptism by immersion.'[58] He cited A. C. Underwood's 'very fair' analysis of the Downgrade Controversy[59] to confirm the Baptist Union's reluctance to adopt a confession of faith rather than a Declaration of Principle.[60]

Kingdon then analysed the modern position of conservative evangelicals in the Baptist Union. Using language remarkably similar to Lloyd-Jones in 1966, he said they were 'in a position of great embarrassment and indeed, of profound inconsistency' by affirming their position as the truth but tolerating those who contradicted it. Those who believed in being 'in it to win it' could only justify their position by getting the Union 'to adopt an evangelical basis of faith, and, should such a basis be adopted, the disciplining of those who do not adhere to the truths set forth in it.' Without these commitments, such evangelicals 'cannot, as I believe, expect the blessing of God in their efforts, for then the reformation which they seek is not reformation according to the Word of God.' Those who argue that 'they

---

[55] Ibid, 7–8.
[56] Ibid, 9.
[57] Ibid, 9.
[58] Ibid., 10.
[59] See A. C. Underwood, *A History of the English Baptists*, (London: Carey Kingsgate Press, 1947), 229–233.
[60] Ibid., 10.

are in the Union to bear witness' but not to change it in this way, 'are saying, in effect, that their evangelicalism is merely one possible point of view among professing Christians, not the Christian faith itself.'[61] In contrast with the Union's unwillingness to stand firmly for any doctrinal standard, Kingdon then compared the Declaration of Principle with the WCC basis as 'a fellowship of churches which confess the Lord Jesus Christ as God and Saviour according to the Scriptures, and therefore seek to fulfil together their common calling to the glory of the one God, Father, Son, and Holy Spirit.'[62] The BU was inconsistent, he thought, in affirming more for the sake of ecumenical unity than it would for denominational unity.

Finally, Kingdon believed that 'the growing ecumenical pressure' required evangelicals to face questions of membership in the 'coming great Church.'[63] Kingdon offered three choices to Baptist Union evangelicals: inaction leading to loss of identity; reformation of the Union if it were possible at all; or separation to stand outside compromised denominations. He offered three possible alternatives to those who chose to separate from the Union – the Fellowship of Independent Evangelical Churches (FIEC), isolation, or – significantly for what would follow in the BRF's plans – to 'form a fellowship of Baptist churches which is ordered by "the faith once delivered to the saints."'[64] It is interesting to note that he did not mention the exclusively Calvinistic Grace Baptist Assembly. Here was exactly what Lloyd-Jones approved – an established denominational grouping upholding the principle of Independency while maintaining throughout its history a strongly conservative evangelical identity.[65] Moreover, it was authentically Baptist and Calvinistic, the very position now of many BRF members. Was this because it would undermine creating a new Baptist fellowship aimed at embracing both Reformed and Arminian evangelicals in the BRF?

---

[61] Ibid., 10–11.

[62] Ibid., 11.

[63] In fact, this was an exaggeration in terms of the BU's official policy. Although there was much discussion, Baptists remained skeptical of reunion. In response to the 'Nottingham Conference' call for reunion, the Union produced *Baptists and Unity*, in which it was clearly stated that Baptists 'are not able to accept the view...that the difference between the Churches concerning the use of standards of belief and concerning the relation between Scripture and Tradition are now insufficient to stand as barriers to unity. *Baptists and Unity*, a report of the BU Council issued in 1967, 58.

[64] Ibid., 11.

[65] Lloyd-Jones at least once declared the Grace Baptists to be the best denominational fellowship available and the one denomination he would be prepared to join. I heard about this in the mid-seventies from the film-maker Norman Stone, who was a friend of mine then through our shared involvement with UCCF activities in London. He recalled it from a visit of Lloyd-Jones to his family home, his father being a Grace Baptist pastor.

The Road to Secession (1966-70)

The secession party, as previously noted, gained control of the BRF in 1967 and adopted a formal stance against ecumenism together with an approving stance towards secession. The BU published a report on ecumenical relations that year which was presented for consideration over a two-year period of consultation with a proposed vote on its adoption at the 1969 Assembly. A collision became inevitable between the BRF and the BU from this point onwards.

The 'Baptists and Unity' Debate

In the late sixties, the most important ecumenical agendum in the BU was the report *Baptists and Unity*, published early in 1967 in preparation for its presentation to the 1967 Assembly. It clearly advocated closer ecumenical relations. The BRF met with Payne in February and asked that either alternative views be presented from the platform or that an open debate should take place. It was reported to the BRF Committee that Payne promised to refer the first suggestion to the Council and of the second said that open debate in an Assembly was 'difficult' and that in any case the Report was being presented only. The plan was to inaugurate a two-year period 'for study and representations by the churches before any decision was taken.' The group raised several further issues about bias in the BU against the conservative viewpoint. None received active consideration.[66] This indicates two interrelated facts. One was a certain naivety in the BRF leadership. They seemed unable to grasp that denominational criticism only carried weight in proportion to denominational loyalty. The other was that their suspicion of bias was correct. Payne had never offered real affirmation to them, and it was evident enough that he was, in reality, courteously ignoring them. Once again, the message seemed to be that conservatives were not on an equal footing with more liberal members of the Baptist family. It is perhaps less surprising under those circumstances that secession was under consideration.

A. Morgan Derham reviewed *Baptists and Unity* in *The Christian and Christianity Today* early in 1968. Derham was a member of the group that had produced *Liberty in the Lord*. He admitted the current independence of Baptist churches and therefore their ability 'to ignore the denominational machine' but commented:

---

[66] Minutes of the BRF Committee, November 21, 1967: Item 9: committee meeting [held the previous February] with Dr. Payne.

> Nevertheless, since Congregationalism changed its nature and abandoned its historic independent principles, Baptist evangelicals have been watching their denominational machine with a wary eye; they have therefore been particularly interested in the contents of the Report *Baptists and Unity*.[67]

Derham warned that any attempt by Baptists to follow the Congregationalist example in order to prepare the way for a united ecumenical Church 'would cause a massive disruption of the Baptist family, and would only further the cause of unity by creating an outsize division.' In fact, *Baptists and Unity* acknowledged the unlikelihood of such a policy, as noticed previously. Nevertheless, this was a deep concern among BRF members. Stanley Voke himself wrote about the report, providing one of three perspectives which were published together in the Baptist ministers' magazine, *The Fraternal*. Voke recognized that the report 'has been sensible to counsel caution' but nevertheless expressed dissatisfaction that the committee that produced it 'does not appear to contain anyone representing the considerable body of Baptists of conservative evangelical outlook who have serious reservations about ecumenical involvement.'[68] The sense of being disenfranchised had become a settled conviction in conservative circles, even for a denominational loyalist like Voke. His main criticism was that unity was posited upon 'the One Gospel' but 'what, we ask, if there has arisen another Gospel…?'[69] He suspected one in sacramentalism and felt that the report 'beclouded' the issue 'by a sacramental emphasis itself.'[70] He believed he represented 'many of us' in his concerns, and called for seeking 'church purity rather than church unity at present.'[71] Thus it may be seen that the BRF contained denominational loyalists who were far more cautious in their criticisms than those who advocated leaving it, yet even they were decidedly suspicious about the ecumenical movement.

In 1969 *Baptists and Unity* was placed before the BU Assembly for adoption as policy. The report had been sent to the associations and churches for their responses, which was published in preparation for the Assembly as *Baptists and Unity Reviewed*. The responses came from 655 of the 2214 churches, together with 17 Associations, 'several fraternals and a number of individuals.'[72] The churches were 'almost all' opposed to organic union,

---

[67] 'Unity: What About Baptists?' by A. Morgan Derham, in *The Christian and Christianity Today*, January 12,1968, 16.
[68] *Fraternal*, No. 146, October 1967, 26.
[69] Ibid., 27.
[70] Ibid.
[71] Ibid., 28.
[72] '"Baptists and Unity" Reviewed': Report to the Baptist Union Council by the Advisory Committee on Church Relations, March 1969.

The Road to Secession (1966-70)

while 164 definitely wished the Union to withdraw from the World and British Councils of Churches compared to 168 who wished it to remain in membership – the remaining 323 not expressing a view. The objectors were reported commonly to present three reasons: that the WCC had an inadequate doctrinal basis, that the WCC was perceived to be 'a vast monolithic Church organization that will tolerate no deviations from its own structure and practice,' and fear 'concerning the influence of the Orthodox Churches ... and the increasing participation of the Roman Catholic Church.' Concern was also expressed over any increased participation in the WCC by the Baptists.[73] This was hardly a ringing endorsement of ecumenism. It signified a wider spectrum of opinion and a larger constituency with reservations than simply the BRF membership.

The 1969 BU Assembly

As the Assembly approached, the BRF sent out a circular letter to its members urging resistance to the adoption of *Baptists and Unity* at the forthcoming Baptist Assembly. The committee felt that this marked an opportunity to make a 'stand for truth that the Union has not known since the days of C. H. Spurgeon who discerned in his day the trends that are now manifest within the Denomination.'[74] They took the view that adopting the report would not only confirm the BU in membership of the WCC and BCC, but would prepare the way for creating a Baptist Church preparatory to reunion and eventual absorption into an authoritative world church. Russell preserved the notes of a speech, presumably given at the 1969 Assembly, upholding this suspicion, in which the unnamed author states that 'despite denials to the contrary it seems obvious that any united church would be centrally controlled.'[75] At the same Assembly, as it happened, the membership of the BU Council was modestly altered as a result of the Report on Association, giving greater representation to the Associations. This was taken to be 'a blow to independency ... of the local church,' as Robert Horn asserted when reflecting upon the Assembly in the *BRF Bulletin*.[76] Some BRF members were convinced that a secret conspiracy existed among the Union leaders to combine ecumenical involvement with the centralization of denominational structures in order to prepare for membership of a hierarchical world church. What certainly existed was a line drawn in the sand by the BRF against continued membership of the World and British Councils of Churches, which 75% of Baptists simply voted to cross by

---

[73] Ibid., 4–7.
[74] Circular letter from Theo Bamber to all BRF members, April 3, 1969 (David Russell's Papers: File Reference A7).
[75] David Russell's Papers: File Reference A9).
[76] *BRF Bulletin*, July/September 1969, 4.

The Baptist Revival Fellowship

adopting the report in question. The 'Spurgeonic stand' materialized only in the determination of a few ministers and churches to regard this as the point of no return that would lead them out of the denomination. The majority of Baptists found nothing significant to fear in *Baptists and Unity*. Local church autonomy had survived and ecumenical engagement was accepted in the knowledge that the envisioned 'world church' would yet have to face the problem of member churches which held such an ecclesiology.

The BRF nevertheless pressed on with its goal of secession, circulating a letter after the Assembly which Horn described as raising 'the possibility of forming some kind of evangelical fellowship of Baptist churches.'[77] From this point onwards, the vision of 1967 became a definite commitment, to withdraw from the BU in favour of a new body. Russell noted that the BRF contained some members who 'felt quite unhappy about the action taken and the attitude adopted by the BRF and resigned from it. These, I believe, included Leslie Larwood and Geoffrey King.'[78] This was significant. It indicates that an open division had now taken place within the BRF. Russell certainly thought so, commenting some months later, at the BU Council meeting of November 11 and 12, that 'those connected with the Fellowship promised to use their influence to combat this trend.'[79] The comment probably reflects discussion of the BRF call for a new denomination at the July meeting of the Advisory Committee on Church Relations. Larwood was a member (despite Voke's opinion that the BRF viewpoint was overlooked) and there stated openly in Russell's hearing that 'he and a number of members of the BRF had written strongly protesting against it.' That committee took the unusual step of sending a deputation to meet the BRF Committee and to request permission to address the annual conference of the BRF.[80] In September, Russell reported to the Officers' Meeting that he, George Beasley-Murray and John Beaumont had met the BRF leaders but 'it had been an unhappy meeting. It had become clear that a number of ministers may withdraw from the denomination.'[81] Nor was the request to address the BRF Conference granted.

Bamber had not been able to attend the meeting with the BU delegation and so sent his own comments in a personal reply to Russell.[82] Referring to the

---

[77] Ibid., 5.
[78] David Russell, Reflections on the General Secretaryship of the BU, 1967–82, (David Russell's Papers, File A1), 3.
[79] Minutes of the BU Council, November 11–12, 1969, Item 13 (p) of the GP&F Report to Council.
[80] Minutes of the Advisory Committee on Church Relations, July 11, 1969, Item II: Baptist Revival Fellowship.
[81] Minutes of the Meeting of Officers, September 8, 1969, Item XIII: Baptist Revival Fellowship.
[82] Bamber to Russell, Memorandum enclosed with reply of July 19, 1969 (Russell's Papers: File Reference A6).

The Road to Secession (1966-70)

adoption by Assembly of *Baptists and Unity*, Bamber said that 'the Assembly has demoted the local church' so that 'it will be easy to make the Baptist Union the Baptist Church.' Bamber spoke of 'a crisis of decision' now reached by many in the denomination, but did not think 'the denomination is really troubled about the possible withdrawal of evangelicals if this should be.' Russell was troubled, however, though perhaps less by the prospect of vocal critics like Bamber leaving than by the thought of those 400 ministers in membership with the BRF following suit with their churches. When the matter was brought to GP&F in October, he reported that he had sent 'a pastoral letter ... to all ministers,' answering the arguments put forward by BRF in favour of secession.[83] In his letter, he had urged that 'it is right that we should hold fast what we have received (2 Tim 1:13); but the danger of dogmatism must be avoided, whatever theological school we may belong to.'[84] He reported to GP&F that he had 'already received some grateful replies,' but evidently so had the BRF, which continued to pursue its plan.

The 1969 BRF Conference and the Adoption of Secession as a Definite Policy

The 1969 Annual Conference was reported at the December Meeting of BU Officers to have agreed the setting up of 'a committee to advise those working to form an evangelical Baptist Union.' *BT* covered the conference both through an editorial by Bottoms and a report from Geoffrey King. King noted that 'some 240 members of the Fellowship attended the conference from all parts if the British Isles' and went on to say that

> In the business session, at which not all members of the conference were present, a decision was taken (to the deep grief of some 60 of us) to set up a sub-committee to explore the possibility of forming a group of Evangelical Baptist Churches for those Baptists who could not be associated with the World Council of Churches. Voting, 101 to 60 against, took place only after a long debate and an adjournment to a second session.[85]

For King publicly to attack the BRF was very significant. He was not a man to renounce his loyalties lightly, let alone publicize them in this way.[86] Walter

---

[83] Minutes of the GP&F Committee, October 7, 1969, Item 85/69: BRF.
[84] 'a special letter from the General Secretary to all ministers', October 1969 (Russell's Papers: File A5).
[85] *BT*, November 27, 1969, 2.
[86] The editor of the *BRF Bulletin*, George Stirrup, subsequently commented on the *BT* coverage and claimed that King 'dissociated himself from the article that appeared under his name' presumably because Bottoms had edited it to his disapproval. *BRF Bulletin* No. 102, January/March 1970, 1.

95

Bottoms headed his editorial 'A Sorry Decision.' He commented that 'fewer than half of those attending voted for it and about 60 voted against' and commented, no doubt repeating the opinion of a disaffected BRF member:

> The more immediate effects of the BRF decision are likely to be a splitting of its fellowship and of some of the churches to which its members belong. A speaker in the discussion at Swanwick who said that the BRF was 'no longer a revival fellowship but a rival fellowship' was voicing what others have felt increasingly in the last two or three years.[87]

Bottoms allowed a reply to his comment about numbers from John Waterman, who had been the conference registrar. Waterman pointed out that the missing 21 people from the business meeting were accounted for by Irish members not voting 'for obvious reasons' and by the women at the conference having their own session at the same time as the business session.[88] There was no hiding the truth, however, that the decision was divisive and deeply distressing to a large proportion of people who had, until that time, accepted the BRF as a legitimate conservative evangelical witness within the Union. This was well expressed by another correspondent that same week, who had joined the BRF only a month before the conference because of his 'increasing concern for revival' and to find people 'who were seeking to experience, in a new and greater dimension, the power of the Holy Spirit.' While he had 'reservations about the ecumenical movement' he hoped 'the time will never come when there is a separate group of Evangelical Baptist churches.'[89] This is an interesting comment, suggestive of an intriguing possibility that never materialized, of the BRF returning to its vision for spiritual revitalization within the denomination by making central its early role in charismatic renewal in the BU alongside a concern for conservative evangelical clarity. Such a policy might not only have influenced BU life considerably but the wider charismatic movement as well. Theo Bamber did not hope the time for secession would never come, however. In the *BRF Bulletin* for July/September 1969, he stated that 'Our ecumenical brethren cannot be surprised if we feel we may have come to the parting of the ways.'[90] The BRF strategy caused its own 'parting of the ways.' The conference decision led three long-standing and senior BRF figures to

---

[87] *BT*, November 27, 1969, 5.
[88] *BT*, December 11, 1969, 3. Remaining confusion led to a restatement of the missing numbers in the *BRF Bulletin* No. 102, January/March 1970, which explained that 216 were present at the Conference, of whom 186 were able to vote. 165 returned ballot papers leaving 21 abstentions. Voting in favour was 101, and against 59 (five of which were blank papers). This indicates serious division by any standard, the essential point Bottoms was making.
[89] Ibid., 3.
[90] *BRF Bulletin* No. 100, July/September 1969, 3.

The Road to Secession (1966-70)

resign their membership: Geoffrey King, Stanley Voke (both of whom were members of the BU Council) and Herbert Ward. Bamber acknowledged of King, 'What BRF owes to him it would be difficult to exaggerate.' He continued to be listed in the *BRF Bulletin* as holding the office of Prayer Secretary, a position he had occupied for many years.

It may therefore be said that, at a critical period of change within the denomination, the BU leadership became less sympathetic to the positions espoused by the BRF, that new trends emerged that were a particular threat to the Spurgeonic tradition, and that the BRF became increasingly doubtful both of their place and their welcome at 'the Union table,' a place that had always been under some degree of scrutiny anyway. Doubt turned to hostility as the BRF came under the dominance of Lloyd-Jones' followers and, after a brief engagement with denominational issues, actively began to pursue a wholesale secession. The denominational loyalists withdrew, leaving the BRF with little or no understanding of active engagement with the BU structures. Even King resigned in dismay. The dominant voice in BRF became the Reformed separatist supporters of Lloyd-Jones. They pressed on with secession by obtaining approval, at the 1969 Annual Conference, to create a sub-committee 'to explore the details of the formation of an Association of Evangelical Baptist Churches,' the membership of which was Robert Horn, Ron Luland, Harold Owen and John Pretlove. All of these men were on the BRF Committee, indicating that although the strategy was kept separate from the BRF's formal programme, it came nevertheless from the Fellowship's key leaders. Bamber was wholly in favour, as may be seen in a resignation letter to him after the Conference from Ernest Rudman, a longstanding BRF activist and minister of the prominent Baptist church Holland Road, Hove. He said of the decision, 'You have secured the vote upon which you had so set your heart that, even while continuing to preside as Chairman, you intimated so clearly ... that a vote otherwise would embarrass the Committee.'[91] Stanley Voke, who had persevered with the BRF up to this point, now resigned from the Committee and openly avowed his intention to advertise his dissociation from the secession policy 'in word and print.'[92] Bamber did not live to see his vision fulfilled, however. He died in his eightieth year in 1970. Despite the parting of their ways, Geoffrey King wrote a gracious obituary for him which was published in the BU Handbook for 1971. He recalled there that Bamber had retired in 1961 following thirty-five years of hugely successful service at Rye Lane Baptist Church, Peckham. King described him as 'the beloved chairman' of the BRF, a role in which he continued until his 'Homecall.' Bamber had died suddenly in his eightieth

---

[91] Letter from E. G. Rudman to T. M. Bamber, November 19, 1969 (BRF Archive, File: T.M.B.).
[92] Letter from S. Voke to T. M. Bamber, November 27, 1969 (BRF Archive, File: T.M.B.).

year 'in a train on the way to a preaching engagement in answer to an emergency telephone call.'[93]

The chairmanship of BRF was given to Harold Owen, minister of Percy Street Baptist Church, Woking, who was by then known as a keen supporter of charismatic renewal, a pro-secessionist, and an advocate of Reformed theology. [94] Under his leadership, the pace quickened towards secession. In August of 1970, the Sub-Committee met to plan a pro-secession meeting at the BRF Annual Conference. It would be 'for those who agreed with the 1969 resolution and had genuine sympathy with the idea of forming some AEBC'[95] and to explore 'the possibility of forming an AEBC soon and to consider future plans.'[96] It was agreed to propose to the meeting that ministers in sympathy with forming the AEBC would be invited to sign a 'Declaration of Intent' to resign from the BU Accredited List, 'perhaps by Spring 1971.'[97]

Denominational Approaches to the BRF

The BRF's ministerial membership made it too significant to be ignored completely within the denomination. There was no real possibility that the leadership of the BU would contemplate the denomination renouncing its ecumenical commitment, but the issue of conserving Baptist tradition was of real concern more widely in the denomination and this gave a certain authenticity to the traditionalist stance of the BRF. David Russell therefore had the unenviable task of trying to include their voice of protest against ecumenism, greater centralization and liberal trends in theology while the denomination was moving in precisely those directions. This resulted in three main strategies: the formation in 1967 of a Union sub-committee on "The Causes of Dissension", the creation by George Beasley-Murray of an 'ad-hoc' group to discuss theological differences between conservatives and liberals, and inviting the BRF to make formal statements in response to denominational reports. These were *The Child and the Church* (1966), *Baptists and Unity* and *Baptists and Unity Reviewed* (1967–9) and *Ministry Tomorrow* (1970–1).

---

[93] *The Baptist Handbook* for 1971, 376: Memoirs of Deceased Ministers and Missionaries.
[94] His church in Woking eventually became identified with the *New Frontiers* movement, a charismatic network with a strong emphasis on traditional Calvinistic theology.
[95] These initials were obviously already understood to be an abbreviation of 'Association of Evangelical Baptist Churches.' In terms of Baptist ecclesiology, this represented a clear intent to establish an inter-church structure of like-minded churches of Baptist faith and order, but something more consultative and less structured than an alternative 'Baptist Union.'
[96] Minutes of the BRF Sub-Committee, August 18, 1970, Item 2.
[97] Ibid., Item 3.

The Road to Secession (1966-70)

The Sub-Committee on "Causes of Dissension" (hereafter 'CoD') had as lay-members Arnold Clark, Sir Donald Finnimore, Gordon Fitch and Godfrey Le Quesne, who took the chair. Ministerial membership comprised George Beasley-Murray, Hugh Butt, A. Ellis, J. Ithel Jones, Leslie Larwood, David Russell, and R. W. Thompson acting as secretary.[98] The BRF was invited to submit a formal statement to the committee, which was tabled in March 1968 and then discussed by CoD in April with George Stirrup and Ronald Luland representing the BRF Committee. The BRF Report covered ecumenism, denominational centralization, the need for a doctrinal basis and the poor spiritual quality of association life. It concluded that unless these matters took a course more acceptable to conservatives in the Union, 'the steady trickle of secessions ... will continue and may even grow.'[99] To prevent this, the BRF proposed five steps: to withdraw from membership of the WCC and BCC; to then hold a referendum on whether or not to apply for membership or alternatively observer status; to adopt a Baptist Confession of Faith; to introduce discipline of those who refused to uphold it; and to adopt a permanent policy in favour of Baptist church autonomy.[100]

In the meeting for discussion the main critics of the BRF stance were David Russell, Gordon Hastings and Arnold Clark. Russell was opposed to doctrinal tests being applied on the basis that it would split the denomination.[101] Hastings was dismissive of the BRF viewpoint, stating that they were not capable among themselves of drawing up a doctrinal basis as 'he had never met conservative evangelicals who believed the same thing.'[102] He judged that the BRF statement 'was in effect an ultimatum,'[103] rather than a contribution to discussions. CoD did not take matters further after these exchanges. It was, ultimately, only a talking shop as far as producing a strategy for greater unity was concerned. David Russell wrote in 1990 a reflection on his years as General Secretary of the BU. In it, he recalled that the committee identified three main problems: 'a difference of attitude within the denomination to the ecumenical movement, the adequacy or otherwise of the Declaration of Principle as a basis of the union, and alleged trends within the Union which might challenge the independence of the local church.'[104] He did not mention the fourth issue raised by the BRF of spiritual

---

[98] This list was provided to the BRF Committee by Ronald Luland in a report on one of its meetings dated April 29, 1968. (BRF Archive: File T.M.B).
[99] Report, 3: Conclusions (in BRF Archive: File T.M.B).
[100] Ibid, 3.
[101] Summary of the discussion for BU records by R. W. Thompson, 7. (BRF Archive: File T.M.B).
[102] Report, 5.
[103] Ibid, 7.
[104] Russell, 'Reflections on the General Secretaryship of the BU,' 5.

vitality in the denomination, but neither did the BRF statement in its Conclusions.

The striking thing about this and other similar statements produced by the Committee after 1966 was the relational vacuum in which they were produced, giving them a cold and confrontational edge that failed to reflect the spiritual vitality of those who led the BRF but more damagingly, was out of place in a denomination small enough for personal relationships to matter. It is doubtful that the BRF leaders could have won the argument, but their lack of participation in the wider Baptist family really meant that they had lost before they started. Perhaps they wanted to.

At the same time as CoD began its meetings, George Beasley-Murray convened an ad-hoc group to overcome the poor relations between conservatives and liberals and the inevitable misunderstandings that caused. The members were George Beasley-Murray, J. Brown, Leslie Larwood, Ron Luland from February 1968 (replacing Leslie Larwood?), David Pawson, Stanley Voke and Morris West.[105] Ian Randall describes it as Beasley-Murray working with David Russell 'and with two ministers trained at the college, Stanley Voke and Leslie Larwood, to seek to address the tensions' over ecumenism, although others were to play a significant role in this attempt.[106] Luland reported to the BRF Committee after his first attendance that he had been invited by Beasley-Murray 'to join an ad-hoc group ... to keep lines of communication open amongst those with a variety of approach to the Ecumenical Movement.'[107] Beasley-Murray's role in this should be noted here. It reveals his concern for conservative evangelicals to be taken more seriously by the Union, and it demonstrates that he was in close touch with the Union loyalists within the BRF leadership.

The third strategy Russell developed was to welcome BRF statements with regard to draft reports to the Union. *The Child and the Church* brought about a published reply by The Radlett Fellowship, a small group of conservative ministers who had joined together to produce leaflets concerning contemporary issues both in Baptist life and in wider society. Although the Radlett Fellowship had no formal relationship with the BRF, its members were also in the BRF and one, John Pretlove, was on the BRF Committee. The BRF Committee requested the Radlett Fellowship to produce a reply to the BU report, which was published in 1967 as *The Gospel, the Child and the Church*. Its main contentions were that *The Child and the Church* misunderstood the doctrines of human sinfulness and the atonement,

---

[105] BRF Committee Minutes, February 12–13, 1968, 2.
[106] Ian Randall, *A School of the Prophets:150 years of Spurgeon's College*, (London: Spurgeon's College, 2005), 121.
[107] Minutes of the BRF Committee, November 20, 1967: Statement on the Ecumenical Movement.

The Road to Secession (1966-70)

favoured universalism[108] and espoused an un-baptistic view of the church by proposing that the church is not simply a fellowship of believers, but of believers and the catechumenate, including the children of the church.[109]

The BRF formally responded to *Baptists and Unity* by means of a Memorandum to the BU General Secretary, the contents of which had been agreed by the BRF Conference of 1967. Four issues were raised: the constitutional legality of Baptist membership of the WCC; a request that churches resigning from the BU should have their letter of resignation published in *BT*; a request that membership of the Church Relations Committee should include two conservative evangelicals; and a request that the BU consider the issue of drawing up an adequate doctrinal basis for the Union.

The constitutional legality of BU membership of the WCC was challenged on the basis that no formal vote had ever been taken at Assembly. The committee minuted David Russell's opinion that the BU Council decision of 1938 to apply for membership was ratified by its inclusion in the Council Report adopted by the 1939 Assembly, although action could not be taken until after the end of the war. The Committee Secretary, Alec Steen, had written to ask for further clarification and this caused Russell to admit to a somewhat less certain situation in 1939 while averring that the validity of the decision-making procedure 'has since been confirmed by use and wont.' The reason for Russell's backtracking was that the Council Report did not in fact mention Council's decision to apply for membership but the Assembly Minutes recorded that attention was drawn to the decision verbally when the Report was presented.[110] The BRF had identified an embarrassing and important deficiency regarding the decision of the BU to join the WCC. Further, the WCC of 1948 was exclusively a Protestant body but had afterwards opened its membership to the Orthodox Churches. These facts caused a degree of unease that the BRF might be successful in challenging the constitutionality of the Union's continuing membership. As a result, a reaffirmation of membership was included in the Report so that adopting *Baptists and Unity* as Union policy was also a vote for WCC membership.

The second issue raised by the BRF, of publishing resignation letters in *BT*, was more ill-considered, since *BT* was editorially independent of the BU and David Russell had pointed out in reply to Alec Steen that such letters were normally private anyway. The third issue was also ill-considered in that membership of Union committees was decided by a vote of Council and not by the officers of the Union. No seats on them could be guaranteed to anyone.

---

[108] *The Gospel, The Child and the Church* (pp. The Radlett Fellowship, 1967), 1–7.
[109] Ibid., 15ff.
[110] BRF Committee, February 12–13, 1968, Item 13: Conference Resolutions.

Russell promised, however, 'to advocate the election of a representative Church Relations Committee, and would bear in mind the possibility of the co-option of evangelicals.'[111] The final matter was, however, something that Russell could take up, as the need for a confessional statement had been raised within the mainstream of BU life already.

David Russell had confessed to Ron Luland after the April CoD discussion with BRF representatives that he was 'very disturbed' by the denominational situation, which prompted Luland to offer a meeting between Russell and the BRF Committee for further discussions.[112] On May 6, that meeting took place. Russell asked for a memorandum of key requests from the BRF. It listed five: that the Officers and Council take note that there were a number of conservatives whose firm intention was to secede rather than remain in a theologically mixed denomination; that there should be a formal and mutual commitment to 'act in a Christian fashion as it takes place'; that seceding churches should not be deprived of buildings held in trusts requiring membership of the BU, and that arrangements be made for ministers not to lose financially through ceasing to participate in the BU Superannuation Scheme; that Model Trust Deeds should be altered so that churches built with denominational funds are not 'tied to the Union for all time'; and that Assembly should be advised to pass an amendment then being advocated by David Pawson in support of ecclesial Independency in order to end doubt as to whether the BU would eventually become a Church rather than a Union of churches.[113] Two things are evident here. The first is that secession had become a matter of 'when' rather than 'if.' The second is that secession seemed imminent. Russell had looked for reassurance over his anxieties, but this meeting gave him only reasons to worry more.

Russell sought a further meeting with BRF leaders on July 24, feeling that the situation was approaching a crisis because of the circular letter to the BRF members exploring the possibility of creating a new Baptist fellowship, sent out in May following the adoption of *Baptists and Unity*. According to the BRF notes of the meeting,[114] Russell called together the BRF leadership and the BU Church Relations Committee, such was his conviction that matters were getting out of hand. It is evident that his patience was wearing thin. He

---

[111] BRF Executive Committee Minutes, May 14, 1968: Item 5: Correspondence with the General Secretary.

[112] Report of the CoD Sub-Committee to BRF Committee by Ron Luland, April 29, 1968 (BRF Archive: File T.M.B).

[113] Memorandum to Russell following the May 6 Meeting (BRF Archive, File: BRF Minutes 1966–75).

[114] Minutes of meeting of signatories of the confidential letter dated May 15, 1969 with representatives of the Church Relations Committee, July 24, 1969 (BRF Archive, File: BRF Minutes 1966–75). [There are no sections in these Minutes to attribute quotations more clearly].

The Road to Secession (1966-70)

challenged the BRF Committee's right to issue such a letter, accusing them of not consulting their members adequately. He confessed to being offended by the BRF's criticism of the denomination (which he no doubt understood to implicate his personal leadership). Beasley-Murray was present at the meeting and expressed his view that the BRF was being misleading, tendentious and unconcerned about the dangers inherent in secessions that might create irreparable breaches and bitterness between fellow believers. His patience seemed exhausted with the BRF's attitude as well.[115] This meeting was highly significant in BU relations with the BRF. For Russell, it marked the end of any hope of reconciliation. For Beasley-Murray it marked the end of his goodwill toward the BRF.

For the BRF it seemed inevitable that secession would happen rather sooner now that the issue had been frankly discussed with the BU leaders. In fact, a sub-committee was formed in July and met for the first time in September to pursue the formation of an alternative Baptist body. At this meeting the name was officially agreed to be 'The Association of Evangelical Baptist Churches' (AEBC),[116] and the BRF Constitution was given a somewhat elastic meaning to its stipulation that the BRF existed for 'giving testimony within the Baptist Denomination.'[117] The sub-committee interpreted it to include secession as an act of witness to the members of the BU.[118] It was thus envisaged that the AEBC should begin as an optional extra within the BRF rather than as a separate body, and that it would develop in ways as yet unpredictable.[119] Nevertheless, discussion covered its method of inauguration, membership clause, doctrinal basis, annual assembly, ministerial recognition and placement, and a ministerial pension scheme. Russell might have ceased his co-operation with the BRF at this point, but he continued a dialogue with them, even concerning requests put to him for alterations to the BU Model Trusts to exclude the requirement that ministers be accredited in view of some ministers resigning from the Accredited List in protest at denominational policy while remaining accepted by their churches.[120] This matter was in fact considered seriously by the Directors of the BU Corporation, leading to a meeting between them and representatives of the BRF.[121]

---

[115] Ibid.
[116] Minutes of the BRF Sub-committee following the Committee Resolution of July 14, 1969.
[117] BRF Constitution, Clause III:6 (see Appendix Two).
[118] Sub-Committee Minutes, September 19, 1969, Item 4: Relationship between BRF and AEBC.
[119] Ibid.
[120] Reported in BRF Committee Minutes, November 16&18, 1970: Item 4f: Model Trust Deeds.
[121] Minutes of a meeting held at Baptist Church House, December 3, 1970 (BRF Archive, File: Committee Minutes 1964–75).

BU Consideration of a New Confession of Faith

In 1968, David Russell addressed the 'Pastoral Session' for ministers at the BU Assembly. His material was subsequently published by the BU as a booklet under the title *Baptists and Some Contemporary Issues*.' Russell explored three paradoxes about Baptist life and thought: 'Independency and Interdependency,' 'Unity and Diversity,' and 'Faith Experienced and Faith Expressed.'[122] In the last of these, he raised the question of whether the denomination needed a credal statement.[123] The *Fraternal* magazine published three articles to further the discussion of these issues.[124] The three contributors, J. J. Brown, W. H. Wragg and Stanley Voke met to discuss their subjects, Stanley Voke's being the third. Voke made no comment on the other issues, but he and Wragg disagreed sufficiently about statements of faith for Wragg to remind readers *en passant* of 'Dr. Russell's warning that when we try to state what many believe we are in danger of drifting into the attitude which states what *some* require *all* to believe' [original italics].[125] Voke, on the other hand, pleaded for a definite credal statement on the basis that 'faith experienced' was 'surely *subjective* faith,' while 'faith expressed' was 'the *objective* content, the original deposit of truth to be believed.'[126] He regarded a statement of the latter as a necessary 'safeguard against error,' as 'a unifying principle,' to 'instruct our people' and 'for the faithful propagation of the truth.'[127] Voke reached out to Baptists of a different theological hue saying,

> Some of us need to repent deeply of our overdogmatism on nonessentials, others of our compromisings on essential truth, some of our conservative pride, others of our radical pride, some need to come down from our intellectual pedestals, others need to come out of our theological defences, and all of us need to gather around the Cross of our Lord Jesus to admit our need, our poverty, our hardness of spirit, our sins against one another. Brethren I speak for myself as one who himself needs to do just this.[128]

Voke no longer belonged to the BRF and probably had them in mind when speaking of 'overdogmatism on nonessentials,' but he nevertheless

---

[122] David Russell, *Baptists and Some Contemporary Issues* (London: Baptist Union Publications Department, 1968).
[123] I have not been able to trace a copy of this publication, but the issues were recorded in *The Fraternal* as referenced below.
[124] J. J. Brown, W. H. Wragg and Stanley Voke, 'Some Contemporary Baptist Issues,' in *The Fraternal*, No. 151, July 1969, 6–21.
[125] Ibid., 11.
[126] Ibid., 17.
[127] Ibid., 19–20.
[128] Ibid., 20–21.

The Road to Secession (1966-70)

maintained a strongly conservative point of view. Wragg was less interested in exact formulations but even he believed that Baptist unity required belief in 'the estrangement of man from God,' 'the Incarnation as God's approach to the human predicament,' 'the Atonement in Jesus Christ,' the 'fact that Christ was raised from the dead,' 'salvation ... in no other way,' and 'that the Sacraments of Baptism and the Lord's Supper can only be fully meaningful when the recipient is already a believer.'[129] The discussion of a statement of faith was taken up more widely, prompting a group drawn from the Yorkshire and the Lancashire and Cheshire Baptist Associations to propose one which was published in *The Fraternal* in 1970.[130] The issue became established on the Union's agenda.

Russell called together a Denominational Conference in May 1970, and included for discussion the question of a doctrinal basis. He asked a young minister and Baptist historian, Roger Hayden, to contribute a briefing paper. Hayden recognized that the early Baptists associated together on the basis of confessions of faith, acknowledged that in the nineteenth century Baptists had 'whittled down' the denomination's doctrinal basis to the point of 'theological vagueness,' and admitted that in the early twentieth century J. H. Shakespeare had used 'freedom from an adequate theological base' to pursue policies in the Union that would prepare the way for a United Free Church.[131] Hayden was refreshingly candid. Whilst acknowledging that Confessions had often divided as well as united denominations, he asked, 'Despite this, how long can Baptists go on stumbling into disorder rather than look honestly at the root of our fundamental differences?'[132] He advocated the adoption of a BU Confession as the basis of unity, as an evangelistic tool (because converts needed to understand at least minimally the confession that 'Jesus is Lord'), and as 'an ecumenical necessity.'[133] However, he did not venture a form of words and nothing was to come of this idea, even though it would be advocated again during the Christological controversy of 1971, of all people by the leading liberals Leonard Champion and Ernest Payne.[134] It would nevertheless come to nothing then as it did now, even with their stamp of approval.

---

[129] Ibid., 14.
[130] *The Fraternal*, No. 155, January 1970, 33–36.
[131] 'Confessions of Faith as a Basis for Associating Together,' by Roger Hayden, in Third Denominational Conference of the Baptist Union of Great Britain and Ireland at 'The Hayes,' Swanwick, Derbyshire, 12–15th May 1970: Handbook for Delegates (David Russell's Papers: File B8), 41.
[132] Handbook, 42.
[133] Ibid., 42–43.
[134] See below, 163–164.

Conclusions

Lloyd-Jones' call for evangelicals to leave their denominations became a critical but divisive influence on the BRF. The Fellowship entered upon an internal dispute that ended with a number of BU loyalists leaving the movement when the secessionists gained control and made the BRF a platform for the policy of secession from 1967 onwards. As a result, the BRF ceased to have any real credibility as a force for conservative influence within the denomination. Even its early openness to radical change through charismatic renewal failed to inspire an alternative and more positive agenda. In 1969, the BRF went further in response to the Assembly affirmation of WCC membership and adopted a definite plan for secession.

Intransigence was not the sole preserve of the BRF, however. The BU pursued a policy whereby dialogue clearly had only one main purpose in seeking to preserve the semblance of fellowship without any corresponding respect for conservative opinion. In fact, there does not appear to be any identifiably conservative influence at all on Baptist policy during the later sixties. Perhaps there was a moderating effect informally, especially on the question of any alteration of Baptist Independency. As for the BRF as a movement, the Union would appear to have been frankly dismissive of it, beyond giving its representatives a polite hearing. The result was unsurprising: growing conservative alienation and marginalization. Nor was that only at a theological or academic level. Hesters Way demonstrates how division could become personal, bitter and intransigent. It drove a Baptist Superintendent to prophesy divine judgment upon a colleague to his face, and a conservative theologian to declare that God could not bless a denomination that disagreed with him. Division was an experience, not just a debate.

CHAPTER FIVE

'HOW MUCH OF A MAN WAS JESUS?': THE CHRISTOLOGICAL CONTROVERSY OF 1971

The subject of this chapter will be the Christological controversy of 1971 which began at the 1971 Baptist Assembly and its development until the November 1971 BU Council Meeting. It arose in reaction to some liberal theological views concerning Christ expressed by Michael Taylor, the Principal then of Northern Baptist College. Taylor rejected the traditional formulation of Christ's Deity and humanity in an address entitled 'How Much of a Man was Jesus?'[1] He was widely understood to have effectively denied the orthodox doctrine of the Deity of Christ, which led on the one hand to conservatives asserting traditional orthodoxy as denominational policy and on the other, to the Union leadership resisting them in favour of allowing greater theological diversity.

The importance of this controversy in a study of the BRF is at least threefold. First, some explanation is needed of the BRF mounting a self-contradictory campaign of protest by reclaiming their representative status in the BU after having declared the time for such dialogue to be over. Secondly, an assessment is needed of the BRF plan to create a conservative evangelical alternative to the BU, a plan that was taken very seriously at the time both by its supporters and detractors. Thirdly, it is necessary to consider how and why this episode brought about the end of the BRF as a denominational movement. These issues are so completely interwoven that the controversy will be considered chronologically and in two chapters, the first covering the period from the 1971 Assembly to the November BU Council, and the second covering the period from then until the 1972 Assembly.

The 1971 Assembly and the Beginning of the Controversy

The 1971 Baptist Assembly was held at Westminster Chapel from April 26 to April 29. The Assembly Programme Committee was chaired by the Regent's Park Baptist College Principal, Gwynne Henton Davies (1906–1998), in his position as the BU Vice President for that year.[2] Russell was on the committee as General Secretary and in view of the aftermath it is notable that so were

---

[1] The full text of Taylor's address is contained in Appendix Eight.
[2] The BU Presidency was an annual appointment preceded by one year in the Vice-Presidency during which the candidate joined senior BU meetings and planned the Assembly at which he or she would take office. Presidents then became life members of the BU Council so that their experience was not lost and their influence, such as it might be, became permanent.

Geoffrey King and Sir Cyril Black (1902–1991), the latter a leading conservative evangelical layman who had retired the previous year after twenty years as the Conservative MP for Wimbledon.[3] King and Black were also prominent in the work of the Evangelical Alliance, where the controversy would also make its presence felt and so were important links in the chain of events that would unfold.[4] The Programme Committee was convened with a struggle already taking place between Henton Davies and Russell to control the 1971 theme. Russell wanted to focus on his first major strategy paper, *Ministry Tomorrow* while Henton Davies wanted 'some theocentric thought' because he felt that the assemblies had for too long been focused 'on the human element of our situation.' He proposed several themes, one of which was 'Centrality – the Centrality of God, of Christ, of the Holy Spirit, and the Cross.'[5] Davies won the day, though Russell did obtain some time for his report.

The Assembly Programme Committee next met on September 7.[6] The theme and the addresses had been modified, building now on the *motif* of 'God's "Presence"' with three questions. Of the Father it would be asked, 'How dead is God?' The question regarding the Son would be, 'How much of a man was Jesus?' And regarding the Holy Spirit, the issue would be, 'Is the Holy Spirit a Ghost?' No clear preference is indicated by the Committee minutes concerning the various names proposed as speakers. It was only at its December meeting that the result was announced: John Huxtable, the United Reformed Church leader, had agreed to give the first address; Michael Taylor, the young Principal of Northern Baptist College would give the second; and B. R. White, the Baptist historian who was then a junior colleague of Henton Davies, the third.[7] John Stott, the leading Evangelical Anglican, would also speak at the Assembly, but had been invited separately by the BMS for its usual Valediction Service at the event.[8] It has sometimes been suggested in retrospect, by conservative evangelicals and others, that Henton Davies deliberately engineered the controversy in order to discomfort traditionalists.[9] The evidence from the committee minutes indicates otherwise. It is true that among the proposed speakers was the

---

[3] BU Council Minutes (held at the Angus Library, Regent's Park College, Oxford): Minutes of the Assembly Programme Committee held on Thursday, June 25, 1970.
[4] Information obtained by a comparison of the Council Minutes of the Evangelical Alliance for the years 1965 until 1972 (held in the EA archives).
[5] Ibid.
[6] Minutes of the Assembly Programme Committee, Monday, September 7, 1970.
[7] Minutes of the Assembly Programme Committee, Friday, December 11, 1970.
[8] The Baptist Missionary Society had secured John Stott as their speaker for the 1971 Annual Missionary Sermon, but this had been done over a year before, according to the Minutes of the BMS General Committee for April 1970 (10).
[9] This has been repeated to me several times in the course of this research.

Anglican New Testament scholar Denis Nineham, whose views would have been remarkably radical for a Baptist Assembly,[10] but the speaking panel was subject to the usual uncertainties about who would finally accept an invitation.[11] Nor is there any evidence that a controversy was anticipated. The Committee clearly did not, there being no reference to any concern during its last meeting before the Assembly, on Friday, February 12. Michael Taylor would later confess that he also had not foreseen the outcome, stating in one of only two press statements he would issue about his address that 'he was surprised at the extent of the reaction to what he had said.'[12] *BT* produced a rare prophetic utterance in view of this. A few weeks later and just before the Assembly began, it began its pre-assembly coverage with the words, 'The 1971 Baptist Assembly, in London next week, promises to be more than a cosy get-together.'[13]

The Assembly began well with the Presidential Address on the opening night. Henton Davies gave a stirring appeal for a higher view of Christ than he felt was to be found in the denomination. In contrast with titles of Christ that denoted his 'rank' in relation to believers, Davies called attention to 'another series of titles … which describe being, rather than rank, and relate mainly to God.' Among these, he included that 'Christ is the Second Person of the Trinity.' Using these as his foundation, Davies went on to deplore the 'Jesus-Unitarian tendencies' of traditional Baptist preaching, and demanded new attention to the Incarnation and the resulting establishment of God's Kingdom among men.[14]

In his address, 'How Much of a Man was Jesus?' Michael Taylor created widespread concern concerning the extent to which he adhered to the traditional doctrine of the Deity of Christ. He acknowledged the Nicene affirmation that Christ was 'true God of true God' as a statement made in 'very different circumstances' but thought it necessary to recast for the modern mind the relationship of Deity to humanity in Christ thus: 'God is

---

[10] Adrian Hastings has commented on the radical-traditionalist theological debate that 'perhaps the deepest divide did lie between naturalists and supernaturalists.' *A History of English Christianity 1920–1990*, 583.

[11] Paul Beasley-Murray, however, in his biography of his father, confidently reports that Henton Davies himself was responsible for the invitation to Michael Taylor as well as for the subject of the address. P. Beasley-Murray, *Fearless For Truth: A Personal Portrait of the Life of George Beasley-Murray* (Carlisle: Paternoster Press, 2002), fn. 77, 148.

[12] *BW*, May 7, 1971, B4. It should be noted that Michael Taylor was in his early thirties and new to senior leadership in the BU at the time of the Assembly, while Henton Davies and David Russell shared many years of experience. Though the conspiracy theory seems unlikely, the possibility remains that Russell and Henton Davies knew his views but were far too complacent about the effect of Taylor stating them at an Assembly.

[13] *BT*, April 21, 1971, 3.

[14] Reported in *BT*, April 29, 1971. 6: 'Put The Kingdom First.'

present in that human life as He is present in all human life. God was there in Palestine 2000 years ago and He is here in the world of the twentieth century.' His thesis was that Jesus was uniquely different from us 'to the extent to which we actually see in Him what human life can become when lived in co-operation with God.' His language was reminiscent of Friedrich Schleiermacher (1768–1834), the theologian who pioneered the liberal theological project, including the rejection of Christ's Deity as traditionally understood.[15] Paul Beasley-Murray discussed Taylor's address in the biography he produced of his father (George Beasley-Murray, who was chairman of Council that year and who would become a key figure in the ensuing controversy). He assessed the address as having 'appeared to question the very basis of the Christian faith ... in an attempt to restate in a contemporary manner the Nicene Creed.'[16] Taylor had denied the Deity of Christ as far as both Beasley-Murrays were concerned.[17] What was at stake here was not simply one speaker's personal beliefs, however, but the acceptability of such liberal views of Christ in the Baptist Union.

Reaction at the Assembly itself was covered for the June edition of *Evangelical Times* by George Stirrup, editor of the *BRF Bulletin*.[18] He noted other voices as well as those within the BRF expressing concern, however, reporting that 'the address had startled the congregation and led the President, Mr. Henton Davies, to state that he personally disagreed with Michael Taylor. On the Thursday morning, the Rev. J. Nainby publicly dissociated himself from the vote of thanks to Michael Taylor.'[19] Stirrup was correct about the reactions to the address. At the post-assembly Council meeting of Thursday, April 29, Stanley Voke 'raised the question of the theology of one address during the assembly.'[20] The minutes record that 'he urged that the Council repudiate the views expressed in the address, and re-affirm its acceptance of the Declaration of Principle.'[21] A 'lengthy discussion' took place, which in the language of the BU Minute Book usually indicates dissension. Voke was opposed by Ernest Payne, who moved that 'the matter be adjourned, and this was agreed. Any follow-up was left to the discretion of the General

---

[15] Alan Spence, in *Christology: a guide for the perplexed*, (London: T&T Clark, 2008), 106, provides this quotation as typical of Schleiermacher's approach, taken from *The Christian Faith* (Edinburgh, T&T Clark, 2007), 385: 'The redeemer, then, is like all men in virtue of the identity of human nature, but distinguished from them all by the constant potency of his God-consciousness, which was a veritable existence of God in him.'
[16] *Fearless For Truth*, 145–6.
[17] Ibid., 195–197.
[18] As a monthly periodical, the June edition would have been the first to be prepared after the assembly took place.
[19] Evangelical Times, June 1971, 1.
[20] Minutes of the BU Council, April 29, 1971.
[21] Minutes of the BU Council, April 29, 1971.

Secretary.' However, Paul Beasley-Murray records that his father, looking for a more neutral response than Voke, unsuccessfully proposed that a notice be put in *The Baptist Times* assuring people that the views of speakers at the assembly were not necessarily representative of the Baptist Union Council.'[22] The Council Minutes record Payne's reason for adjourning the discussion as the fact that 'the speaker concerned had not been informed that the matter was to be raised.'[23] Beasley-Murray records another reason that was put forward: that the post-assembly meeting was not a full Council and was held only for the purpose of co-opting new members[24] (though in fact there was a fuller agenda than that). The variation perhaps indicates something of the content of that 'lengthy discussion.' What is clear is that the lines of the controversy were already forming. The denominational leaders sought to combine official neutrality with defending Taylor from criticism while a wide spectrum of conservative opinion began to unite in opposition to the public acceptability of unorthodoxy regarding Christ. It will be shown that such unity would not emerge about how to answer it, however.

The Christological controversy was first and foremost theological. However, it quickly became obvious that it posed a constitutional problem for Baptists because of the Declaration of Principle. Thirty years previously the overt confession of Christ as 'our God and Saviour' had been replaced with the more equivocal description 'God manifest in the flesh.' The Union had not discouraged its large conservative wing from believing that the new phrase was an adequate confession of the Deity of Christ, but as the 1971 controversy developed it became obvious that conservatives and liberals could appeal to this phrase with diametrically opposite interpretations of it. The focus therefore widened from a purely theological to a constitutional debate. *British Weekly* (or *BW*), for example, carried a letter from a Baptist layman, Alec Russell, who made the point that the Declaration of Principle did in fact allow for Michael Taylor's statements, and permitted liberty of interpretation to the churches, so that anyone who criticized him should be seen as 'abrogating to himself an authority which is Christ's alone.'[25] This was a telling criticism in that he, an obviously thoughtful person but apparently not a trained theologian, regarded it as the most straightforward way of reading the Declaration of Principle.

---

[22] *Fearless For Truth*, 146.
[23] A. A. Pain, in a private interview dated September 20, 2009, recounted to me that George Beasley-Murray had discussed the meeting with him at the time. Pain recalled Beasley-Murray saying that there were a number in the meeting who objected that Voke should have spoken to Michael Taylor personally before raising the matter in council. Pain was a leaving student of Spurgeon's in 1971.
[24] *Fearless For Truth*, 146.
[25] *British Weekly* (or *BW*), May 27, 1971, 7.

The Baptist Revival Fellowship

The Development of a Denominational Policy

Bottoms very quickly developed an editorial policy in *BT* of studied neutrality as to whether Taylor was theologically right or wrong, of defending the Declaration of Principle as a sufficient affirmation of honour to Christ, and of defending the Baptist tradition of liberty of thought. It was exactly the position Russell urged on the denomination, analyzing the situation as a protest from a comparatively small number of 'individuals, churches, and groups' on the right of the denomination.[26] At the May 7 Officers' Meeting, Russell reported that 'on the whole there were fewer than he expected and the general tone was kind but critical. One or two favourable letters had been received.'[27] Russell hoped to contain the protest by willing it to be what he wanted and by writing personally to each correspondent rather than be forced into making a formal statement.[28] Bottoms reinforced this version of events in *BT*.

Regarding Taylor, Bottoms (correctly) portrayed him as an individual expressing his own opinion only, and not an official position: 'One question which puzzles many people is how far, in an official assembly or conference called by a body like the Baptist Union, that body is responsible for views expressed by speakers. The answer is, not at all.'[29] Yet Bottoms appears to have had more sympathy for the position in which Principal Taylor found himself than for Taylor's many critics, pleading for him:

> At times most, if not all, of us have made statements which would have failed us in a theological examination, or even have been deemed by others as unorthodox. But that does not make us heretics. Rather it emphasizes that finally our faith is not in words but in a Person.

A few weeks later he responded to a criticism of Taylor expressing in public his doubts about orthodoxy with the comment, 'According to the script of Principal Taylor's address there was no "airing of doubt", but a definition of

---

[26] Ibid.
[27] Minutes of the Officers Meeting, May 7, 1971, Item VI: The Michael Taylor Address.
[28] The Minutes of the Churches Advisory Committee for May 20 (with George Beasley-Murray in the chair) state (V. AFTERMATH OF ASSEMBLY, 1971) that David Russell reported his 'fears and feelings.' He mentioned 'the letters he had received, and the fact that he had replied to each one individually,' as a routine letter might be seen as a policy statement. Russell also reported that Taylor was going to write to the *BT* 'in reply to questions raised'; it was felt to be wise if David Russell could see this beforehand. 'The committee gave warm approval to David Russell's handling of the matter.'
[29] *BT*, April 29, 1971, 3.

limits beyond which he refused to be categorical – which is different.'[30] Taylor was portrayed as misrepresented and misunderstood.

Regarding the Declaration of Principle and liberty of interpretation, Bottoms argued in a leading article on May 6 the need for 'grace enough to allow one another liberty to hold and express their views.' Sir Cyril Black, perhaps the leading evangelical layman of the time in Baptist life, was driven to challenge Bottoms a week later. He urged that 'there must clearly be some limit upon the toleration to be exercised,' citing as examples a minister who ceased to accept believer's baptism or who became a Unitarian.[31] The Declaration of Principle was under scrutiny despite Bottoms' defence of it.

By the middle of May, the debate showed no sign of abating yet no pronouncement had been made by David Russell on behalf of the Union. This official silence meant that the Union was unable to steer the debate significantly, but Bottoms was then left fighting a losing battle to damp down the controversy. Russell remained silent, wanting to preserve the official neutrality of the Union, but his immediate predecessor, Ernest Payne, could speak without compromising that policy while conveying a sense that the established leaders were expressing grace rather than uncertainty. He used *British Weekly* on May 14 to downplay adverse reaction to the address.[32] Referring to Henton Davies dissociating himself publicly from Taylor's views, Payne claimed that the previous week's report in the paper was wrong to state that 'the many hundreds of Baptists who were present' applauded Mr. Davies' reaction, contending that the applause came from a minority. He also stated of Taylor that:

> In the opinion of many he gave an address which was not only orthodox, but one of great courage, notable in manner, spirit and content. He refused to take refuge in a mere repetition of the phrases of the creeds and confessions, but he expressly said he had no wish to disown them and affirmed the phrases in the Baptist Union Declaration of Principle.

Payne reinforced the line Bottoms had adopted in *BT*.

The Emergence of Protest Among Baptist Loyalists

At this point, Russell and Bottoms, in their different denominational spheres, shared a similar analysis of the situation. They acknowledged the existence of enraged traditionalists and also of liberal supporters of Taylor, although

---

[30] *BT*, May 13, 1971, 3.
[31] Ibid., 3.
[32] *BW*, May 14, 1971, 1.

the latter were few in number in comparison with the former. They responded with studied neutrality as to whether there was a serious problem with Taylor's views, by defending the Declaration of Principle as a sufficient statement of the Deity of Christ, and by asserting Baptist freedom to interpret it otherwise. However, their interpretation required them to brand any complaint against Taylor as from a small number of hard-line conservatives and fundamentalists. Walter Bottoms did this by regularly portraying critics of Taylor as bigots.[33] But the fact is they were both guilty of wishful thinking. The voice of protest had grown beyond hard-line anti-denominationalists in the BRF and encompassed a much larger number of people, such as Voke, who had left the BRF; Sir Cyril Black, who had never joined it; and George Beasley-Murray, who had always been an ecumenical enthusiast.

Up and down the country churches and associations were beginning to produce resolutions to affirm the traditional orthodoxy about Christ's divine nature, and usually also to protest against allowing it to be contradicted within the Union. Only the second week after the assembly, *BT* reported on Bromham Baptist Church, a village church in Bedfordshire with no connection to the BRF or other theologically right-wing affiliation. The previous week, the church had passed a resolution expressing concern about Principal Taylor's reported views, and calling on the officers and council of the Union 'to publicly repudiate the view reportedly expressed by Michael Taylor.'[34] The case was noted by Russell in his personal papers because of its early response to the Assembly.[35] The resolution, which was printed in *BT*, stated:

> If in fact Michael Taylor holds such a view, we call upon the Officers and Council of the Union to consider whether or not they are able to continue to recognize a college of which he remains Principal, and we ask Michael Taylor to consider whether he can with all conscience continue to fill that office. We would at the same time ask Michael Taylor in a spirit of Christian love and concern, to seek before God and in the light of the Scriptures, a cleansing of his own

---

[33] Walter Bottoms developed a way with headlines and articles that were obliquely but obviously related to attacking conservative views, e.g., a book review by David Goodbourn of 'Student Witness and Christian Truth' (IVP) headed 'You Must Believe As We Do Or Else' (*BT*, May 27, 1971,4); a front page banner concerning a liberal theologian's speech, 'Stop Misusing the Bible Plea' (*BT*, June 10, 1); and a Southern Baptist Convention speaker discussing minor disagreements of theology in the denomination: 'We Almost "Hate One Another" Over The Scriptures.' (*BT*, June 17, 1971, 5).
[34] *BT*, May 13, 1971, 12.
[35] Letter from Bromham Baptist Church to David Russell, (David Russell's Private Papers, held at the Angus Library at Regent's Park College, Oxford, (File: Assembly Address/M.T.Debate/Resignations/Resolution Assembly 1972/Correspondence and Cuttings).

heart from heresy, by faith in the Lord Jesus Christ, Divine Son of God, and Saviour.[35]

This was the voice of a small country church without a pastor (it was led by two elders),[37] but nevertheless it highlights a number of important issues that the Union faced, even if not particularly well thought-out at that moment: that the controversy was not confined to the BRF committee or even to its members; that there was widespread concern that the denomination should unequivocally affirm its adherence to the Deity of Christ; and that the affirmation should be a real test of membership in the Union and not just a form of words. Bromham was only the first of many churches that would communicate similar concerns either to *BT* or to Russell's office over the months to come.[38]

The most ominous sign of serious discontent among usually loyal Baptists came from the London Baptist Association. The LBA was predominantly conservative in its ethos but as a denominational body it could hardly be labelled institutionally disloyal or extreme. The first objection came from its Western Group of churches. Interestingly, the Group co-operated with *ET* to give publicity to their action, which was covered in its June edition, the first to deal with the Assembly controversy.[39] This underscores the impression that *ET* had the ear of denominational loyalists at first. The Western Group was reported as having sent a letter objecting to Michael Taylor's views to the BU Council, the Council of Northern College, and the LBA Council, in which it was stated that the committee had concluded that his words were:

> contrary to the teaching of the New Testament, to the claims of Christ Himself, and to the witness of the apostles, and that this view is inconsistent with the Declaration of Principle ... in our view, anyone who doubts the Deity of Jesus Christ should not be an accredited Baptist Minister and should not participate in the training of men for the Baptist Ministry.[40]

That an Association committee should issue such a statement was a warning that Russell's analysis of the situation was seriously flawed. The silent majority was finding its voice as it perceived a genuine crisis of faith in the denomination.

---

[36] *BT*, May 13, 1971, 12.
[37] Information obtained from Mark Hatto, the present pastor, in a personal conversation on March 4, 2010.
[38] It is impossible to know the exact number of such letters because Russell did not preserve a comprehensive record of them in his papers, and *BT* did not archive letters it declined to publish.
[39] Evangelical Times, June 1971, 2
[40] Ibid.

The Baptist Revival Fellowship

To make matters worse, the Congregationalists were at that time passing through the final stages of changing from a 'Congregational Union' to membership of a new 'United Reformed Church' in which they would finally lose their traditional ecclesiology of Independency. The first step had taken place in 1967 when churches were invited to affiliate with a temporary 'Congregational Church.' At that point, an evangelical secession had taken place to form an 'Evangelical Fellowship of Congregational Churches.' When the second re-affiliation became necessary, the EFCC leafleted the churches to remind them that having the freedom to choose offered a second opportunity to consider joining the EFCC.[41] Their success in 1967 and their stability since then was evidence enough that a minority conservative secession could succeed, and could unite not only supporters of Lloyd-Jones but a wider spectrum of conservatives. Lloyd-Jones' appeal had stirred considerable debate about forming such evangelical church affiliations but only a handful of BU churches had thus far acted upon the vision. The BU, after all, was founded upon Baptist and evangelical convictions that had not formally changed. Taylor, however, was something approaching a last straw for many more conservatives than Russell realized, after ten years of feeling undervalued by a leadership that had cast doubt on both Baptist Independency and traditional evangelical convictions in the name of ecumenical advance and theological liberalism. Taylor represented at last a 'clear and present danger' while in the EFCC there was a successful secession body. The lesson was no more lost on the BU than the BRF leaders. The evangelical magazine *Crusade* provided an alternative, and more sympathetic, platform than *BT* for denominational loyalists to speak out. David Pawson, the Cambridge educated Methodist-turned-Baptist minister, was recognized among the moderate conservatives as an outstanding communicator and an able thinker who was not tainted by anti-denominationalism. He began a five-part series in the June edition, entitled *The Character of Christ*,[42] developed from a series of sermons he had preached in response to the Christological controversy. Pawson set out an alternative treatment of the humanity of Christ, dwelling not only on his human life on earth, but on his continuing humanity as the mediator in heaven:

> Now why isn't it enough just to remember his character: his compassion, his obedience, his anger or his honesty? Why should we remember his body; what is the importance of this? I want to take

---

[41] *Crusade*, September 1971, 30. Peter Brain, who would become a leading URC minister, wrote to accuse the EFCC of schism, saying, 'It is, in my belief, a burden on those who wish to divide any church by further separations, to prove their several reasons for doing so ... I hope that, although this new grouping announces itself as Evangelical, it will be clear that this label conceals as much as it reveals.'

[42] *Crusade*, June 1971, 24f. The magazine was edited by the Evangelical Anglican David Winter.

The Christological Controversy 1971

you through three stages of Our Lord's existence as a person. Stage number one: he had no body at all. Stage number two: he had a natural body just like ours. Stage number three: he had a new body, which one day we may share.[43]

Tension Begins to Mount as Moderates Reconsider their Loyalties.

It should be noted that division was not only a threat from conservatives. Some on the liberal wing felt alienated by perceived attacks on their liberty of thought. The same week that Payne had written to *British Weekly* about its Assembly coverage, another Baptist did so. John Radford felt far less compunction about attacking conservatives than the ever-cautious Payne. Radford wrote a vitriolic letter, declaiming that 'we are not all yes men,' that the anonymous minister who suggested that Taylor should not be an accredited minister 'was being plain silly,' that Stanley Voke should 'define the Deity of Christ in other than pre-Victorian terms,' and that Henton Davies was 'being no denominational leader on this occasion but a neo dictator ... redolent of theological clichés ... scathing, bitter and illiberal.' In Radford's opinion 'his strictures only underline the increasing feeling that the Baptists are the most divided of denominations.' One wonders what Radford meant by this dividedness when the Anglican Communion was in the throes of a battle between liberals and Anglo-Catholics, and the prospect of a new United Reformed Church had occasioned not one but two divisions in Congregationalism.[44] Did he think there were irreconcilable differences between conservative and liberal theologies? If so, he was the unwitting supporter of Peter Masters, who was about to publish exactly the same message in the June edition of *Evangelical Times*.

The BRF Strategy

Meanwhile, the BRF constituency was pursuing its own campaign. George Stirrup, as noted above, reported the Assembly in *ET* under the front-page banner headline 'Dilemma of Discipline.' His main focus, though it was shrouded in alarmist rhetoric, was the implication for the Declaration of Principle as a confession of the Deity of Christ if the address by Taylor was not challenged. He asked:

> What of the future? The Baptist Union is once again on the horns of a dilemma for it must surely decide what is going to be done. Can a

---

[43] *Crusade*, October 1971, 19.
[44] i.e., the Congregational Federation, which retained the theological openness of the Congregational Union and the Evangelical Fellowship of Congregational Churches, which was exclusively conservative.

scholar who has made such a plain confession of deviation from Christian doctrine remain as Principal of a Baptist Theological College? Will local churches within the Union continue to support the Northern College if Michael Taylor remains? Can the Union continue to recognize men trained at the Northern College under Michael Taylor's leadership? Only time will be able to answer these questions, but further issues arise.

Someone Must Go

To be a minister on the accredited list one must sign the Declaration of Principle of the Baptist Union. Michael Taylor has signed this stating that he agrees with what it says. Many Evangelicals have also signed this Declaration. The question must be posed "What does the Declaration mean?" If it means what Michael Taylor believes, then many men could not agree with it. Churches have also agreed to this Declaration, and therefore they too, must surely ask the same question and demand some answers. What precisely does it mean?[45]

Stirrup also used the *Bulletin* to pursue this issue. He wrote an open letter about it to Russell, sent copies to Geoffrey Haden and Michael Taylor, and then published it in the *BRF Bulletin*.[46] Stirrup stated his understanding of the phrase in the Declaration of Principle, 'God manifest in the flesh,' to be an affirmation of the Deity of Christ; stressed that ministers had to affirm the Declaration in order to be accredited; and argued therefore that either action should be taken to remove the accreditation of Michael Taylor or the meaning of the phrase should be clarified officially since 'many Baptists would assume it to be orthodox.' Russell was reported to have replied that there was no question of the Union failing to stand by the Declaration of Principle, but 'it is not for the Union to require an interpretation of these words from those who subscribe to them.' Stirrup commented on Russell, 'So to my understanding of his letter he virtually claims that the Declaration of Principle has no meaning because it can be capable of many meanings.' Stirrup replied to Russell to assert that in a Union of independent churches 'it is not for the hierarchy to make the final decision regarding the meaning of the Declaration of Principle but rather the local Churches.' Stirrup concluded that:

> everything seems to revolve around the Declaration of Principle – what does it mean? If Michael Taylor has violated this, then he must be removed from the Accredited List, if Michael Taylor has not violated the Declaration of Principle then my own place on the List

---

[45] *Evangelical Times*, June 1971, 1.
[46] *BRF Bulletin* No. 108, July/September 1971, 4–5.

must be considered – for I refuse to acknowledge such an ambiguous Declaration of Principle.' [47]

Concern that allowing doubt about the Deity of Christ led also to uncertainty about the Trinity emerged in a second open letter, this time from a church connected with the BRF. It was reported in the *BRF Bulletin* for July 1971 that the pastor and deacons of South Lee Baptist Church, London SE 12 had written, and published as a circular, a letter to David Russell focusing on the implications for Trinitarian belief of denying the Deity of Christ They accused Michael Taylor of views 'quite heretical in that he denies the essential Deity of our Lord and Saviour Jesus Christ.' *Evangelical Times* reported the letter and noted that the writers 'believe this also denies the doctrine of the Trinity which is "fundamental to the basis of our faith. To deny the Deity of our Lord is to deny our faith in Him."' [48]

These were personal actions of BRF members. The committee took its first official action by writing, on May 25, a formal letter of concern to Russell, signed personally by all its members. [49] Rather belatedly, they wished to be heard once more in their traditional role of representing conservatism in the BU, despite having denounced such dialogue since 1967 and while still threatening to leave even in the letter. Claiming that they were 'being led of God' the committee called for a denominational response to certain demands, without which they 'could not remain in fellowship' with a denomination that equivocated over the Deity of Christ. [50] The first was that Russell should bring their letter before the General Purposes and Finance Committee at its next meeting, with the request that they authorize him to make an official statement 'in their name categorically affirming that they believe Jesus is God.' Their reason was the conviction that:

> This doctrine of the Person of our Blessed Lord existing eternally co-equal with the Father and the Holy Spirit in the mystery of the Trinity, has been the fundamental issue facing the Church again and again through the centuries and is so today. There can be no hope for the true blessing of God upon the Church, nor for revival in the Church, where there is any ambiguity and uncertainty here.

---

[47] Ibid., 5.
[48] Ibid.
[49] These were stated in the letter as Harold Owen (Woking), C. P. Collinson (Dudley), R. M. Horn (Horley), E. M. Kirk (Cheam), R. S. Luland (Bedford), P. Nuttall (Liverpool), J. L. Pretlove (Sheffield), G. Stirrup (Sidcup), H. C. Tyler, (no placement was stated for some reason, but he had been since 1966 at Clementswood, Ilford), A. J. Waterman (Barnet), J. Wood (Crewe).
[50] Letter to Russell dated May 26, 1971 (Russell's Private Papers: Michael Taylor Controversy 1971, File: MT/1).

The Baptist Revival Fellowship

Their second demand was:

> that the Rev. Michael Taylor be invited to make and publish an equally clear statement that Jesus is God. If he cannot do that, or refuses to do that, we submit he should not be allowed to retain his positions as Principal of the Northern Baptist College, or as a member of the BU Council and on the BU Accredited List [note: that is, of Ministers].

This appeal was obviously inspired by high spiritual and doctrinal ideals, but it was ill-conceived as a strategy. The most obvious strategies would have been to press for a Council debate on the meaning of 'God manifest in the flesh' and for Michael Taylor to be examined by the Ministerial Recognition Committee. Russell's reply to Stirrup appeared to close those avenues off, but the committee accepted too readily that Russell's view would prevail when put to the test. Instead, they opted for an obviously wrong procedure. In the first place, they did not understand that the GP&F Executive had no means of authorizing a statement on behalf of the denomination. This could be done only by the BU Council and even then was subject to ratification by the Assembly. In the second place, they could not issue an invitation to Michael Taylor to take the step required. Russell might do that informally or the Council formally, but not a committee of the Council.

Russell somewhat impishly pointed out to them his confidence that the GP&F members 'I am sure will wish to reaffirm' their acceptance of the Declaration of Principle, 'although they may well be surprised that you feel the need for them to do so.' Regarding the inappropriate demand made by the BRF Committee, Russell had rather more to say:

> I would further point out that the members of the General Purposes Committee will probably be most hesitant to take upon themselves responsibilities which by the constitution are the right only of the Council and Assembly. Be assured that they are as concerned as you yourself are for the honour and glory of our Lord Jesus Christ and for the wellbeing of His Church.[51]

The wrong-footed approach of the BRF Committee is a significant indicator of the poor relationship with the BU to be found in BRF circles. No-one among the committee members was experienced in Union affairs and procedures, despite half of them having solidly BU backgrounds, some of them being senior ministers and some of them having exceptional

---

[51] Reply to BRF Committee, May 26, 1971, (Russell's Private Papers: Michael Taylor Controversy 1971, File: MT/1).

The Christological Controversy 1971

qualifications. According to the *BU Handbook* for 1971,[52] three were Manchester trained (Kirk and Owen together in the forties, and Stirrup a decade later). Harold Owen, the chairman, led a church of 250 members at Woking. Edward Kirk was at Cheam with a membership of 425. Lulard and Tyler had trained at Spurgeon's and held pastorates of just under 200 members. Horn and Pretlove were Cambridge graduates before training for the ministry and Horn would go on to significant leadership in the wider evangelical scene, editing *ET* and then its breakaway rival (when his policy was deemed too soft-line), *Evangelicals Now*. Eventually he would become General Secretary of the Universities and Colleges Christian Fellowship (formerly IVF). Collinson, Nuttall, Pretlove, Waterman and Wood were non-collegiate entrants to the Baptist ministry but Collinson, like Owen, ministered to a 250-member church while the others were in churches with memberships mostly between 100 and 150. It is of further interest to note that Kirk, Luland, Nuttall and Owen had all been in Baptist ministry for over twenty years in significant pastorates without holding office in Association or Union structures.

Owen and his colleagues had clearly been out-manoeuvred by Russell but on June 10 Owen wrote a second time. Now he turned to the real issue, which was the proper interpretation of the Declaration of Principle:

> Since Principal Taylor presumably assents to this Declaration while still holding his views, we have to ask for a clarification of just what is meant by "Christ, God manifest in the flesh". We had taken this to be an unequivocal statement of the Deity of Christ, but now we are not at all convinced that this is what is clearly meant ... for the sake of His glory, any doubts as to His essential Deity must be removed, and be seen to be removed.[53]

David Russell would seem to have sensed that this time neither flippancy nor force of personality would suffice. He responded with some diligence, writing a lengthy reply on June 16 after reading through the Council Minutes relating to the adoption of the phrase 'God manifest in the flesh' at the 1938 Baptist Assembly.[54] He also checked Ernest Payne's account of the discussion in his history of the Baptist denomination. As a result, he had two points to make, which are significant for being rare exceptions to his usual avoidance of comment:

---

[52] Information drawn from the *BU Handbook 1971*: List of Ministers, 249ff.
[53] BRF to Russell, June 10, 1971, (Russell's Private Papers: Michael Taylor Controversy 1971, File:MT/1).
[54] Russell to BRF, June 16, 1971, (Russell's Private Papers: Michael Taylor Controversy 1971, File:MT/1).

1. Prior to the Assembly of 1936 [sic] the relevant words in the Declaration of Principle were 'the Lord Jesus Christ, our God and Saviour.' At that juncture, they were changed to read 'Our Lord and Saviour Jesus Christ, God manifest in the flesh.' The Minutes do not record in so many words the reasons for this change, but Dr. Payne in his book 'The Baptist Union' (page 163) states that 'the new phrase clearly excluded the Unitarian interpretation of the person of Christ.' It had been pointed out in a previous debate that the phraseology as it stood lent countenance 'either to Swedenborgianism or to tritheism ... which should receive no encouragement in the Union's official Declaration of Principle.' In a council debate preceding the submission and acceptance of the new clause moreover, reference was made, with full approval, to 'the Deity of Christ as of one nature with God, the unique manifestation, the incarnation of Deity and verily and in effect one in the quality of his being with the eternal God.'
2. It is not for me to defend Principal Taylor's use of words: but let me say this. When he stated, 'I cannot categorically affirm that Jesus is God' he had, I imagine, the support of reputable theologians who would assert that for those who believe in the Trinity such a statement is to be deemed theologically inadequate. This is quite different from saying that such a statement is a denial of what is termed in classical theological language, the Deity or divinity of Christ.... I believe furthermore that he adheres to the Declaration of Principle in its affirmation of faith in 'Father, Son and Holy Spirit' and in 'Jesus Christ, God manifest in the flesh.'

Russell had the high ground regarding the original and naïve proposals made by the BRF. He was not quite so secure when it came to the history of the BU adopting the phrase 'God manifest in the flesh.' In fairness, he followed Payne's published line of thought, but he also manipulated the quotations he discovered in the BU Minutes of the time. The 'previous debate' from which he drew some of them was not, as he implied, the Council discussion of the Declaration of Principle but the examination of E. J. Roberts concerning his disavowal of the Deity of Christ. Neither were they all drawn from the orthodox side, but some of them from Roberts himself – in criticism of the statement that Jesus was 'our God and Saviour.' Had the BRF committee been able to read the original Minutes for themselves, Russell would have been exposed to considerable difficulty. The Roberts case had resulted in precisely the outcome he was seeking to avoid – the trial of a respected and scholarly minister for unorthodoxy and the eventual requirement by the BU Council that he should formally recant or lose his accreditation.

The Christological Controversy 1971

Peter Masters and the Metropolitan Tabernacle

An even less sympathetic voice than the BRF was about to be heard. Peter Masters, the founding editor of *Evangelical Times* in 1967, was appointed to the pastorate of the Metropolitan Tabernacle in 1970. The Officers' Meeting on May 7 considered the church's resignation. The minutes record that:

> One item was the subject of a suggestion for the GP&F's consideration. This was the matter of the resignation from the Union of the Metropolitan Tabernacle. It was agreed to recommend that a deputation consisting of the President, Vice-President, and the ex-President should join the General Secretary in interviewing a deputation from the Metropolitan Tabernacle.[55]

Peter Masters had accepted a call to the Metropolitan Tabernacle on condition that the church would leave the BU. The Metropolitan Tabernacle took a formal decision to do so at a church meeting held on February 22, 1971 and had immediately written to inform the Union.[56] It is not clear why Russell was responding to it only now. Perhaps in February the impending Assembly had so pre-occupied committee business that the matter had been deferred only for it to become the more urgent in the aftermath of Principal Taylor's address. That Peter Masters should take such a stand was not surprising, however. He had previously been a member of Martyn Lloyd-Jones' congregation at Westminster Chapel; and was a willing and earnest champion of Lloyd-Jones' call to leave the mainstream denominations with whom 'the Doctor' was in frequent contact over the period under review. Masters was not however, a member of the BRF.[57]

The deputation was to consist of the newly-elected President (Henton Davies), the immediate ex-President (Sir Cyril Black), the Vice-President (Godfrey Robinson [1913–1971], minister of the large congregation at Bromley Baptist Church), and the General Secretary. This would have meant that the deputation consisted of two well-known conservatives in Black and Robinson, and two who were associated with the more liberal element in the denomination. In the event this arrangement failed, because Godfrey Robinson died suddenly just hours before the planned meeting, and the ensuing crisis required both Henton Davies and Sir Cyril Black to be elsewhere on behalf of the Union. Russell therefore went with only the

---

[55] Minutes of the Officers Meeting, May 7, 1971, Item XI: G. P. Agenda.
[56] *The Sword and The Trowe*, (London: Metropolitan Tabernacle Church, 1971): February:6ff.
[57] In an email dated September 3, 2009, Mr. Masters informed me that 'I never had any real connections with BRF.'

The Baptist Revival Fellowship

London Area Superintendent for support, Geoffrey Haden (1909–1990).[58] The deputation failed to persuade Masters and his deacons.

In the early summer, the BRF moved closer to the completely uncompromising outlook of Peter Masters and *ET*. This requires full consideration here in view of its consequences for the BRF and for conservative protest in the BU. The June edition of *ET* has already been noted for its front-page coverage of the 1971 Assembly. In July, coverage continued with a two-page spread,[59] written (it was revealed in the next edition) by three unnamed BU ministers who quite obviously were knowledgeable about, and supportive of, the BRF's plan to form a secession group of churches. Under the headline, 'Is The Union Baptist Any Longer?' the article presented an argument that would prove highly damaging to the BRF and deeply hurtful to many evangelical loyalists in the BU.

It began by presupposing that Baptists should be committed to an evangelical theology and spirituality based on 'the inspired, infallible and inerrant Word of God in its totality.' This was a contentious beginning even towards fellow conservatives in the BU, since the BRF doctrinal basis maintained only the infallibility and not the inerrancy of Scripture. The authors continued in a similarly provocative manner by presenting Principal Taylor's address as symptomatic of a widespread rejection of orthodoxy in the BU. The Declaration of Principle was declared unsatisfactory as a defence, not 'because of the things in it, but because of the things it leaves out'[60] and the authors believed it was not only possible to sign it as 'an extreme Modernist' but that many had in fact done so. Consequently, the Union was 'as mixed as the Church of England communion – able to boast all shapes and sizes of heresy, including the view of the former Bishop of Woolwich[61] and Hugh Montefiore.' The true state of things, the writers asserted, was that 'the great majority of Union pastors would repudiate' the infallibity of Scripture, so that 'the prevailing opinion is non-Evangelical.' Their drastic conclusion was that the denomination had ceased to preach the gospel and that any evangelicals who remained within it were thereby guilty themselves of betraying the gospel, a view for which they claimed the authority of Spurgeon, who 'sincerely believed that for Christians to be

---

[58] Reported to the GB&F Committee June 8, 1971.
[59] *ET*, July 1971, 4–5.
[60] This comment is reminiscent of Martyn Lloyd-Jones. I recall him saying from time to time at meetings of the Westminster Fellowship in the 1970s that, when judging someone's convictions, one should listen for what a preacher or theologian chose not to say, as well as what he did.
[61] The bishop referred to was John Robinson, author in 1963 of *Honest to God*.

linked in association with ministers who do not preach the Gospel of Christ is to incur moral guilt.'[62]

The argument contained several falsehoods. Inerrancy was not the undisputed position of conservative evangelicals. Michael Taylor's address was not representative of a majority – far from it. There was no available evidence (then) for gauging the views of 'the great majority of Union pastors' on Scripture or anything else. Even the reference to Spurgeon was misleading in that it failed to mention his continuing personal relations with those who did not agree with him (with John Clifford, for example). Spurgeon was not a supporter of 'second degree separation' despite his name being associated with it here. However, the most outrageous claim was yet to come:

> Equally serious is the way in which the Baptist Union has thrown out one of the two pillars of Baptist witness. In addition to the basic doctrine of the Gospel, early Baptists stood out for their practice of Baptism by Immersion, and their belief in the *Independence of each local Church* [italics in original]. It is the latter which has been gradually eroded so that the Union HQ body is *not legally Baptist at all.*[63]

The next section of the article portrayed all its assertions as contributing to an inter-related and conspiratorial whole by describing an imaginary church. This fellowship was pictured as having been founded recently using one of the Model Trusts of the BU in the belief that they were joining with an evangelical denomination in which their church was independent in status and voluntary in involvement. A crisis was then pictured in which, during a denominational pulpit exchange, a visiting preacher denies the atonement. The new church decides to withdraw from the BU only to find that they cannot, and that their building can be taken from them and sold, but 'meanwhile, those who continue to deny Christ continue to preach – unhindered.'[64]

In the concluding section of the article, the authors claimed that although the church was imaginary the problem was not because in the Baptist Union heresy predominated, Independency had ceased, and 'the BU HQ' was cynically betraying the Baptist cause. According to this analysis the denomination was now 'swamped' by men who did not accept traditional

---

[62] Ibid., 4.
[63] Ibid.
[64] It is very likely that the situation described was in fact an oblique reference to the Hesters Way case, which had been used in ET to argue that the BU no longer practised its commitment to local church independence (*ET*, November 6, 1969, 1: 'Facing Eviction.'

evangelical doctrines such as the virgin birth, the atonement, and the bodily resurrection of Christ. They believed in 'little more than the divinity of Christ. Now even this last shred of truth is being thrown aside.' In contrast to such a general betrayal of Baptist principles and evangelical truth, the BRF was presented as a 'lone voice' of opposition, notably through their booklet *Liberty in the Lord*. The authors claimed to be in touch with the Chairman of BRF who 'informs us that their committee is making representations to the Union. The matter is being vigorously pursued by them.' However, the authors believed there had finally come 'a point where true believers MUST separate from those who deny that basis.'[65] Once again, *ET*'s coverage was a thinly disguised message from an increasingly aggressive and ebullient BRF.

This was the moment when, if any doubt lingered as to the validity of the BRF as representative of the wider conservative constituency, it was comprehensively destroyed. It was inevitable that many conservative evangelicals in the BU would be incensed by the article and it was equally inevitable that some Baptists of broader convictions would come across it, including Russell, who kept a file of press cuttings for himself as articles appeared concerning the controversy. An official reply was sent to *ET* co-signed by Russell, George Beasley-Murray, Stanley Turl, Geoffrey King and Stanley Voke. All of these, except Russell, were known as conservative evangelicals and the latter two, of course, were significant for their earlier prominence in the BRF. *ET* continued its coverage of the Christological controversy in similar vein until the BRF broke with the BU and the alternative Baptist fellowship was established in 1972, but if anything it contributed to the resurgence of conservative loyalty to the Union by its coverage.

The July issue of *ET* would appear to have made some within the BRF join the moderate protest as well. On July 30, Cheam Baptist Church issued a circular letter of its own to fellow members of the London Baptist Association. Earlier that month on July 8, the church meeting had agreed a resolution which was in direct contradiction to the dire picture of heresy rampant in the Union to be found in the columns of *ET*. The minister of the church, Edward Kirk, had been a signatory to the BRF committee letter addressed to Russell at the end of May but he was changing his mind. The resolution called not for discipline against Principal Taylor or for a stronger confessional statement by the Union, but rather the united affirmation of the:

> divine nature of Jesus Christ, i.e., that Jesus is God. This we find to be the clear, repeated teaching of the Scriptures.... Moreover we acknowledge the Lord Jesus Christ as the sinless One who offered

---

[65] *ET* July 1971, 6.

up Himself a sufficient sacrifice and atonement for sin and thus procured for every believer the gift of eternal salvation ... we call upon our brethren everywhere to acknowledge Him as God and Saviour and so to worship Him for who He is and what He has done. We plead also for a renewed and strengthened proclamation to needy men and women all around us of Christ, the Divine Son of God, the only Saviour of the world.[66]

This resolution had been offered for publication to *BT* but was refused, and so a covering letter was then circulated to the members of the LBA explaining the circumstances for their doing so, and that the resolution had been drafted with the two purposes of avoiding 'a purely negative and critical attitude ... we considered would not be helpful' and to affirm a 'positive attitude to the vital issue at stake.'[67] Kirk evidently did not support the direction of BRF and the next letter to the BU from the whole BRF committee (in early October) would not include either his name or that of George Stirrup. That Stirrup backed down is really rather remarkable given his close involvement in the rightward swing of the BRF over the previous five years. The BRF's tactics were losing it support.

The *BRF Bulletin* for July/September contained a statement from the chairman in which he sought to clarify the essential issue as a battle between conservative and liberal theologies. He declared that 'unless the Baptist Union, through its Council, clearly and categorically states that 'Jesus is God,' I for one can no longer remain associated with it.' However, in the September 9 edition of *BT*, the venerable conservative minister T. Wilkinson Riddle (1886–1983), a Spurgeon's student whose ministry began in 1911, wrote a letter to *BT* in response. He pointed out that, in the fundamentalist publication *Zondervan's Bible Dictionary*, 'Professor Everett-Harrison writes: "Some moderns, about whose orthodoxy there is no question, have, nevertheless, expressed the feeling of restraint in referring to Jesus as God, though they do not doubt His essential Deity" (page 160).... Perhaps it would be wise to keep closely to the words of Holy Scripture, and be content that "every tongue should confess that Jesus Christ is LORD, to the glory of God the Father." What was inferential, according to the writer, could not always be stated "clearly and categorically" without transgressing the bounds of

---

[66] Resolution adopted at Church Meeting, Thursday, June 24, 1971, (Russell's Private Papers: The Michael Taylor Controversy: File MT/1
[67] Circular letter from Cheam Baptist to the LBA dated July 31, 1971, (Russell's Private Papers: The Michael Taylor Controversy 1971, file: MT/5 (attached to a bundle of correspondence between Russell and Cheam Baptist Church).

accuracy.[68] The BRF once again had failed to sound a representative Baptist note in its protest against Michael Taylor.

The First Official Attempt to End the Controversy

The usual summer hiatus in Baptist life provided David Russell with the opportunity to attempt a greater measure of control over the controversy. First of all, he and Bottoms drew correspondence on the subject to a close in the July 15 edition of *BT*. A letter from Michael Taylor was published in which he stated that he saw 'little wisdom in pursuing this theological debate in public.' He stressed the need for openness in theological discussions and wondered whether it was possible in the BU:

> The question which remains unanswered in my own mind is whether or not we are free to make this kind of exploration within the circle of the denomination unaccompanied by the drama of a doctrinal crisis which can prove to be both inhibiting and exhausting. [69]

Russell contributed a final word alongside Taylor's letter, acknowledging 'deep concern for the truth of the gospel and the honour of Christ by individuals, groups and churches,' but calling for protestors to 'refrain from precipitate action that would damage the Church of God' and for all Baptists to 'keep in perspective internal disagreement' about doctrinal truth on the basis of 'sharing our common conviction that Jesus Christ is Saviour and Lord.'[70] Alongside this strategy, Russell issued a circular letter to the churches calling for 'restraint and graciousness in dealing with the remarks about the Divinity of Christ made by the Rev. Michael Taylor.'[71] *BT* sought to move the controversy away from an open discussion through correspondence to a series of five articles on Christology by well-informed contributors representative of a fairly wide theological spectrum, the first appearing on July 29 when George Beasley-Murray addressed 'The New Testament Witness to Christ.[72] This was followed by some historical perspective from Gordon Pearce, a survey of current Christological thought by Neville Clark, a more popular article about the present reality of Christ from David Pawson, and finally a consideration of the biblical and spiritual place of Christ in worship contributed by Stephen Winward.

---

[68] *BT*, September 9, 1970, 8.
[69] *BT*, July 15, 1971, 2.
[70] *BT*, July 15, 1971, 2.
[71] Reported in 'Baptist News,' *BW*, July 23, 1971, B7.
[72] *BT*, July 29, 1971, 7.

The Christological Controversy 1971

The strategy was solid enough, but it was completely upstaged by the July article in *ET*. The rebuttal issued by Russell and his fellow Baptists served only to fuel the controversy again during August. It was reproduced in the August edition of *ET* under a front page banner: 'Union Defends Downgrade' together with a running commentary printed alongside.[73] The letter complained that the June article 'makes allegations which are unfounded in fact, indulges in unworthy innuendos and utters statements which are inaccurate.' The signatories professed particular outrage at the portrayal of the Union as controlling and of its ministers as mainly anti-evangelical. The first point, regarding control, was rebutted by the *ET* editor by reference to Hesters Way Baptist Church being evicted from its building when it left the Union in 1969. This was not a well-managed event in Union life, and the Union certainly caused ill-feeling among many of its more theologically conservative members. The latter accusation, that the Union was dominated by a majority of non-evangelicals, was patently undermined by the letter bearing the names of leading conservatives, two of them well-known for having been associated for many years with the BRF. Masters nevertheless stood by the accusation of 'complete doctrinal confusion' without apology. Had he claimed that the Union was dominated by a *minority* of non-evangelicals, it is likely that many conservatives in the Union would have agreed, if not actually supported him; but as it was, Masters succeeded in further alienating conservatives in the Union rather than galvanizing them to stand with him.

Perhaps the August edition of *ET* also provoked Walter Bottoms to a reaction. What is certain is that he broke the hoped-for cessation of hostility himself with a lengthy editorial in the August 12 edition of *BT*. Headed 'Orthodoxy And Heresy,' the article first asserted the danger of confusing 'trust in God and faith in the risen Lord with trust in our own professions, confessions, traditions and creeds.' It went on to describe various traditions in which that happened, ranging from the Roman Catholics to the Jehovah Witnesses, who all shared the same misguided conviction that 'they alone understand the Book.' Baptists, by contrast, were 'born in freedom, they did not ignore the need for an unshackled search for truth.' He described the process of preserving one orthodoxy alone, as having 'a long and tortuous history,' going so far as to say that 'any who claim to have found some fixed form are in danger, like Lucifer, of mistaking themselves for God.'[74] He thus reached the remarkable position of equating conservatism in theology with the satanic. It is safe to say that Bottoms was incensed by the attitude he found in *ET*. Matters were getting out of hand on both sides of the debate.

---

[73] *ET*, August 1971, 1.
[74] *BT* August 12, 1971, 5.

The Baptist Revival Fellowship

As September approached it was altogether evident that the controversy would not die down. Protest did, however, settle into clearer streams. One of them was that of Peter Masters and *ET*. A second, close to Masters in spirit though not in overt argument, was that of the BRF. The third was a new and determined campaign by the moderates of the Union.[75] Indeed, they would entirely take the initiative away from the anti-denominationalists.

The Loyalist Campaign for Orthodoxy

September saw a group of loyalists take decisive action. Unlike the BRF's strategy of confronting perceived unorthodoxy, this group chose a public celebration of traditional orthodoxy. *BT*, on September 2, carried an advertisement for a rally to be addressed by David Pawson in October, on the subject 'How Much of a God Was Jesus?'[76] Block bookings were invited; these were obtainable by contacting C. N. Moss, (minister of Wimbledon Baptist Church, London). In addition, Kirk's reversal of loyalties went on public view in the 'Baptist News' column of *British Weekly* for September 10, 1971, which reported the circular letter to all churches in the LBA from Cheam Baptist Church.[77] The London Baptist Association added its official voice through a special Council Meeting to express concern for orthodoxy, which was reported by *BT* on September 30 and by *British Weekly* a week later in the October 8 edition, under 'Baptist News.' *British Weekly* noted that it was 'following the closure of the correspondence on this subject in *The Baptist Times* that the LBA decided to adopt a resolution calling for further action by the BU Council. It criticized Michael Taylor as appearing 'to throw doubt on the Authority, Deity and Sinlessness of Jesus Christ, and to be inconsistent with the Declaration of Principle.' It called on the Council of the BU:

> To take all necessary steps to repair as far as may be possible the harm done to our Denomination, by making clear the intention of the Union to maintain inviolate the Declaration of Principle, and of insisting that those who serve the Denomination should clearly understand and be willing to give loyal support to it. This Council is of the opinion that the Declaration of Principle represents the minimum requirement for fellowship in the Baptist Denomination and places on record the importance it attaches to the loyal and

---

[75] From the liberal wing, it should be acknowledged that a trickle rather than a stream of protest also emerged against Union policy over its perceived failure to defend liberty of thought.
[76] *BT*, September 2, 1971, 1
[77] *BW*, September 10, 1971, B4

wholehearted acceptance of the Declaration, both in letter and in spirit.[78]

In early October, the Bloomsbury rally took place to celebrate the Deity of Christ. *British Weekly*, on October 8, 1971, reported:

> Bloomsbury Baptist Church, London, was packed last Saturday when 900 Baptists from London and the Home Counties met to hear an address by the Rev. David Pawson, minister of Guildford Baptist Church, entitled, 'How Much of a God was Jesus?' [79]

The report went on to state that 'the meeting was arranged by three London ministers, Charles Moss, Wimbledon, Douglas McBain, Streatham,[80] and Andrew McKie, Norwood.' *BT* covered the meeting on October 7, noting that the chairman was a fourth leading conservative in the Union, Stanley Voke. Like King, Voke was finding ways other than the BRF he had once supported to express solidarity with fellow conservatives. His presence was not so much the evidence of a link between them as of a gulf between them. Walter Bottoms chose the headline 'Baptists Challenged To Produce Statement Of Belief.'[81] Pawson, he reported, had 'challenged the denomination to produce a Scriptural statement of its beliefs' while the 'capacity congregation' stood at the end of the meeting to confess unequivocally their faith in Jesus Christ as 'their Lord and their God.'

On October 22, *British Weekly* reported that the address had been published within the remarkably short period of two weeks by another Baptist minister, Derek Moon, who secured funding to rush through the printing of 6000 copies, on sale at 10p each to recoup the cost. 1700 copies were mailed free of charge to every minister and probationer minister in the Union, and to some one hundred Christian bookshops.[82] This might have provided an opportunity for the conservatives to seize the high ground in the denomination, but the booklet was sent out with an accompanying letter which referred to the forthcoming November Council. Russell had asked in his *BT* letter of July 15, for a moratorium on public debate until the November Council was able to consider the issue formally. Four liberal ministers accordingly co-signed a letter to *BT* on November 11, to re-open the denominational debate, accusing Moon of 'a breach of faith' against Russell's

---

[78] *BT*, October 8, 1971, 3.
[79] Ibid.
[80] An interesting connection between McBain and Kirk lies in McBain having been a member of Cheam Baptist Church before entering the ministry.
[81] *BT*, October 7, 1971, 16, continued 11, column 1.
[82] *BW*, October 22, 1971, 6.

policy.[83] They now candidly expressed their 'hope for a different outcome' from Derek Moon's.'[84]

These events signalled the full recommencement of hostilities. The conservative voice had previously descended to vitriol over the summer but had been rescued by the Bloomsbury meeting and David Pawson's skill in dealing with the controversy with good grace. Now it was the liberal side that seemed to cast off a proper restraint. To begin with, Henton Davies joined the controversy. He had remained fairly silent until now, a fact all the more remarkable considering the substantial role he had played in its origin. He wrote a letter to BT about David Pawson's address, published on October 28. It was a poor contribution – intending cleverness and wit but achieving neither. He criticized the title of the address, noting its derivation from the Assembly title 'How Much of a Man was Jesus?' He thought it either amusing or clever to attack the change to 'How Much of a God was Jesus?' by suggesting that Pawson 'has given the appearance of committing himself to an Arian Christology of a splendid God-like man, and of course this was the very thing he was seeking to avoid.' The lowest level of his wit was reached when he wrote 'Mr. Pawson's title speaks of a god, and as such it is a polytheistic howler.' Such a crude attempt at humour seemed incredibly inept in view of the theological storm now raging around him. Secondly, on October 14, two letters appeared in BT concerning the LBA Council resolution about the Deity of Christ, both of them extremely critical of the further publicity given to the Christological controversy. Paul Ballard, a respected minister on the liberal wing of the Union, displayed belief in the kind of evil conspiracy long suspected of liberals by conservatives. He detected:

> a deliberate campaign not to allow the matter to rest and to use the denominational structures as a means of demanding some sort of action.... The whole episode appears sinister and dangerous for a number of reasons, not least because the politics of the situation have obscured the real issues at stake.[85]

He went on to suggest that the freedom 'inherent in Baptist tradition' was at stake, through 'the introduction of a credal confession and a limitation of the range of interpretation.' He believed the denomination should realize what was happening: a 'heresy hunt' that was a denial of the greater reality that 'in the Gospel love, concern and long suffering are the truth.' The second letter was a tirade against the London Baptist Association. The writer was a

---

[83] The four ministers referred to above were Robert J. Paul, A. R. Barker, Hugh D. Logan, and Hugh G. Cross, and was addressed from Hemel Hempstead.
[84] BT, November 11, 1971, 5.
[85] BT, October 14, 1971, 3: 'Let Us Realise What Is Happening.'

The Christological Controversy 1971

minister who chose to remain anonymous as he wished to protect his congregation 'from the viciousness of such "conservative" attacks' as he was condemning.[86]

The Second Attempt to End the Controversy

The Union was by now working through the autumn cycle of meetings preparatory to the November Council. Up until this point of time, its only policy was studied neutrality. It was now faced with a dilemma. Conservatives were interpreting the Union's silence as theological weakness while liberal voices were seeing it as a failure to defend liberty of thought. The lead committee to deal with this was the General Purposes & Finance Committee, which met on October 5, and was chaired by Stanley Turl. On its agenda was 'a suggested statement for submission to the Council' which had already been drawn up for presentation to the meeting.[87] No authorship is indicated, but David Russell presented a complete draft to the committee. The statement would become the basis of the official response of the Union to the Christological controversy and so had very great importance, a fact that merited, perhaps, a more complete minute of how exactly it came into being. The draft was eventually adopted for presentation to the November Council. In essence, it sought to preserve the policy of neutrality by neither criticizing nor absolving Taylor, to avoid defining the meaning of the Declaration of Principle, and to acknowledge the commitment of the Union as a whole to the Deity of Christ without ruling out more liberal standpoints.[88]

The committee meeting was a difficult one. George Beasley-Murray, the Council chairman, revealed his settled opposition to Russell's policy of neutrality. He proposed an amendment to make clear that 'this Council records its belief that the address of the Rev. Michael Taylor does not apparently do justice to the teaching of the New Testament concerning our Lord Jesus Christ.'[89] He was defeated then and would continue to be on later occasions. More extreme voices were to be heard as well. The committee noted that some churches had called for a stronger statement against Michael Taylor, and even for disciplinary action against him. They decided that such matters should be left for Council members to raise on behalf of their constituencies should they feel inclined to do so. When the content of the statement and of the policy to be adopted at the forthcoming Council were eventually settled, Beasley-Murray was sufficiently committed to open

---

[86] Minutes of the Baptist Union GP&F Executive, October 5, 1971, Item 75/71.
[87] Ibid.
[88] See Appendix Nine for the full text as it was finally proposed to Council.
[89] GP&F Minutes, November 5, 1971, Item 75/71, 12.

disagreement with it that he 'suggested he should not preside in Council while the matter of the Rev. Michael Taylor and his address were under discussion. The committee thought that he could express his views in Council without leaving the chair.' This decision was appended to the Minute Book in retrospect,[90] perhaps because at the November Council meeting the permission granted by GP&F had not been revealed to the Council so that Beasley-Murray, when he spoke against the proposal as he had indicated, was accused of abusing his position as chairman (see further the discussion of the Council meeting below).

The BRF had remained remarkably silent in terms of official communications with the BU after the two letters of May 26 and June 10 demanding that both the Union and Michael Taylor should unequivocally state that 'Jesus is God.' Perhaps the thoroughness of Russell's research had caused them to question their thinking more carefully, but in any case, the actions of the London Baptist Association, and various individuals within the LBA, had set the pace of protest far more effectively than the BRF. Perhaps also, the primary activity of the movement's leaders was at that stage to prepare for the possibility of large-scale disaffiliations from the Union. These plans would be revealed publicly in the forthcoming Annual Conference in November. However, on October 6, Alec Steen, the recently appointed secretary of the committee, wrote again to Russell – somewhat incredibly in view of the long interval – 'to acknowledge your letter of 16th June to our chairman Harold Owen.' It was the committee's view that 'the Declaration of Principle needs to be defined. It is obvious that the words can be used to give quite distinct and indeed opposing views of the Person of our Lord Jesus Christ.' Steen requested that Russell should return to the first letter and its demand for the Union and Principal Taylor to affirm that 'Jesus is God.' This was the line drawn in the sand as far as the BRF was concerned. Nothing less, apparently, would convince them that the denomination was committed to the Deity of Christ.

Conclusions

The Christological controversy of 1971 caught not only the BRF but the whole denomination unawares. The position espoused by Michael Taylor was neither novel nor eccentric in academic circles, but stating them at a Baptist Assembly not only distanced him from most other Baptist theologians but, more importantly, from the great majority of Baptist church members and their ministers. The outcome, expressed in widespread protest, was so

---

[90] Ibid., 14, loose leaf adhered to the page as an addendum to Item 75/71.

predictable that it is surprising, to say the least, that he was neither forewarned nor able to anticipate it.

Members of the BRF were among many who responded individually from the outset, but the BRF did not formally respond until late May, and when it did it adopted unworkable methods and unhelpful stances for a denominational campaign. It used *ET* as a mouthpiece when *ET* was already committed publicly to Lloyd-Jones' call for secession. It called for actions that were either unconstitutional or so unrealistic they were bound to fail. It took until June for the BRF to engage the Union over the fundamental constitutional question of what meaning should to be attached to 'Christ, God manifest in the flesh.' However, the July edition of *ET*, so obviously the work of BRF members, managed to alienate completely the loyalist conservatives who might have gathered around the BRF to press that issue. Instead, the loyalists became hostile to the Fellowship even as they wondered how to take an effective stand against Taylor.

The autumn brought with it Russell's worst nightmare. The moderate conservatives who comprised the mainstay of BU membership found their own voice in the Bloomsbury Rally, and in representative leaders who could not be pigeon-holed as conservative extremists. The organizers of the rally either had nothing to do with the BRF or had explicitly repudiated it. David Pawson's address galvanized more widespread opposition. Beasley-Murray and Sir Cyril Black combined to give voice to it within the corridors of Baptist House. The BRF Committee, by contrast, having fumbled their initial approach, then delayed for nearly four months before further communication with Russell. When they did eventually reply, they returned to their wrong-headed initial letter calling upon the Union to request from Taylor an affirmation that 'Jesus is God,' rather than pressing for clarification of the phrase 'God manifest in the flesh.' However, the *ET* articles over the summer had made them pariahs not only to the Union leadership but also to the loyalist conservatives who were now prepared to make a stand. The Bloomsbury Rally was as much a rejection of the BRF as it was of Michael Taylor's address. The BRF strategy undoubtedly helped to keep the controversy before the denomination and the wider public, and its policy of secession was sufficiently determined to cause considerable concern. However, it was obvious by the end of the summer that the Fellowship had lost not only the ear of the Union leadership but even of its own conservative evangelical constituency in the denomination.

CHAPTER SIX

'WE CANNOT IN CONSCIENCE REMAIN': THE SECESSION OF THE BAPTIST REVIVAL FELLOWSHIP AND THE RESOLUTION OF THE CHRISTOLOGICAL CONTROVERSY

This chapter will consider a period begun by the November BU Council and ended by the inaugural meeting of an 'Association of Evangelical Baptist Churches.' Three interwoven themes will be discussed: the attempt by David Russell to preserve his policy, the campaign against him led especially by Sir Cyril Black and George Beasley-Murray, and the culmination of the BRF's plan to create an alternative Baptist body.

The November Council and Its Aftermath

At the November BU Council 193 members were listed as present with 17 apologies for absence.[1] The item that dominated the proceedings was the draft statement from the GP&F Committee intended for debate at the next Annual Assembly in 1972. Essentially, this acknowledged the concern of 'some in the denomination' over Michael Taylor's views, affirmed the Deity of Christ as the predominant position of Baptists, but maintained that the Declaration of Principle needed neither clarification nor alteration. The resolution represented a major concession to conservative protesters by its affirmation of the Deity of Christ but held the line regarding any reconsideration of the Declaration of Principle. This ambiguity was attacked in amendments. Four were expressions of a more emphatic doctrinal conservatism. One sought to make liberty of thought more central, although it did endorse the Deity of Christ, and came from Ernest Payne and Leonard Champion. In view of its complexity, its new contribution to the debate, and its central place in the escalation of the controversy, this amendment needs particular discussion.[2]

The wording proposed by Champion and Payne was complex, but distanced Principal Taylor's views from any 'official policy or doctrine' of the Union and affirmed the undisputed fact that the address did not depart from belief in 'the full and complete humanity of Jesus' (which no-one had questioned). Commitment to the Deity of Jesus Christ was next affirmed through Baptist

---

[1] BU Council Minutes, November 9 &10, 1971, 38–45.
[2] See Appendix Nine.

approval of various ecumenical statements between 1926 and 1961.[3] Clause 2(d) was an historical note recognizing that 'the Union has always contained within its fellowship those of differing theological opinions and emphases believing that its claim for toleration involves tolerance and mutual respect within its own ranks.' It concluded with a call for a Baptist Confession of Faith to be drawn up by the Conference of Baptist Principals and Tutors, and an appeal to avoid controversy at Assemblies.

All the amendments received very limited support, that of Payne and Champion receiving more than most, but with only 43 votes in favour.[4] It was clear that the Council was anxious to avoid taking any stance that would either promote further divisions or avoid the real difficulties felt over Taylor's opinions. There the matter might have rested, but in the closing discussions about the final wording to be presented to the Assembly, P. J. Cooke, seconded by Walter Fancutt, made a supplementary proposal that the Payne and Champion historical explanation of liberty should be added as an addendum to the original proposal. The Minutes record that 'this was put to the meeting and carried with two against.' The addition of a comment concerning Baptist history may have seemed innocuous to the meeting, but Sir Cyril Black immediately realized that this addition – the addendum – would weaken the original proposal by recognizing the legitimacy of contradictory opinions about the Deity of Christ.[5] He therefore proposed an additional phrase to the call for mutual toleration by adding the qualification 'consistent with acceptance of, and loyalty to, the doctrinal clauses of the constitution.' Ronald Armstrong seconded him but the Minutes record, without giving numbers, 'It was put to the meeting and lost.'[6] Council then agreed by consensus some minor alterations, deleting two ambiguous phrases about Michael Taylor's statements being 'variously interpreted' or 'however the address is to be interpreted.'[7] At the conclusion of the discussion, David Russell expressed the prayerful hope that the resolution 'will do something to allay the fears of all parties,' both those who 'have been

---

[3] Payne and Champion were perhaps trying here to show that conservatives had good reason to affirm ecumenism.

[4] Council Minutes, November 9 &10, 1971, 39–42.

[5] An interesting historical parallel exists here with the Downgrade Controversy. As previously mentioned, in response to Spurgeon's concerns, the BU adopted a Doctrinal Basis but added to it a similar addendum acknowledging as an historical fact that disagreement existed among Baptists concerning eternal punishment. See Iain Murray, *The Forgotten Spurgeon* (Edinburgh: Banner of Truth, 1966), 218–219, where the 1888 BU Statement of Faith is reproduced as per Appendix Two. Just as Black now rejected the modern one as a negation of the resolution, Spurgeon rejected the earlier one as a negation of adopting the Doctrinal Basis. Iain Murray, *The Forgotten Spurgeon*, 155.

[6] Ibid., 43.

[7] Ibid.

concerned that the truth of the gospel might have been undermined' and those who 'felt deeply that the principle of liberty might have been placed in jeopardy.'[8] He could not have been more wrong.

Black's consternation has been noted and the aftermath will be discussed in due course. Another senior leader now expressed his disagreement. Beasley-Murray abruptly resigned as Council Chairman. There is no minute to that effect in the official record, but it happened at some point after the resolution had been debated. In a private communication to Paul Beasley-Murray dated June 2000, Russell recalled that 'As General Secretary, sitting by his side, I confess I was greatly taken aback by this unexpected announcement, given without warning.'[9] Sir Cyril Black wrote to Russell in support of Beasley-Murray the next day, confessing that 'I found yesterday afternoon's debate deeply distressing, culminating as it did with the resignation of Dr. Beasley-Murray.'[10]

George Beasley-Murray confirmed his resignation in writing to David Russell on November 17. In it he expressed his profound conviction concerning Michael Taylor's address:

> that what was expressed was not faith in the living Christ of the Bible, and that its implications demand radical changes in Baptists' attitudes to the New Testament, to the God we worship and the Gospel we preach. Not least on such a basis our understanding of baptism would be an anachronism, and therefore the continued existence of our denomination unwarranted.[11]

He wrote another letter that same day, a personal message to Michael Taylor. He candidly stated that:

> you have set in motion forces that will continue to move for a long time. My concern will be to try to direct some of them at any rate in a right direction. If the end of it all is a greater understanding of Christ and the gospel and a better communication of our message to the world, that will be a wonderful gain. But in the process there will certainly be hurt, for many feel that their faith and the Baptist Denomination in particular is threatened, and people in that situation are not used to quiet speaking. They feel above all that the

---

[8] Reported in *BT*, November 18, 1971, 7.
[9] Quoted in *Fearless For Truth*, 162.
[10] Letter from Sir Cyril Black to David Russell dated November 10, 1971, (Russell's Private Papers: Michael Taylor Controversy 1971: File MT/6).
[11] Copy of George Beasley-Murray's letter of November 17, 1971, (Russell's Private Papers: Michael Taylor Controversy 1971: File MT/6).

honour of the Lord is at stake, and they must see that we give him his rightful place in our thought and message.[12]

These words explain the depth of feeling and conviction within George Beasley-Murray concerning the implications of the denomination not rejecting publicly Taylor's address. For him, the issue was not simply that people might leave the Union. It was that the Union might leave Christ.[13]

Ernest Payne was sharply critical of Beasley-Murray, stating in a letter to him some months later that 'you have been stirring up trouble instead of calming it, and have contributed therefore, more than perhaps any other individual, to the very difficult and dangerous situation we now face.'[14] Beasley-Murray replied by accusing Payne of being far more guilty because he had led opposition at the end of the 1971 Assembly against issuing a statement regarding Taylor's address 'embodying the perfectly obvious observation that speakers at our assembly bear the responsibility for their utterances themselves.'[15]

Payne was the only senior Baptist figure who made public statements strongly supportive of Michael Taylor, although the radical Baptist Renewal Group went into print in defence of Taylor at that point.[16] *British Weekly*, on November 26, reported the more usual view, presenting Beasley-Murray as a defender of evangelical belief who 'wishes to dissent in the strongest terms from the Council's action' of refusing to dissociate itself from the views of Michael Taylor.[17] Moreover, Sir Cyril Black, in his post-Council letter to Russell noted above, bluntly declared that the Council was 'unrepresentative of the state of opinion in our rank and file membership, and is becoming increasingly so.' Walter Bottoms nevertheless gave strong approval to the Council's actions, hoping that the resolution affirming Russell's hope that the outcome 'will have gone a long way to allay the misunderstandings and fears aroused in recent months by the discussion of an assembly address.'[18] Of the addendum he claimed it was nothing more than a statement which 'emphasizes the place the denomination claims in the Evangelical tradition and the holy universal church and its heritage of religious liberty.'

Bottoms expressed the hope that the controversy was now over, but in fact he had already made sure it was not. The week of the Council meeting,

---

[12] *Fearless For Truth*, 150.
[13] See Appendix 12: George Beasley-Murray, *The Christological Controversy in the Baptist Union* (pp. and circulated to Baptist Ministers and Church Secretaries, January 1972), 4.
[14] *Fearless For Truth*, 155.
[15] A letter dated April 20, 1972, quoted in *Fearless For Truth*, 156.
[16] *BW*, December 10, 1971, p. B4.
[17] *BW*, November 26, 1971, 3.
[18] *BT*, November 18, 1971, 5.

Bottoms had made a fresh attack on David Pawson's address 'How Much of a God was Jesus?' in a review of the published address in *BT* on November 11. He slated Pawson for a host of perceived errors, including the Appollinarian heresy of denying the genuine humanity of Christ.[19] Sir Cyril Black felt it necessary to write to David Russell about the review, stating his amazement at its contents and concluding that 'if there was any glimmering of hope after the debate on Tuesday afternoon last' it was now 'completely torpedoed.' He expostulated:

> What induced the Editor, without waiting to see the result of the Council debate on Tuesday last, to write and publish his review, and the letters to which I have referred, passes my comprehension. If ever there was a case of pouring fuel on the flames, this is it.[20]

Bottoms' review was attacked by others. On November 25, two lengthy letters were published in *BT*, with an editorial note that three more in similar vein had not been included: from Revs. Clifford Fryer (Merton), John Pretlove (Sheffield), and Bryan Harrison (Liverpool).[21] The first of the two published letters came from Stanley Voke. The second was jointly penned by the organizers of the Bloomsbury rally. Both letters took the editor to task for accusing David Pawson of Apollinarianism for his assertion that Christ could not commit an error of judgment. Voke went on to make a broader point about the Christological focus of the Declaration of Principle. Baptists might sometimes question 'the Holy Scriptures as inerrant' but cannot do so of Christ when He is declared to be the 'sole and absolute authority' in Baptist belief:

> Sir, we cannot have it both ways. Either He is errant, in which case He is not wholly trustworthy, or He is inerrant and He is trustworthy. In the light of our Lord's own words and claims I suggest it is not Mr. Pawson who presents us with "a defective Christ", but his critics and his reviewer.[22]

The second letter, jointly signed by Douglas McBain, Andrew McKie and Norman Moss, reacted strongly to a communication from four Hemel Hempstead ministers who had criticized the circulation of a letter, sent with the published address by Pawson, calling for action at the November Council meeting. The Hemel ministers considered this a breach of faith against David Russell's request for patience until the Council was convened:

---

[19] *BT*, November 11, 1971, 3.
[20] Letter from Sir Cyril Black to David Russell, November 12, 1971, (Russell's Private Papers: Michael Taylor Controversy, 1971: File MT/6).
[21] *BT*, November 25, 1971, 3.
[22] Ibid.

> To have a meeting five months after the assembly is surely not lacking in restraint; its objective and achievement has not done harm to the church of God and no one has yet accused us of a lack of graciousness in anything we have said or written. If, however, Dr. Russell's plea to us in *The Baptist Times* of July 15 last was to be interpreted as a call to silence then we are guilty, but of a guilty silence we are not.[23]

Russell soon had another protest on his hands. On December 2, he had to acknowledge a letter from the prominent and wealthy Baptist benefactor, Sir Herbert Janes. Sir Herbert had received many letters from concerned Baptists but was finally moved to speak out after a report of the Council controversy appeared in *The Daily Telegraph* on Saturday November 28. He believed that 'it was a great mistake to have invited Michael Taylor to speak on this subject. Our assembly is such a great occasion that it ought to be treated with greater respect.' He went so far as to say, 'The Michael Taylors would cut the tap root of [laypeople's] faith. Tell them to shut up and let us get on with our work.'[24] Russell's policy was proving unworkable.

The November BRF Conference and the Decision to Secede

The BRF held its 1971 Conference at Swanwick from November 15–17. David C. Potter, one of those who were present, wrote a report of the event for *Evangelical Times*.[25] He recorded that the conference had produced an official resolution, committing BRF members to withdrawal from the Union because of the November Council's lack of clarity in affirming the Deity of Christ.[26] This included a further statement:

> We now ask other churches and ministers who feel as we do and are in sympathy with our assessment of the denominational situation to give the most serious consideration to these matters and to make a stand with us for the truth concerning Christ.[27]

Robert Horn, one of the committee members, recorded 'a remarkable sense of the Lord's presence' before the vote, with 155 votes in favour, 14 against, and with 24 abstentions.[28] Horn went on to report the resignation from the BU List of 'perhaps around 20' before the Council meeting, with more known

---

[23] Ibid.
[24] Letter from Sir Herbert Janes to David Russell, November 30, 1971, (Russell's Private Papers: Michael Taylor Controversy 1971: File MT/6).
[25] *Evangelical Times*, December 9, 1971, 1.
[26] See Appendix Ten for the full resolution.
[27] Reported in *Evangelical Times*, December 1971.
[28] *Grace Magazine*, No. 19, January 1972, 4–5.

The Baptist Revival Fellowship

to him afterwards, and 'various churches and ministers' still considering their position. Of this resolution David Russell commented waspishly to Michael Taylor, in a letter dated November 25:

> The BRF has gone to town on the business of the Council's statement, and no doubt you have seen their reply on the back page of *The Baptist Times*. Beasley-Murray has also insisted that a paragraph or two be inserted in *The Baptist Times* to make clear his position and announce his resignation as chairman of the Council. This, I feel, is most unfortunate, but he has, as I said, insisted on this being done.[29]

The BRF moved forward its plans for secession. On December 7, the GP&F Executive Committee formally noted the BRF Conference Resolution and received a report from Russell of his discussions with the BRF in its light. Included in this was a letter from the BRF dealing with various practical issues such as pension arrangements for those who left.[30] Then, as noted above, in January a circular letter was sent out (followed by a public response from Russell) to advertise a secession meeting on January 22 at the Metropolitan Tabernacle at which a more public consultation would take place on the constitution and progress of a new 'Association of Baptist Churches.' *BT*, on January 27, carried a report in which it was said that a hundred people attended, and 'among them were 82 ministers.'[31] *Grace Magazine*, in its March issue, noted that 'letters were received from other ministers and churches'[32] that could not be present or represented. The meeting was explained as arising from the 1971 BRF Conference Resolution.

A Doctrinal Basis was agreed informally after some discussion, and the aims of the association were derived from the original statement of purpose in 1812–13 at the founding of the 'General Union of Particular Baptists' – to afford the means of fellowship and to disclaim any superiority or control over member churches. Harold Owen was reported by *BT* as saying that 'we are not trying to pull people out of the Baptist Union or offer a bait to get them out, but to provide a haven of fellowship for those who no longer belong to the Union and would otherwise be isolated.' However, it would be a haven only for churches and their appointed ministers. No membership or accreditation would be available for ministers who resigned from the Union but whose churches did not, for any reason, follow them. It was decided to hold a further meeting in the autumn, at which the AEBC would have its formal inauguration. When Russell reported on this event to the BU Officers'

---

[29] David Russell to Michael Taylor, November 25, 1971:(Russell's Private Papers: Michael Taylor Controversy 1971: File MT/6).
[30] See Appendix Eleven for the full text of the letter.
[31] *BT*, January 27, 1972, 12.
[32] *Grace Magazine*, No. 21, March 1972, 18.

Meeting on February 4, he expressed concern that 'it could become a rallying point to encourage others to leave the BU.'[33] It was agreed to wait and see what its formal name would become and how many churches would join it, before taking any definite course of action as a Union. 'In the meantime, a friendly attitude should be maintained.' Russell was concerned that it might become a significant alternative to the BU. It will be shown below how close that would come to happening, not because the BRF moved towards the loyalists but because Sir Cyril Black began to move toward them.

Sir Cyril Black's Campaign Against Russell's Policy

The BRF had given up any serious intention to influence denominational policy by its choice of secession. Conservative loyalists, however, had no intention of surrendering. At the December 3 BU Officers Meeting, Russell conceded that neither the 'conservatives' nor the 'liberals' were happy with the result of the November Council. The liberal minister Gordon Hastings, who been nominated for the Vice Presidency of the Union, now wished to withdraw 'in view of the fact that were he elected to office he might very well be unable to represent to the country the policies which he believed stemmed from certain decisions made at the Council meeting in November last.'[34] At the same time, Russell had to report that the conservative wing was even more roused:

> he had received a number of resignations and also other correspondence including a letter from Sir Cyril Black indicating that he intended bringing forward a notice of motion for the forthcoming assembly. It would appear that quite a number in the denomination were dissatisfied with the Council's statement in view of the fact that it had not explicitly dissociated itself from the address given by Mr. Taylor.[35]

Sir Cyril had decided to play for all or nothing and had announced his campaign to defeat the resolution.

The opening manoeuvre of this campaign consisted of a letter from Sir Cyril Black to *BT* concerning the addendum. This meant that the whole Baptist denomination was being put on alert that he would fight against the official policy. He believed the addendum meant only one thing:

> there is no limit to the 'tolerance and mutual respect' to be accorded to people within our own ranks. The warning given by Jesus and His

---

[33] Minutes of the BU Officers, February 4, 1972, Item IV.
[34] Ibid: Item V.
[35] Minutes of the Officer's Meeting held on December 3, 1971, Item IV.

> apostles regarding 'false prophets' and 'false teachers' are no longer to be heeded. No heresy can be so great that 'tolerance and mutual respect' are to be withdrawn.
>
> I find it amazing, as I think will many other people, that this clear-cut and reasonable amendment should have been rejected. This may well prove to be the issue by which, more than any other, the 'parting of the ways' will be reached.

For the first time, a highly respected figure from within the establishment had declared the Union to be in imminent danger from heresy. Even George Beasley-Murray, despite his actions, had avoided such a blunt accusation. It is not surprising that both David Russell and Ernest Payne thought it necessary to reply publicly to Sir Cyril's letter, and these were published by *BT* on December 9.[36] Russell sought to undermine Black's conclusion that the consequence of the addendum would be to open the door to every kind of false teaching and he attacked those who claimed that the Union was '"unorthodox" and "unevangelical".' Virtually quoting Sir Herbert Janes, he appealed for peace in the Union 'by getting on with the task He has given us to do.' Ernest Payne's letter expounded his personal interpretation of toleration in the history of Baptist life:

> Baptists have shown themselves opposed to subscription to theological statements as a test of discipleship or even of orthodoxy. The Baptist confessions of the 17th Century, the Covenants of local churches and the various formulations of the basis of the Union have never been intended for use in this fashion. They offer corporate testimony, but words are "daughters of earth"[37]

Payne was making a determined stand for the addendum and its protection of what he conceived to be the Baptist tradition of liberty. The attack on the addendum gathered pace, however, when Spurgeon's College Council met in December and resolved:

> The Council of Spurgeon's College welcomes the statement of the Baptist Union Council in so far as it re-affirms the Baptist Union Declaration of Principle, but regrets that in the course of its proper desire to preserve liberty, the Baptist Union Council failed to make it clear that such liberty must be within the bounds of its Constitution. Spurgeon's College Council therefore asks the Baptist Union Council to reconsider its statement in view of its ambiguity.[38]

---

[36] Both letters appeared in *BT*, December 9, 1971, 2.
[37] Ibid.
[38] Reported in *BW*, January 29, 1971, B5.

Russell continued to defend the addendum, stating later that month in reply to a critical letter from A. R. Watts, secretary of Gorse Hill Baptist Church, Swindon, that 'This ... has been misunderstood by many. I would stress that it was intended to be a factual historical observation and not an attempt to justify any or every doctrinal expression.'[39] The LBA Council evidently shared this 'misunderstanding,' adding its own voice to that of Spurgeon's by unanimously resolving at its December meeting that:

> The Council of the London Baptist Association welcomes the statement approved by the Baptist Union Council at its meeting on November 9, 1971, in so far as such statement unequivocally confesses the Deity as well as the humanity of Jesus Christ, and explicitly reaffirms that the basis of the Baptist Union is the Declaration of Principle set out in the constitution.
>
> It regrets, however, that the Baptist Union Council feels unable to make it clear that any statement which fails to do justice to the Deity of our Lord Jesus Christ offends such Declaration of Principle as generally understood among us, and thereby goes beyond the bounds of liberty of opinion and theological statement.
>
> It invites the General Purposes & Finance Committee of the Association to consider the Addendum to the Baptist Union Council's statement with a view to bringing a further resolution before the Council of the Association for consideration.[40]

The issue had become a battle between two groups and two visions: the Baptist establishment with its vision for a denomination in which the centre of gravity was located in liberal tolerance, and an increasingly militant body in which the centre of gravity was located in traditional evangelical belief. Both parties professed a capacity for tolerance towards those who dissented, but both had in mind a limit to it. The conservatives frankly set the limit at rejecting the Deity of Christ, although a more comprehensive evangelical faith was clearly implied in that. The establishment leaders apparently held a more tolerant position, but a private exchange of letters between Black and Russell suggests otherwise. In December, Russell had written to Sir Cyril raising a number of issues. The original letter is not preserved in his papers, but Black's reply included a response to some critical comments from Russell about conservative evangelicals. Black had read 'with interest' his views, and expressed the judgment that:

---

[39] Letter from Russell to A. R. Watts, December 21, 1971, (Russell's Private Papers: Michael Taylor Controversy 1971: File MT/5).
[40] Reported in *BW*, January 14, 1972, B5.

those in the Union who are opposed to the Conservative Evangelical position must necessarily differ among themselves as to the extent to which they would wish Conservative Evangelicals to withdraw. They are, of course, faced with the dilemma that, while they would like to be rid of the Conservative Evangelicals, they are naturally concerned about the loss of support for the Union, financial and otherwise, that would be caused by their withdrawal.[41]

Sir Cyril was very close to resignation from the Union. He referred to a previous comment to Russell that he would leave the denomination 'in the event of an unsatisfactory decision by the assembly.' Now he was in no doubt that 'a number of Ministers, laymen and churches will withdraw, and it is certainly my intention to be among them.'[42] This was very bad news for Russell. The BRF might inspire enough secessions to make a dent in the Union but Black, backed by Beasley-Murray, Spurgeon's College and the LBA could rip it apart, perhaps even leaving only a minority of more liberally-minded members in the existing Union. The controversy had escalated to the point that only a victory for the traditionalists would prevent a major division. Black warned that the Baptist Union leadership 'might try to persuade themselves that things are in fact as they would like them to be' but 'they have now to face the harsh reality' that the denomination was facing serious crisis. Black had decided that the popular voice of protest would not influence Russell and he felt driven to fight him on territory that had not been contested for nearly sixty years – the public humiliation of a General Secretary's recommendation to the denomination.

Russell still thought, however, that it was possible both to reassure the denomination that the Deity of Christ was sacrosanct and also to avoid any real questioning of the claim. Bottoms reinforced the official line once again by placing alongside the letters from Russell and Payne five others decrying further disagreement, including one from Humphrey Vellacott (East Ham), a well-known Union minister.[43] It was too late for such a hope. Not only did letters continue to appear in BT despite a public appeal from both the current and former General Secretaries to move on, but Sir Cyril Black responded to

---

[41] Sir Cyril Black to David Russell, December 20, 1971 (David Russell Archive: Michael Taylor Controversy, File MT/5).

[42] Sir Cyril had remained aloof from the BRF to this point in the controversy. His attitude changed sufficiently to write 'a sympathetic letter' to the BRF Committee in January 1972 on hearing of progress towards the establishment of an alternative Baptist group in which, according to a BRF Committee Minute 'his long-term assessment of the situation seemed to be similar to our own' (BRF Committee Minutes for 27.3.72, Item 10: Correspondence following the meeting of January 17, to progress towards founding the Association of Evangelical Baptist Churches).

[43] BT, December 9, 1971, 3.

their criticisms without reserve. On December 30, a letter from him appeared in *BT* in which he stated, 'their arguments, in my view, only confirm my statement. They reject the Declaration of Principle as a limiting factor.'[44] He quoted from the rules for Ministerial Recognition and the ordination service included in the Baptist *Orders and Prayers for Church Worship*, to demonstrate that Payne was wrong to assert that Baptists were opposed to 'verbal tests' (and had the temerity to point out that the verbal test sworn at ordination vows was co-written by Payne himself!). He warned that the Council decision, 'far from healing divisions, has created more serious misunderstandings. It was an ambiguous statement that satisfied none, 'and for this ambiguity the statement is surely to be condemned.' In response to the accusation of Payne that there was a spirit of heresy hunting in the denomination, Black accused Michael Taylor's address of having 'cast doubt upon the authority, Deity, and sinlessness of Jesus' without which 'there would have been no occasion for the concern' being expressed. His final word was to reiterate his determination that 'it is to the assembly we must now look.'

January brought a new year, but nothing to cheer David Russell. That month's edition of *Crusade* reported at length on the November BU Council meeting. The Baptist controversy would be kept before a wider circle than the readership of *BT* or even the Free Church newspaper *British Weekly*. *Crusade* covered the situation with the headline 'Council Debate Fails to Heal Divisions.[45] Meanwhile, the issue continued to demand attention within the Union structures. On January 7 David Russell was obliged to report to the Officers' Meeting that 'he had received a number of letters which obviously showed a misunderstanding of the addendum to the Council's statement.'[46] (His critics were concerned, however, about its consequence rather than any supposed intention). Russell had drafted a supplementary statement for consideration by the GP&F Committee. In addition, the BRF had sent a circular letter to all churches and ministers, and Russell had also drafted a public reply. Russell was authorized to meet again with Sir Cyril Black to discuss what motion he might put before the Assembly. The impression of open-handed co-operation was somewhat blighted, however, by the decision that, should Black not be dissuaded from opposing the official resolution, 'a group of people ought to meet and discuss tactics concerning the presentation of this whole affair to the Assembly.'[47]

---

[44] *BT*, December 30, 1971, 3.
[45] *Crusade*, January 1972, 7.
[46] Minutes of the Officers' Meeting, January 7, 1972, Item IX: Assembly Address.
[47] Ibid.

Russell was fighting fires in several directions, but a new one now erupted from a completely unexpected quarter. At the GP&F Committee held on January 11, 1972, Henton Davies interrupted the agenda to circulate a surprise personal statement saying, among other things, that although he had approached Taylor to speak at the 1971 assembly, he had not appreciated how different were Taylor's views from his own until a few weeks before the assembly, when he chanced to have a conversation with him at the College Principals' and Tutors' Conference: 'That was the first inkling that I received that I could expect in the Assembly address something radically different from what I anticipated from him.'[48] Henton Davies had apparently been accused of deliberately setting up the possibility of a controversy. He praised Taylor for 'the clarity and appeal of the address'[49] but he considered him 'to have departed from the theme he was given, and from the point of view which I was personally expecting'[50] in three ways.

First, Davies believed that Taylor had departed from his given theme of God's 'Presence' because 'he abandons that particular theology of the Incarnate Presence which was the starting point'[51] for Davies' understanding of Jesus as the second Person of the Trinity. Second, Davies felt that Taylor 'democratizes the Presence of God, e.g., "So first, Jesus is a man like me and you."' His judgment was that 'Mr. Taylor apparently means "God is <u>only</u> present and active in Jesus, as he is present and active in us all" … if that is what he really means I am bound to reject this statement. A doubt exists as to what he really does mean.'[52] Third, Davies criticized Taylor's belief that God's presence in Jesus was not essentially different from His being "actively present on every occasion."' Davies' conviction was, 'If the statement denies that an incarnate fullness of God began in Bethlehem and ended on the cross, then I am bound to reject it.'[53]

Davies concluded that, theologically, Taylor's Christology was 'insufficient and defective … the real difficulty lies in his conception of God, and in what I conceive to be his rejection of some aspects of the Biblical teaching about God.' Later, he states that 'Mr. Taylor's view of God makes it impossible for him to believe that God was incarnate in Christ in a form different from the divine incarnation in any and every man.' Davies provided here what had been strikingly absent in the whole controversy – a scholarly Baptist assessment of Taylor's Christology. Beasley-Murray had informally and privately shown the address to two theologian friends (I. Howard Marshall

---

[48] Ibid.
[49] Ibid., 2.
[50] Ibid
[51] Ibid., 3.
[52] Ibid.
[53] Ibid.

and T. F. Torrance, both of whom were Scottish university professors), but had received only a similarly informal response supporting his conviction about Taylor. Henton Davies put his views in writing and circulated them to what was, in effect, the executive committee of the Council. His opinion was pure dynamite. It frankly sided with those who accused Taylor of denying the Deity of Christ.

Henton Davies was not, perhaps, entirely altruistic in providing a careful assessment of Taylor's orthodoxy. He had been hurt by criticism, so that he expostulated at one point. 'Am I not entitled to the recognition that Mr. Taylor really did depart from the theme and its terminology which I first proposed?'[54] His final remark was that Taylor's modification of the original theme and what he effectively described as his deviant theology had 'led to our present difficulties. For this neither the Baptist Union Council, nor the Assembly Programme Committee, nor the President are responsible or blameworthy.' It would seem that the President had not until then been included in that list. The statement would never publicly be revealed. Had it been, Michael Taylor would have been formally accused of unorthodoxy.

Even so, the January 1972 Officers' Meeting marked an abrupt change in David Russell's position. Sir Cyril Black was not present at this meeting, so that Russell wrote to him. Henton Davies had evidently made a considerable impact, as Russell now asked for a meeting of Henton Davies, Sir Cyril and himself 'to discuss amicably together possible future procedure for handling the Michael Taylor affair.'[55] He then revealed that he had changed his view that opposition to the addendum was only a misunderstanding. This had amounted to insisting that such people were either unable or unwilling to comprehend its proper meaning. Now Russell told Black that he was willing to go 'further than the Council itself went last November, particularly with reference to the Declaration of Principle' and assured Sir Cyril that his own convictions in this respect 'reflect truly the mind of the Council as a whole.' The general feeling now was 'that those who adhere to it ought to abide by it.' What he did not want was that candidates should be asked to submit 'not only to the statement there printed but also to particular interpretations given to it by members of the committee concerned.' This concession might, he hoped, 'influence you in what you have been contemplating saying to the assembly.'

This letter crossed with one from Sir Cyril to him that same day. Had he seen it, he would have been even more perturbed. Black was responding to Russell criticizing him for the tone of his statements concerning the Council

---

[54] Ibid.
[55] Letter from Russell to Black, January 13, 1972, (Russell's Private Papers: Michael Taylor Controversy, 1971: File MT/6).

decision. Black had had enough. He stated that 'there is really very little I can add to our correspondence.' He allowed himself to tell Russell, 'I think you have put yourself in the position of gravely lessening your ability to do anything in this matter. Your letter in reply to mine in *The Baptist Times* virtually denies that there is any real substance in the point that concerns me and a great many other people.' However, Black did further the correspondence on January 19 by taking up at some length the concession from Russell that the Declaration of Principle should be adhered to. He was unimpressed by such a general assurance:

> In my view, every organisation or society must have some rules by which members are bound, and no-one has yet been able to tell me what the Baptist Union would do, if anything, if we had a case like that with which the Methodist Conference recently had to deal affecting, I believe, a certain Mr. Billington, a Minister in the Church who, by reason of his statements was deemed to be an Atheist. I understand he was removed from the Methodist list of ministers. If we had a Baptist Billington, what should we do? We have, I think, to consider the matter in the alternative of what we would do if the man concerned claimed to accept the Declaration of Principle, while making statements which in other people's views were clearly inconsistent with it, and in the alternative, the man himself admitted that he did not accept the Declaration of Principle. If we assumed that something must be done in such a case, then we have to decide what is the test by which the man's orthodoxy will be judged, and what are the steps that can be taken.[56]

Sir Cyril pressed ahead with his resolution, and David Russell shared the contents of it at the February Officers' Meeting. They did no more than suggest 'a few slight amendments' in order to gain unanimity.[57] It is obvious that by this stage, any resistance to Black had all but dissolved. The question was no longer whether to stop him, but how to join him. The Officers treated the resolution as if it were an official one coming from the Union committees, even agreeing that Black should move it with their stated approval. Russell suggested that Henton Davies second it to show that the Council was identified with it (though in the event Beasley-Murray would do this), and Davies himself 'stated that he was very grateful for the action Sir Cyril proposed to take and hoped he would look at the few amendments suggested.' Sir Cyril promised to seek 'the consent of his colleagues.' What is even more remarkable is that 'the General Secretary stated that the Officers

---

[56] Letter from Black to Russell, January 13, 1972, (Russell's Private Papers: Michael Taylor Controversy, 1971: File MT/6).
[57] See Appendix Thirteen for the finally agreed version.

were deeply indebted to Sir Cyril for his efforts.'[58] GP&F met on Tuesday February 15. Russell reported the motion due to be presented at the assembly by Black, and it was agreed to recommend to Council that it 'readily give permission for Sir Cyril Black's resolution to go forward to the Assembly.'[59] January had produced a *volte face* by Russell. Sir Cyril had defeated Russell's policy but at a cost. At some point, the demand for a disciplinary process was dropped.

The March Council and the 1972 Baptist Assembly

Council met on Tuesday and Wednesday, March 14–15, 1972. The final test of the turnabout policy would be whether the less conservative Baptists would support it when the policy itself was what they had been resisting all along. Some at the Council still wanted the addendum to be removed from the previous Council statement. This would require the suspension of Standing Orders and the requisite majority was not achieved to do so. Then Ernest Payne put forward an amendment changing the phrase 'readily gives permission' to 'readily agrees to provide a place upon the agenda.' This may have been simply a procedural correction, as Council had logically first to approve resolutions for discussion at the assembly and then to find space within the agenda for them. It reads, however, more like some kind of lower level of approval for the proposal – merely making space for it rather than approving of it. A further amendment was proposed to remove the word 'readily' from Payne's phrase, but was lost and Payne's wording was accepted.

Attention now turned to Russell making a statement about the purport of the addendum. Again, an amendment was proposed to weaken the statement so that any specific mention of limiting the meaning of the addendum would be removed. However, Beasley-Murray persuaded the proposer, E. B. Grant, to second his own form of words, formulated as follows:

> In the light of observations made to the Union concerning the Council's resolution relating to the address given at the 1971 assembly on the theme of 'How Much of a Man was Jesus…?' it would appear that there has been widespread misunderstanding of the purport of the addendum to the statement. In the body of the resolution itself the Council made an unequivocal profession of belief in the Deity and humanity of our Lord Jesus Christ, and in God as Father, Son and Holy Spirit. The addendum which originally belonged to a different document, in no way sought to weaken this

---

[58] Ibid., Item V.
[59] Minutes of GP&F Committee, February 15, 1972, Item 24/72.

declaration of faith. It was a plea for tolerance of general theological differences. The Council regrets that this statement has occasioned confusion regarding its faith in Jesus Christ.[60]

British Weekly carried a substantial analysis of the issues surrounding the Christological controversy in the lead-up to the 1972 Baptist Assembly. The author, John Capon, indicated that 'on the eve of this year's Annual Assembly ... there has been a new development in the continuing controversy within the denomination concerning the Deity of Christ.'[61] Russell was also asked to make clear at the Assembly that the addendum was 'not intended to govern or invalidate the preceding statement nor is the toleration of which it speaks intended to range beyond the basis of the Declaration.' Capon refers here to the publication of an article by George Beasley-Murray and sent to every BU minister.[62] Beasley-Murray had written this article, entitled 'The Christological Controversy in the Baptist Union,' in the hope of it being published by *BT* in the weeks preceding the Assembly. However, Bottoms had rejected it, on the basis that it was 'misleading' because the assumption on which it was based was 'judged to be false,' because he had already contributed an article on the subject, and because the article was considered to be unfair in claiming that 'the denomination stands on the brink of some possible theological plunge.' Beasley-Murray therefore had it printed and sent to every Union minister. He was indeed very pessimistic about the future. His final judgement of whether Michael Taylor's convictions were consistent with Baptist life was:

> The answer is plain: we must recognise that this interpretation we have considered is not one we can embrace, and preach that Gospel of Christ to which we are committed. But in view of the confusion that exists, we must declare where we stand. If we fail to do so we call in question our existence as a Christian denomination today. And maybe forever.[63]

Capon reported on the most public demonstrations of protest: that at least 40 ministers had resigned from the Union, that a new Baptist grouping had emerged from the BRF in the Association of Evangelical Baptist Churches, that Beasley-Murray had resigned as Council Chairman, and that David Pawson's 'much-disputed' booklet had been published and distributed to every minister in answer to Michael Taylor, entitled 'How Much of a God

---

[60] Minutes of the BU Council, March 14–15, 1972, Administration Department Item 7.
[61] *BW*, April 21, 1971, B11.
[62] See Appendix Twelve: George Beasley-Murray, *The Christological Controversy in the Baptist Union*, (privately published and circulated to Baptist Ministers and Church Secretaries, January 1972).
[63] Ibid., 4.

Was Jesus?' Capon continued his coverage in another lengthy report in the April 28 edition of *British Weekly*. Under the headline 'Baptists Move To The Right?' Capon began with this statement:

> At around 12 noon on Tuesday, April 25, British Baptists made a slight but significant move to the Right. It was not far enough for some, too far for others, but for the vast majority it was just right.[64]

The resolution under discussion had been proposed by Sir Cyril Black, the full text of which was given in the *British Weekly* article.[65] Capon recorded that Sir Cyril emphasized the third and fourth paragraphs of the resolution as requiring special notice because failure to include them, as one amendment proposed, would 'be regarded as meaning that acceptance of the Declaration was no longer necessary, or that the Assembly was so doubtful about it that it was unwilling to let the words go in.' However, he specified, according to Capon, that he wanted to avoid 'an inquest' on the past. This effectively meant that he definitely excluded the possibility of disciplinary action against those who signed the Declaration of Principle but did not assent to his statement concerning the Deity of Christ. Or to put it more bluntly, he sought to avoid a witch-hunt with Michael Taylor as the chief suspect. The resolution was seconded by George Beasley-Murray, taking up the theme that 'faith and freedom' should not be seen as opposites.

Capon also reported that a leaflet, signed by Eric Blakeborough and John Matthews, both of whom were ministers from the more radical wing of the denomination, had been distributed to the audience as they entered the building. This was a call to the denomination that 'We should leave the Declaration as it stands, we should keep room in the Baptist Union for conservatives and radicals, we should not vote on Christology at an Annual Assembly of the Baptist Union.' According to the *BW* report, Paul Rowntree Clifford, President of the Selly Oak Colleges, supported this sentiment during the debate, and a number of people called out from the audience to express agreement with his view. However, Douglas McBain, Norman Moss, and Stanley Voke all spoke in favour of Black's resolution. Capon records them asserting that 'The resolution was necessary, and particularly paragraphs three and four, because there were many within the Union who wanted more clarification on these issues than the BU Council's statement last November had given.'

Various amendments were tabled and had now to be considered. The first called for discipline against those who denied or contradicted the Declaration of Principle as qualified by Black's motion. Derek Moon, George

---

[64] *BW*, April 28, 1972, 1.
[65] See Appendix Thirteen for the full text.

Stirrup, John Pretlove and Paul Bevan spoke for this, but it was defeated on a show of hands by a proportion of four to one, according to Capon. The second amendment wished to insert into Black's proposal a definite recognition that the Deity of Christ had been denied by Michael Taylor, rather than that churches and ministers had left due to a 'misunderstanding,' as implied in the substantive motion as proposed by Black. This was also defeated by the same proportion. Finally, Leonard Champion, the retiring President of Bristol Baptist College, seconded by Bernard Green (who would later become the BU General Secretary), proposed deleting the two controversial paragraphs altogether. They spoke in favour of greater freedom of expression than Black wished to see. Their amendment also was lost 'by a large majority.' At this point, Paul Rowntree Clifford proposed that the next question be put – that Black's proposal should not, in other words, be put to a vote. J. J. Brown, the chairman, refused to accept his proposal and he proceeded to take the vote. The result was that Black's proposal was carried with only 46 votes against but with 72 recorded abstentions. Capon mentioned, in his coverage, a *BT* report the previous week to the effect that under the Union's constitution, a further amendment would be put without the usual 15 days notice. This would be to delete the two offending paragraphs in favour of a less specific declaration accepting the 'Trinitarian sense' of the preceding paragraphs. It was not called by the chairman and Capon speculated as to whether the officers of the Union had decided to draw back from their own attempt at opposing Black.[66]

Conclusions

After the summer, there was a groundswell of support for the conservative evangelicalism long espoused and defended by the BRF. By then, however, the Fellowship was really no longer interested in receiving it unless it was accompanied by a commitment to secession. They were intent on leaving, not on remaining a representative movement within the denomination. Meanwhile, the conservative reaction was increasingly being given focus and direction by the London Baptists, led especially by George Beasley-Murray and Sir Cyril Black. This brought about an attempted compromise resolution at the November Council, which came under attack in the form of amendments both from the right and the left. Even so, it looked likely to unite the Council until the addendum was adopted suggesting a greater liberty than at first appeared with regard to affirming the Deity of Christ as a denomination.

---

[66] *BW*, April 28, 1972, B5.

We Cannot in Conscience Remain

From that point onwards, conservative opposition to David Russell hardened in two apparently disparate directions. The BRF openly moved towards establishing an alternative Baptist body while Sir Cyril Black and George Beasley-Murray chose a public fight for the theological direction of the denomination. The establishment leaders were no more willing to concede to the loyalists than to the secessionists, however. This drove Sir Cyril Black not only to an outright conflict with David Russell but also to the brink of secession himself. The BRF then returned briefly from the fringes of this controversy as the body with a definite plan of action. Sir Cyril went so far as to write sympathetically to them and that potentially opened the way to a major secession in which the more moderate conservatism of the loyalists would characterize the new body rather than the more hard-line attitudes by then dominant in the BRF. The secession might well have become less right-wing and more attractive to a wider circle of Baptists. Perhaps the BRF leaders would not have welcomed that, but certainly Russell did not relish the prospect. He had, in the end, to back down.

Russell's predicament dawned on him in the New Year. He was backing a policy doomed to failure because the denomination was not behind him. There was an imminent danger of the Baptist Union collapsing. It may have occurred to him how similar was his position to J. H. Shakespeare's in 1917. Shakespeare, the General Secretary then, had proposed ecclesiastical re-union in a United Church with Baptist ministers being episcopally re-ordained. This was so out of step with denominational opinion that a leading layman (T. R. Glover) co-operated with the venerable Baptist minister John Clifford to defeat him and so effectively to censure him. Like Shakespeare, Russell was opposed by the partnership of a leading layman and a greatly respected minister and faced a similar public humiliation at the forthcoming Assembly. Shakespeare never recovered from the blow and Russell might not have done either. There was a quinquennial review of his post due that year which raised, however remotely, the possibility of Russell losing his position if the denomination turned decisively away from him.

Russell led the Union in a complete reversal, backing the alternative resolution devised by Black and Beasley-Murray which affirmed without equivocation that the phrase 'God manifest in the flesh' should be understood exclusively in terms of traditional orthodoxy concerning the Deity of Christ. New and more moderately conservative leaders were emerging who would go on to senior roles in the denomination in years to come, while the more liberal element of the denomination faced the reality that they were not sufficiently representative to maintain their previous ascendancy. However, it was a partial victory through avoiding any definite policy within the Union for policing adherence to the Declaration of Principle. The conservatives won the day with regard to official doctrine, but the liberals had their compensation with regard to practical policy. This satisfied the vast majority, and in the end, a comparatively small number of ministers and their churches, probably somewhere in the region of a hundred, left the Union over a period of some years.[67] Robert Horn again wrote a commentary on the controversy for *Grace Magazine*. He expressed the opinion that the end result amounted to something rather different from what it appeared:

> The significant event here was that the younger radicals said virtually nothing in the debate. Was this discretion on their part? If they had spoken as vigorously against the resolution as a pre-Assembly handout from two of them had done, then the Assembly in passing the resolution would have been voting against them [sic]. Their silence allowed the resolution to be fired off into thin air and ensured that it certainly could not be applied to them or their views. So the Assembly's vote was not overtly anti-radical.[68]

Whether it was intended or not, the episode returned the Baptist Union to where it had been earlier in the century, that carefully balanced 'central evangelicalism' espoused by leaders such as Aubrey, in which traditional evangelicalism was recognized as the mainstream but not exclusive tradition in BU life.

The BRF, meanwhile, pressed on with founding that year the Association of Evangelical Baptist Churches. It attracted mostly the supporters of Lloyd-Jones' outlook, but not even all of them. Some churches which left the BU joined the Fellowship of Independent Evangelical Churches, some joined charismatic networks, and some remained independent. Some of those who had been part of the drive towards secession remained in the Baptist Union when faced with taking the ultimate step of seceding. The evangelical unity dreamed of by D. Martyn Lloyd-Jones did not become a reality even among the Baptists who were his most loyal followers.

---

[67] It is not possible to provide a definite number because letters of resignation were not always specific about the reason, they occurred over a period of some years after the controversy, and no specific record has been kept of them in the BU Archives. Some of them were prominent Baptist causes, such as Kensington Baptist Church in Bristol, Carey Baptist Church in Reading, Mount Pleasant Baptist Church in Swansea, and Lansdowne Baptist Church in Bournemouth (regarding all of which I have checked for their reasons through personal conversation with current or past leaders).

[68] *Grace Magazine*, No. 24, June 1972, 11.

CHAPTER SEVEN

CONCLUSIONS

Four general conclusions may be drawn from this study. First, the Baptist Revival Fellowship was a reaction to wider trends in twentieth century church life which were inevitably manifested in the Baptist Union. The second conclusion is that the BRF reflected trends in British evangelicalism, initially in reasserting the declining influence of pietism, then in moving towards fundamentalism, and finally by coming under the remarkable influence of D. Martyn Lloyd-Jones, an influence more widely represented among conservative evangelical Baptists than in any other denomination. This in itself was manifested in three ways: by adopting the new evangelical conservatism, in particular a more intellectually rigorous faith informed by Reformed theology, and therewith making a serious contribution to the denominational debate; by embracing early charismatic renewal; and finally, by embracing as its official policy Lloyd-Jones' call for secession in favour of some kind of exclusively conservative evangelical fellowship of churches. Thirdly, the BRF represented something distinctively Baptist that the denominational establishment did not after the era of M. E. Aubrey, until the BRF agenda ceased to be informed primarily by its denominational heritage. As such, it performed an important function, although one which was never welcomed by the post-war leadership of the denomination, either because they suspected it of harbouring disloyalty or because they were trying to depart from the traditions advocated by the BRF. Finally, the BRF must be judged never to have fulfilled its promise as a renewal movement within the denomination.

Reaction to Wider Trends in British Church Life

The first of the wider trends requiring notice was the impact of liberalism, which twice threatened to dominate theology in Britain, in the liberal movement that somewhat dissipated under the massive influence of the Swiss theologian Karl Barth before the Second World War and then in the radical movement of the 1960s that was answered by more cautious voices in the 1970s.[1] During the nineteenth century, the greatest challenge to western Christianity had been the 'modern' rejection of traditional Christianity in favour of scepticism and materialism.[2] Across the whole

---

[1] Cf. Hastings, *English Christianity 1920–1990*, 651–652.
[2] B. G. Worrall, in *The Making of a Modern Church* discusses this period in chapters devoted to the advance of science, the rise of biblical criticism and the Liberal and Modernist movements (pages 63–133).

ecclesiastical spectrum conservative forces reacted by defending traditional positions while liberal ones advanced various forms of accommodation. In Catholicism, conservatives reasserted traditional dogma such as papal infallibility, while accommodation emerged in Catholic Modernism. In Anglicanism, some conservatives sought a greater Catholic identity while the Evangelical party asserted the Protestant heritage of the Church of England. In the mainstream Free Churches of Britain, conservative voices essentially upheld the reliability of Scripture, traditional orthodoxy in doctrine, and the reality of evangelical experience. The voice of accommodation came mainly in the form of exploring the liberal Protestant project that began and developed in Germany, especially under the influence of Friedrich Schleiermacher.

Baptists in the twentieth century were less affected by liberalism than the other mainstream churches, certainly because of their exceptionally strong evangelical identity and possibly because their scholars tended to focus more on Biblical Theology than Systematics. The BRF was nevertheless founded as a conservative reaction to perceived liberal tendencies in the BU and there is no doubt that after World War Two the denomination became less secure about its earlier 'central evangelical' identity, and the appointment of Ernest Payne as General Secretary signalled a move to the left. The BRF was the obvious voice of conservatism and spearheaded resistance to Payne's vision. It was a more temperate kind of conservatism at heart than was to be found in some wider evangelical circles because of the Baptist Christological focus that has been traced both to C. H. Spurgeon and F. B. Meyer at the end of the nineteenth century. This at first provided a more attractive reaction to liberalism than the fundamentalist stance, with its focus on the ultimate authority of an inerrant Bible rather than the living Christ. It was this older Baptist evangelicalism, and even Meyer's strategies for promoting it, that Bamber sought to rescue in founding the Baptist Revival Fellowship. His fundamentalist tendency was not the dominant influence upon him at the beginning. However, in the late fifties Bamber changed towards a more fundamentalist agenda and to this was added at the same time the rising influence on younger Baptist ministers of the anti-denominationalism and anti-ecumenism of D. Martyn Lloyd-Jones.

The second wider trend to affect Baptist life and stimulate reaction from the BRF, especially in its early years, was the secularisation of society that accelerated after the First World War. Traditional Christian faith and church life lost their popular appeal and church attendance began to decline. It has been noted that the Baptist Union, like other denominations, sought to come to terms with this through various strategies, all of which failed to prevent the process. Hindsight may inform us that the forces at work were too great for any strategy put forward but that was not nearly so obvious at the time.

Conclusions

The Free Churches became respected and respectable in a new way through public recognition, especially during the inter-war period, so that numerical decline did not seem as drastic a problem as it really was. Furthermore, Baptists remained open to the possibility of a revival movement. The Welsh Revival of 1904–5 was a powerful memory even in the 1930s, and had there not been a Baptist-led revival in Suffolk in the 1920s? The trend within the BU was certainly not to give in to failure but rather to examine itself rather critically and to attempt new measures as a result. The failure of those strategies confirmed to Theo Bamber that they were the wrong response. His personal success at Rye Lane appeared rather to confirm that what was needed was not something new but something old: a return to the pietist message of spiritual empowerment to proclaim the gospel as in times past. The BRF thus celebrated the past in Baptist life and practice as it did the past in conservative evangelical life.

The third wider trend in British Christianity to impact Baptist life and the creation of the BRF was the birth and growth of ecumenism. This offered an alternative to maintaining distinctive identities which largely owed their origins to the Reformation and Puritan eras and depended upon theological principles which now seemed discredited, as much by recent scholarly developments as by changes in the secular world. Ecumenism also appeared to promise in what was often summarised as 'the unity God desires': a new spiritual vitality, restored Christian credibility, the authentic ecclesial identity willed by Christ and the prospect of renewed success in mission. All the denominations took this seriously – more seriously on the whole than did the Baptists. It was entirely predictable that the Baptist Union, perceiving itself as belonging within the mainstream of British church life and sympathising with the vision of Christian unity, would wish to participate in so exhilarating a venture as restoring the church to Christ's stated will and purpose 'that they all may be one.'[3] Closely related to this in Baptist life has always been the question of central authority and local church independence. Shakespeare had made sure that the issue of reunion was wedded to that of central control by his advocacy of Episcopal authority over a United Church. Free Church conservatives in general did not warm to his vision but Baptists were entirely hostile, seeing an imminent threat to their credo-baptist views and their insistence that the true church was to be found in the local fellowship of believers living under the headship of Christ, present by his Spirit. Evangelical conversion was never far away from the Baptist mind. As the Baptist Union began officially to engage in the ecumenical movement in the late thirties, Bamber found another reason to

---

[3] John 17:21, a saying of Jesus long regarded within the ecumenical movement as its most fundamental biblical warrant.

believe that his denomination needed to hear again the pietist message, with its traditional preference for spiritual over structural unity. For Bamber, 'all one in Christ Jesus' was a spiritual fact, not an ecclesiastical dream. After the founding of the World Council of Churches, ecumenism grew in importance both to its supporters and detractors. To the first it appeared the greatest spiritual movement of the century. To many conservative evangelicals it seemed almost the entire opposite. Brian Stanley has pointed out that 'although the anti-ecumenical stance of the BRF received little support from the denominational leaders, it appealed to large numbers of British Baptists who viewed the ecumenical movement with suspicion, if not hostility.'[4]

BRF Reactions to Trends within Evangelicalism

The BRF was self-consciously out of step with wider trends in British Christianity. It was less consciously out of step with new trends within conservative evangelicalism. In part, this was because of the distinctive spirituality present in Baptist life, a spirituality which for conservatives did not so much stand in opposition to the inerrancy of Scripture as to the affirmation of its supreme authority without the qualification that the rule of Christ Himself was an existential necessity and reality for a living faith. The closer post-war Baptist conservatives grew to the new evangelical conservatism of the period the less this distinction probably mattered. The most significant issue is the relation of evangelicalism to Romanticism. A distinction must be made between pietist evangelicalism and what followed. Pietism was Romantic in its ethos, but the IVF pioneered something new precisely because it affirmed modernity in a way that pietism did not in being intellectually more engaged and culturally more open. That is not to say that there was a clear breach between the two, for there was not. For example, the IVF held a large student camp at the Keswick Convention so that the Keswick message could be reinforced to Christian Union members. The Higher Life teaching was the default understanding of being truly spiritual and 'worldliness,' defined in pietist terms, long remained a subject of IVF books and talks. As the Evangelical Anglican leader Michael Green observed of his student experience in 1950s Oxford, 'a whole host of activities were then regarded as somewhat – or very – taboo.'[5] The new conservatism was more a hybrid than a pure species. Indeed, it was some while after World War Two that it began more definitely to emerge as something distinctive and energised by a different vision from its older manifestation. Integral to that process was D. Martyn Lloyd-Jones.

---

[4] Stanley, *History of BMS*, 417.
[5] Michael Green, *Adventure of Faith: Reflections on Fifty Years of Christian Service* (Grand Rapids: Zondervan, 2001).

Conclusions

In place of pietist-premillennialism Lloyd-Jones advocated Reformed theology and a 'baptism' in the Holy Spirit for spiritual authority. He opposed not only premillennialism and pietism but the Arminianism that usually accompanied it. In their place he advocated intellectually serious and culturally engaged Christian living in which the first coming of Christ was more important to understand than the Second Coming. He opposed Keswick conventions as a rarefied experience based on wrong theology, and as an affront to the local church.[6] His influence was immense over post-war evangelical life. He developed several power bases which have been well observed. The IVF and its sister movements provided him with a national platform to influence young people. The founding of the Puritan Conference gave him a means of propagating Reformed theology in partnership especially with J. I. Packer. The Westminster Fellowship created a network of local ministers and churches that welcomed his leadership.

Another reason for the BRF's ambivalent relationship with wider evangelicalism must be attributed to Bamber's personality. He was an individualist most at home with building a large personal following, as he undoubtedly did in his own congregation. This was his approach to leading and speaking for the BRF. He was less at home with those outside his sphere of influence. He joined the Westminster Fellowship but did not attend regularly. As Lloyd-Jones grew in influence among BRF members, Bamber grew more defensive and his position was diminished with the introduction of an elected committee through the constitutional changes of 1964. Bamber represented the old pietism tinged with fundamentalism, and it was only around 1960 that the BRF definitely opened itself to newer influences in IVF style conservatism, Reformed theological vigour and charismatic renewal. Had not so many BRF members become so completely involved with Lloyd-Jones' vision for secession, the BRF might then have reinvigorated its role as a more contemporary renewal movement within the Baptist Union. At that very moment, however, it came to view denominational involvement as a waste of energy and a theological compromise, consequently making secession rather than denominational renewal its central policy. Ironically, its decision once more distanced it from the wider conservative evangelical scene, where Lloyd-Jones' call for secession from the mainstream denominations was generally rejected.

The BRF as Keepers of a Baptist Heritage

The BRF preserved a Baptist identity that came under scrutiny from Baptist leaders before World War Two and which was nearly repudiated afterwards.

---

[6] See for example in Murray, *D. Martyn Lloyd-Jones: The Early Years*, 235–237.

The Baptist Revival Fellowship

It comprised three parts: Independency, pietism, and the distinctive Christological spirituality of Baptist life. This Baptist identity was, in short, the experience Leonard Champion described as a personal faith built upon the inner authority of Christ and the outer authority of the Bible, producing serious commitment to the church and to a disciplined lifestyle. What undermined this particular 'Baptist way' was a combination of changes in evangelical life, Baptist life and society at large. The BRF was determined not to see it die and succeeded in maintaining a witness to it after World War Two. Although the BRF was born looking backwards when it was claiming to look forward, it did identify some important issues. Firstly, Baptists in general remained committed to their Independency as local churches despite every General Secretary since Shakespeare trying to convince it otherwise to one degree or another. Secondly, Baptists remained essentially conservative in their evangelicalism while the denominational leaders who dominated post-war Baptist life did not. In representing the majority conservative wing of the denomination, the BRF gave it both voice and momentum. Thirdly, the BRF enabled conservative Baptists to identify more definitely with new conservative emphases without surrendering their Baptist identity. In the period between 1960 and 1966 this led to the BRF engaging at a serious theological level with the Baptist denominational agenda. These are no mean achievements.

The BRF and Exclusivity

It may appear that the BRF adopted secession almost against its Baptist instincts through following the leadership of Lloyd-Jones. It is possible, however, to view the appeal of secession in two broader contexts.

In the first place, spiritual exclusivity has a long history among English Protestants. In some circles in the sixteenth century there was talk of forming 'a church within the church.' In the generations following, the Puritans and Separatists continued to endure hostility from government and church. The eighteenth century Evangelical Revival produced converts whose piety was scorned as 'enthusiasm' by many Establishment leaders. Whereas evangelicalism became respectable by the nineteenth century, it also produced Brethren teaching which condemned the existing churches. Holiness, said the Brethren, was required among the faithful 'remnant,' the spread of which teaching Bebbington associates with the rise of Keswick.[7] The acceptance of liberalism in the mainstream churches appeared to be yet another attack on the faithful.

---

[7] Bebbington, *Evangelicalism in Modern Britain*, 157–159.

Conclusions

This offers a broader context in which to view the BRF's mission as a denominational renewal movement. Bamber repeatedly presented a contrast between the BRF and the BU establishment as one between the spiritual and those who depended instead on outward forms and structures. If he did not directly identify the BRF as a persecuted 'faithful remnant,' he certainly did represent them as a faithful evangelical minority in the Last Days, existing in a denomination fast losing its spiritual foundations. It also offers an explanation of Lloyd-Jones' appeal. His diaries indicate that for some years in the 1950s, he met regularly with ecumenical leaders before declaring publicly that there was no prospect of evangelicals finding a safe haven in a re-united church. When Lloyd-Jones then called upon evangelicals, especially from the Free Churches, to separate from their denominations on the basis that they had sold their evangelical heritage for the sake of a mess of ecumenical potage, he appealed to a deep evangelical instinct The evangelical experience has been profoundly shaped by a tendency to spiritual certainty, even superiority, combined with an experience of rejection even within Protestantism. If the twentieth century produced so severe a solution as secession it was in reaction to the shock of evangelicals finding themselves under suspicion even in the historically evangelical Free Churches.

Secondly, as Adrian Hastings points out, there is in English Free Church life 'a born-again congregationalism which was long part of English religion.'[8] He characterises it as 'a church here, a church there' but says, 'All in all, there were far more of them than one easily realises, because next to nothing has ever been written about them.'[9] He notes particularly the Congregational ecclesiology that permitted such churches to exist but identifies also wider groupings such as the Wesleyan Reform Union and the General Assembly of Unitarian and Free Christian Churches; and he associates with this tradition the modern emergence of the Congregational Federation – the main body of those churches which declined to surrender their Independency to become part of the United Reformed Church in 1972.[10] Hastings regards these as examples of a long-established minority tradition in English church life of standing apart, even from churches in the same tradition, for the sake of either a doctrinal principle or a strictly local identity. For Hastings, this phenomenon should be seen as 'representing the basic characteristics of the English Protestant tradition in its unestablished form.'[11] He includes within

---

[8] Hastings, *English Christianity 1920–1990*, 620.
[9] Ibid.
[10] Ibid.
[11] Ibid., 621.

it contemporary renewal movements in British church life and believes the tradition has achieved a surprising new relevance in modern society:

> It fitted not at all with the Establishment culture of modern society but rather well with a mass of other ill-financed structures engendered by the increasing multitude of people repelled by the syndromes of centralised control.[12]

The BRF's choice of secession appears in this light not only as a more coherent and established expression of English Protestant life than their rejection of the BU makes it appear, but even as a (perhaps unarticulated) step towards seeking cultural relevance in an anti-establishment generation.

The Failure of the BRF

Yet the final word must be that the BRF was a failure. It sought to renew the denomination but it ended by abandoning it. It sought to represent conservatism but the conservatives in the denomination finally rejected it. It failed in its two most basic visions. It is possible to identify the main reasons. The Baptist establishment under Payne and Russell certainly resisted conservative influence within the BU, but the BRF was deeply flawed as a denominational movement. First of all, it was too much of a personality cult around Theo Bamber to be trusted, especially when Bamber was all too often outspoken against fellow Baptists. When Bamber's influence waned, it was replaced by one that was even less acceptable to the Baptist establishment, that of D. Martyn Lloyd-Jones. In the second place, the BRF's leadership was insufficiently engaged in denominational life so that its policies were by turns incompetent, naive and arrogant, despite the Fellowship's spiritual vigour, vision for mission, and high ideal of Baptist renewal. Thirdly, whatever verdict is passed upon charismatic renewal, the BRF failed to notice its significance as a new manifestation of its distinctive message. Had it not done so, it might have spearheaded and shaped what would become a major force in modern Baptist life. Instead, it adopted secession as a policy and so made itself a denominational pariah.

---

[12] Ibid.

Bibliography

Primary Sources

Archive of the Westminster Fellowship, (lost prior to the 1980s, but the remainder held by Basil Howlett, c/o Fellowship of Independent Evangelical Churches, Market Harborough, England).

Baptists and Unity. London: BUGB Publications Department, n.d.

'Baptists and Unity' Reviewed. London: Baptist Union of Great Britain and Northern Ireland, 1969.

Baptist Documents 1948–67. Various Baptist Union statements bound and archived at the Angus Library, Regents Park College, Oxford.

Baptist Quarterly. Didcot: Baptist Historical Society, copies held in the Angus Library, Regent's Park College, Oxford.

Baptist Revival Fellowship Bulletin. BRF Archive, Spurgeon's College, London.

Baptist Revival Fellowship Constitution and Rules. Adopted at the Annual Conference of 1964. BRF Archive, Spurgeon's College, London.

Baptist Times. London: copies held at the Angus Library, Regent's Park College, Oxford.

Baptist Union Documents 1948–77. Various Baptist Union Reports bound and archived at the Angus Library, Regents Park College, Oxford.

Beasley-Murray, George. The Christological Controversy in the Baptist Union. London: p.p., 1972.

British Baptist Statements 1948–67. Various Baptist Union Statements bound and archived at the Angus Library, Regents Park Baptist College, Oxford.

British Weekly. London. Copies held at the British Library Newspaper Collection, Colindale, and London.

Christian and Christianity Today. London: Billy Graham Evangelistic Association [BGEA]. Archive held at the Evangelical Alliance Head Office, London.

Crusade. London: Thirty Press. Copies held at the Evangelical Alliance Head Office, London.

Evangelical Library Bulletin. London: Evangelical Library. Copies held in the Evangelical Library Archive, London.

Evangelical Times. Boreham Wood. Copies held at the British Library Newspaper Collection, Colindale, London.

Grace Magazine. London: Grace Baptist Assembly. Copies held in the Strict Baptist Historical Society Library, Dunstable.

Kingdon, D. & Luland, R. *Liberty in the Lord.* Baptist Revival Fellowship, 1964.

Kingdon, D. *Baptists at the Crossroads.* Baptist Revival Fellowship, 1967.

Minutes of East London Tabernacle. Mile End, London. Held at the Church Office.

Minutes of the Baptist Missionary Society General Committee. Held at the Angus Library, Regent's Park College, Oxford.

Minutes of the Baptist Revival Fellowship Committee. Held at Spurgeon's College, London.

Minutes of the Baptist Union. Held at the Angus Library, Regent's Park College, Oxford.

Minutes of the Evangelical Alliance Council. Held at the Evangelical Alliance Head Office, London.

Private Papers and Diaries of D. Martyn Lloyd-Jones: Preaching Diaries. Held at the National Library of Wales, Aberystwyth, Wales.

Private Papers of Basil Howlett: Hesters Way File. Held by Basil Howlett, c/o, Fellowship of Independent Evangelical Churches, Market Harborough, England.

Private Papers of D. R. Russell. Held at the Angus Library, Regent's Park College, and Oxford.

Private Papers of M. E. Aubrey. Held at the Angus Library, Regent's Park College, and Oxford.

The Baptist Handbook. London: Baptist Union of Great Britain, published annually.

The Baptist Union Directory. London; Didcot: Baptist Union of Great Britain, published annually.

The Evangelical Fellowship of Congregational Churches Website: http://www.efcc.karoo.net/history.html

The Fraternal. Privately Published. The Baptist Ministers Fellowship. Copies held in the Angus Library, Regents Park College, Oxford.

The Sword and The Trowel. London: Metropolitan Tabernacle Church Archive.

Unity in Diversity: Evangelicals, the Church and the World. Ten Papers Given at the National Assembly of Evangelicals at Westminster, London, in October 1966. London: The Evangelical Alliance, 1967.

Bibliography

Secondary Sources

Aubrey, M. E. *A Minister's Manual*. London: Carey Kingsgate Press, 1927.

Bamber, Theo. *His Glorious Appearing*. Privately Published, Rye Lane Chapel, Peckham, 1927.

Bamber, Theo. *His Personal Return*. Privately Published, Rye Lane Chapel, Peckham, 1939.

Baptist Church Hymnal. London: Psalms and Hymns Trust, 1900.

Baptist Church Hymnal. Revised Edition, 1933. London: Psalms and Hymns Trust, 1933.

Baptist Hymn Book. London: Novello, 1962.

Barclay, Oliver. *Evangelicalism in Britain 1935–1995*. Leicester: IVP, 1997.

Barclay, Oliver. Whatever Happened to the Jesus Lane Lot? Leicester, IVP, 1977.

Barr, James. *Escaping From Fundamentalism*. London: SCM, 1984.

Barr, James. *Fundamentalism*. London: SCM, 1977.

Bartholomew, C., Parry, R., West, A., eds. *The Futures of Evangelicalism*. Leicester: IVP, 2003.

Bartles-Smith, Douglas. *Fighting Fundamentalism: A Spiritual Autobiography*. Shrewsbury: Saxty Press, 2007.

Beasley-Murray, Paul. *Fearless For Truth: A Personal Portrait of the Life of George Beasley-Murray*. Carlisle: Paternoster Press, 2002.

Bebbington, D. W. 'Baptists and Fundamentalism in Inter-War Britain.' Pages 95–114 in *Protestant Evangelicalism: Britain, Ireland, Germany and America, c1750–c1950*. Edited by K. Robbins. Oxford: Blackwell, 1990.

Bebbington, D. W. 'Oxford Group Movement Between the Wars." *Studies in Church History* 23 (1986): 495-507.

Bebbington, D. W. *Evangelicalism in Modern Britain*. London: Unwin Hyman, 1989.

Bebbington, D. W. *Baptists Through The Centuries: A History of A Global People*. Waco, TX: Baylor University Press, 2010.

Beckwith, Francis J. *Return To Rome: Confessions of an Evangelical Catholic*. Grand Rapids: Brazos Press, 2009.

Bendor-Samuel, T. H. *Keeping the Faith*. Croydon: FIEC, 1992.

Berkouwer, G. C. *A Half Century of Theology*. Grand Rapids: Eerdmans, 1977.

Bloesch, Donald G. *The Evangelical Renaissance.* Grand Rapids: Eerdmans, 1973.

Bonser, H. 'Recollections of a General Superintendent.' *BQ*, Vol. XIII (1949–50).

Borg, Marcus J. *The God We Never Knew: Beyond Dogmatic Religion to a More Authentic Contemporary Faith.* New York: HarperCollins, 1997.

Brackney, William H. *Historical Dictionary of the Baptists.* Lanham: Maryland; London: The Scarecrow Press, 1999.

Brackney, William H. *The Baptists.* New York; London: Greenwood Press, 1988.

Brackney, William H., Fiddes, Paul S., and Briggs, John H. Y. *Pilgrim Pathways: Essays In Baptist History In Honour Of B. R. White.* Macon, GA: Mercer University Press, 1999.

Brencher, John. *Martyn Lloyd-Jones (1899–1981) and Twentieth Century Evangelicalism.* Milton Keynes, Paternoster, 2002.

Briggs, J. H. Y. *The English Baptists of the Nineteenth Century.* Didcot: Baptist Historical Society, 1994.

Briggs, John H. Y. ed. *A Dictionary of European Baptist Life and Thought.* Milton Keynes: Paternoster Press, 2009.

Briggs, John H. Y. *Studies in Baptist History and Thought. Vol. 33. A Dictionary of Baptist Life and Thought.* Milton Keynes: Paternoster Press, 2009.

Brown, C. G. *The Death of Christian Britain.* Abingdon: Routledge, 2001.

Bruce, F. F. *In Retrospect: Remembrance of Things Past.* London: Pickering & Inglis, 1980.

Bush, L. Russ and Nettles, Tom J. *Baptists and The Bible.* Chicago: Moody Press, 1980.

Calver, Clive. *Where Truth and Justice Meet: Tracing the Roots of Evangelical Belief.* London: Hodder, 1987.

Campbell, R. J. *The New Theology.* London: Chapman & Hall, 1907.

Capon, John. *Evangelicals Tomorrow.* London: Collins Fount Paperbacks, 1977.

Carlile, J. C. *My Life's Little Day.* London: Blackie, 1935.

Catherwood, Christopher. *Five Evangelical Leaders.* London: Hodder, 1984.

Chidester, David. *Christianity: A Global History.* London: Allen Lane The Penguin Press, 2000.

Bibliography

Child, R. L. *Baptists and Christian Unity*. London: Carey Kingsgate Press, 1948.

Clements, K. W., ed. *Baptists in The Twentieth Century*. London: Baptist Historical Society, 1983.

Clements, K. W. *Lovers of Discord: Twentieth Century Theological Controversies in England*. London: SPCK, 1988.

Clements, K. W., ed. *Baptists in the Twentieth Century*. London: Baptist Historical Society, 1982.

Coffin, H. Sloane. *The Public Worship of God*. London: Independent Press, 1950.

Cook, H. *Charles Brown*. London: The Kingsgate Press, 1939.

Cook, H. *Speak: That They Go Forward. A Report on the Spiritual Welfare in the Churches of the Baptist Denomination*. London: Baptist Union, 1946.

Cook, H. *The Theology of Evangelism*. London: Carey Kingsgate Press, 1951.

Cook, H. *What Baptists Stand For*. London: Carey Kingsgate Press, 1947.

Cross, A. R. 'Service to the Ecumenical Movement: The Contribution of British Baptists.' *BQ*, Vol. 38, No. 3 (1999).

Cross, A. R. *Baptism and the Baptists: Theology and Practice in Twentieth-Century Britain*. Carlisle: Paternoster Press, 2000.

Davies, D. R. *Theology and the Atomic Age*. London: Latimer House Publishers, 1947.

Davies, D. R. *On To Orthodoxy*. London: Hodder and Stoughton, 1939;

Derham, Morgan, ed. *Unity in Diversity: Evangelicals, The Church and the World*. London: Evangelical Alliance, 1967.

Dickson, Neil T. R. and Grass, Tim. *The Growth of the Brethren Movement*. Milton Keynes: Paternoster, 2006.

Douglas, J. D., ed. *Twentieth Century Dictionary of Christian Biography*. Carlisle: Paternoster Press, 1995.

Dudley-Smith, Timothy. *John Stott: A Global Ministry*. Leicester: IVP, 2001.

Dudley-Smith, Timothy. *John Stott: The Making of a Leader*. Leicester: IVP, 1999.

Duriez, Colin. *Francis Schaeffer: An Authentic Life*. Nottingham: IVP, 2008.

Edmonds, G. *The Free Church Fellowship, 1911–1965: An Ecumenical Pioneer*. Gerrards Cross: Free Church Council, 1965.

Evans, Percy. *The Cross as a Tree*. London: Marshall, Morgan & Scott, 1950.

Fiddes, Paul S., ed. *Under the Rule of Christ: Dimensions of Baptist Spirituality.* Macon, GA: Smyth & Helwys, 2008.

Fielder, Geraint D. *Grace, Grit and Gumption: Spiritual Revival in South Wales.* Fearn: Christian Focus Publications, 2000.

Fielder, Geraint D. *Excuse Me, Mr. Davies – Hallelujah! Evangelical Student Witness in Wales 1923–1983.* Bridgend: Evangelical Press of Wales, 1983.

Fielder, Geraint D. *Lord of The Years: Sixty Years of Student Witness.* Leicester: IVP, 1988.

Fountain, D. G. *E. J. Poole-Connor, 1872–1962: Contender for the Faith.* Worthing: Henry E. Walter, 1966.

Freeman, Curtis W., McClendon, James Wm., and Ewell, C. Rosalee Velloso. *Baptist Roots: A Reader In The Theology Of A Christian People.* Valley Forge, PA: Judson Pres, 1999.

Fullerton, W. Y. *Souls of Men.* London: Carey Press, 1928.

Fullerton, W. Y. *F. B. Meyer: A Biography.* London: Marshall, Morgan & Scott, 1929.

Garrett, Jr., James Leo. *Baptist Theology: A Four Century Study.* Macon, GA: Mercer University Press, 2009.

Gillett, David. *Trust and Obey: Explorations in Evangelical Spirituality.* London: Darton, Longman and Todd, 1993.

Gilmore, A., ed. *The Pattern of the Church.* London: Lutterworth Press, 1963.

Glover, T. R. *Fundamentals.* London: Baptist Union, 1931.

Glover, T. R. *The Jesus of History.* London: SCM, 1917.

Glover, T. R. *The Free Churches and Re-Union.* Cambridge: W Heffer & Sons, 1921.

Glover, Willis B. *Evangelical Nonconformists and Higher Criticism in the 19th Century.* London: Independent Press, 1954.

Goodliff, Paul. *Ministry, Sacrament and Representation: Ministry and Ordination in Contemporary Baptist Theology, and the Rise of Sacramentalism.* Oxford: Regent's Park College, 2010.

Gooch, Henry Martyn. *William Fuller Gooch.* London: World's Evangelical Alliance, 1929.

Gordon, James M. *Evangelical Spirituality.* London: SPCK, 1991.

Gouldbourne, R. M. B. *Reinventing the Wheel: Women and Ministry in English Baptist Life.* Oxford: Whitley Publications, 1997.

Bibliography

Graham, Billy. *Just As I Am: The Autobiography of Billy Graham*. London: HarperCollins, 1997.

Grass, T. 'Strict Baptists and Reformed Baptists in England, 1955–76.' Pages 294–316 in *Baptist Myths*. Milton Keynes: Paternoster, 2005.

Green, Bernard. *Tomorrow's Man: A Biography of James Henry Rushbrooke*. Didcot: Baptist Historical Society, 1997.

Green, Michael. *Adventure of Faith: Reflections on Fifty Years of Christian Service*. Grand Rapids: Zondervan, 2001.

Gribbon, Crawford and Stunt, Timothy C. F. *Prisoners of Hope? Aspects of Evangelical Millennialism in Britain and Ireland, 1800–1880*. Milton Keynes: Paternoster Press, 2004.

Guest, Mathew. *Evangelical Identity and Contemporary Culture*. Milton Keynes: Paternoster, 2007.

Harper, Michael. *A Faith Fulfilled*. Ben Lomon, CA: Conciliar Press, 1999.

Harris, Harriet A. *Fundamentalism and Evangelicals*. Oxford: OUP, 1998.

Hastings, Adrian. *A History of English Christianity 1920–1990*. London, SCM Press, 1991.

Hayden, E. W. *A Centennial History of Spurgeon's Tabernacle*. Revised Edition. Pasadena, TX: Pilgrim Publications, 1971.

Hayden, R. 'Still at the Crossroads? Revd J. H. Shakespeare and Ecumenism.' Pages 31–54 in *Baptists in the Twentieth Century*. Edited by K. W. Clements. Didcot: Baptist Historical Society, 1982.

Hayden, R., ed. *Baptist Union Documents, 1948–1977*. London: Baptist Historical Society, 1980.

Hayden, Roger. *English Baptist History and Heritage*. Didcot: Baptist Union of Great Britain, 2005.

Haykin, Michael A. G., and Stewart, Kenneth J., eds. *The Emergence of Evangelicalism: Exploring Historical Continuities*. Nottingham: Apollos, 2008.

Hebert, Gabriel. *Fundamentalism and the Word of God*. London: SCM Press, 1957.

Hempton, David. *Evangelical Disenchantment*. New Haven: Yale, 2008.

Hocken, Peter. *Streams of Renewal: The Origins and Early Development of the Charismatic Movement in Great Britain*. Revised Edition. Carlisle: Paternoster, 1997.

Hopkins, Mark. *Nonconformity's Romantic Generation*. Carlisle: Paternoster Press, 2004.

Horner, Norman A., ed. *Protestant Crosscurrents in Mission: The Ecumenical-Conservative Divide*. Nashville; New York: Abingdon Press, 1968.

Howard, Thomas. *Evangelical Is Not Enough*. San Francisco: Ignatius Press, 1984.

Howells, George. *The Soul of India*. London: James Clark/Kingsgate Press, 1913.

Hulse, Errol. *An Introduction to the Baptists*. Haywards Heath: Carey Publications, 1973.

Hylson-Smith, Kenneth. *Evangelicals in the Church of England 1734–1984*. Edinburgh: T&T Clark, 1988.

Hylson-Smith, Kenneth. *The Churches in England from Elizabeth I to Elizabeth II. Volume III: 1833–1998*. London: SCM, 1998.

Jeffery, Peter. *Evangelicals Then and Now*. Darlington: Evangelical Press, 2004.

Johnson, Douglas. *Contending For The Faith*. Leicester: IVP, 1979.

Jones, Brynmor P. *The King's Champions*. Cwmbran: Christian Literature Press, 1986.

Jones, Brynmor P. *The Spiritual History of Keswick in Wales 1903–1983*. Cwmbran: Christian Literature Press, 1989.

Jones, R. Tudor. *Congregationalism in England 1662–1962*. London: Independent Press, 1962.

Jones, Rhys Bevan. *Dr. Glover and the Presidency of the Baptist Union*. 4th Edition. Pontypridd: Pontypridd & Rhondda District of the East Glamorgan Baptist Association, 1924.

Jordan, E. K. H. *Free Church Unity: History of the Free Church Council Movement, 1896–1941*. London: Lutterworth Press, 1956.

Kay, William K. *Apostolic Networks in Britain*. Milton Keynes: Paternoster, 2007.

Kidd, R. L., ed. *Something to Declare: A Study of the Declaration of Principle*. Oxford: Whitley Publications, 1996.

King, Geoffrey. *By All Means Save Some: BRF Booklet No.1*. London: Kingsgate Press, 1939.

Bibliography

King, Geoffrey. *Rend the Heavens! Presidential Address given at the Annual Assembly of the London Baptist Association, March 1962.* London: London Baptist Association.

King, Geoffrey. *Truth For Our Time.* London: Lutterworth Press, 1957.

Klaiber, A. J., et al. *The Baptist Union General Superintendents.* London: Baptist Union, 1949.

Laws, G. 'The Edinburgh Conference: What was the Good of it?' *BQ,* Vol. 9, No. 1 (1938).

Lee, G. 'Women in Baptist Ministry in the 20th Century.' Unpublished Paper, 2001.

Leeming, Bernard. 'The Nottingham Conference.' in *The Furrow,* Vol. 15, No. 11, November, 1964. www.jstor.org/stable/27658850

Leonard, Bill J. *Baptist Ways: A History.* Valley Forge, PA: Judson Press, 2003.

Lenwood, F. *Jesus - Lord or Leader?* London: Constable & Co., 1930.

Lloyd-Jones, D. Martyn. *From Fear To Faith.* London: IVP, 1953.

Lloyd-Jones, D. Martyn. *Revival: Can We Make It Happen?* Basingstoke: Pickering & Inglis, 1986.

Lloyd-Jones, D. Martyn. *What Is An Evangelical?* Edinburgh: Banner of Truth Trust, 1992.

Lloyd-Jones, D. Martyn. *Joy Unspeakable: The Baptism with the Holy Spirit.* Eastbourne: Kingsway, 1984.

Machen, J. G. *Christianity and Liberalism.* London: Victory Press, n.d. but reprint of 1921 original.

Marchant, James. *Dr. John Clifford.* London: Cassells, 1924.

Marsden, George M. *Fundamentalism and American Culture.* Oxford: Oxford University Press, 1980.

Martin, Hugh, ed. *Towards Reunion: What the Churches Stand For* London: SCM Press 1934.

McArthur, John F. *Ashamed of the Gospel.* Wheaton: Crossway, 1993.

McBain, Douglas. *Fire Over the Waters: Renewal Among Baptists and Others from the 1960s to the 1990s.* London: Darton, Longman & Todd, 1997.

McBeth, H. Leon, *The Baptist Heritage,* (Nashville, Tennessee: Broadman Press, 1987)

McCaig, A. 'The Pastors' College Jubilee.' *The Sword and the Trowel,* June 1906.

McLeod, Hugh. *The Religious Crisis of the 1960s*. Oxford: Oxford University Press, 2007.

McGowan, A. T. B. *The Divine Spiration of Scripture*. Nottingham: Apollos, 2007.

McGrath, Alistair. *A Passion For Truth*. Leicester: Apollos, 1996.

McGrath, Alistair. *Evangelicalism and the Future of Christianity*. London: Hodder & Stoughton, 1993.

McGrath, Alister. *To Know and Serve God: A Biography of James I. Packer*. London: Hodder & Stoughton, 1977.

Moon, N. S. *Education For the Ministry: Bristol Baptist College 1679–1979*. Bristol: Bristol Baptist College, 1979.

Morden, Peter. *'Communion with Christ and his People': The Spirituality of C. H. Spurgeon*. Oxford: Centre for Baptist History and Heritage, Regent's Park College, 2010.

Morgan, D. *Span of the Cross: Christian Religion and Society in Wales 1914–2000*. Cardiff: University of Wales Press, 1999.

Mountain, J. *Rev. F. C. Spurr and Keswick*. Tonbridge Wells: n.p., 1921.

Munson, J. *The Nonconformists: In Search of a Lost Culture*. London: SPCK, 1991.

Murray, Harold. *Campbell Morgan: Bible Teacher*. Belfast: Ambassador; reprinted 1999.

Murray, I. H. *David Martyn Lloyd-Jones. 2 Vols*. Edinburgh: Banner of Truth Trust, 1990.

Murray, I. H. *Evangelicalism Divided*. Edinburgh: Banner of Truth, 2000.

Murray, I. H. *The Life of Arthur W. Pink*. Edinburgh: Banner of Truth, 1981.

Murray, I. H. *The Forgotten Spurgeon*. Edinburgh: Banner of Truth, 1966.

Neil, Stephen. *Anglicanism*. Oxford: Mowbray, 1977.

Nicholls, M. *Lights to the World: A History of Spurgeon's College, 1856–1992*. Harpenden: Nuprint, 1994.

Noll, Mark A. *The Scandal of the Evangelical Mind*. Leicester: IVP, 1994.

Orr, J. Edwin. *The Flaming Tongue: The Impact of 20th Century Revivals*. Chicago: Moody Press, 1973.

Page, George E. *A. G. B: The Story of the Life and Work of Archibald Geike Brown*. London: Carey Kingsgate Press, 1944.

Bibliography

Parker, L. G. *Francis Schaeffer: The Man and his Message.* Eastbourne: Kingsway Publications, 1985.

Patterson, David Taite. *The Call To Worship.* London: Carey Kingsgate Press, 1930.

Pawson, David. *Not As Bad As The Truth: Memoirs of an Unorthodox Evangelical.* London: Hodder & Stoughton, 2006.

Payne, E. A. *A 20th Century Minister: John Oliver Barrett, 1901–78.* London p.p., 1978.

Payne, E. A. *The Baptist Union: A Short History.* London: Carey Kingsgate Press, 1959.

Payne, E. A. *The Fellowship of Believers: Baptist Thought and Practice Yesterday and Today.* London: The Kingsgate Press, 1944; 2nd Edition, 1952.

Payne, E. A. *The Free Church Tradition in the Life of England.* London: SCM, 1944.

Payne, E. A. and Winward, S. F. *Orders and Prayers for Church Worship: A Manual for Ministers.* London: Carey Kingsgate Press, 1960.

Peaston, A. E. *The Prayer Book Tradition in the Free Churches.* London: James Clarke & Co., 1964.

Pickering, Ernest D. *The Tragedy of Compromise: The Origin and Impact of the New Evangelicalism.* Greenville: Bob Jones University Press, 1994.

Poole-Connor, J. E. *Evangelicalism in England.* Worthing: Henry Walter. Revised Edition, 1966.

Price, Charles, and Randall, I. M. *Transforming Keswick.* Carlisle: Paternoster/OM, 2000.

Proctor, W. C. G. *Evangelical Thought and Practice.* London: James Clarke & Co., 1946.

R. G. Torbet. *A History of the Baptists.* Pennsylvania: Judson Press; Revised Edition, 1973.

Randall, I. M. '"Arresting People for Christ": Baptists and the Oxford Group in the 1930s,' *BQ,* Vol. 38, No. 1 (1999).

Randall, I. M. *A School of the Prophets: 150 years of Spurgeon's College* London: Spurgeons College, 2005.

Randall, I. M. '"Capturing Keswick": Baptists and the Changing Spirituality of the Keswick Convention in the 1920s,' *BQ,* Vol. 36, No. 7 (1996).

Randall, I. M. 'Look To Jesus Christ': English Baptists and Evangelical Spirituality.' *American Baptist Quarterly*. Vol. 25, No. 1, Spring 2006. King of Prussia, PA: American Baptist Historical Society.

Randall, I. M. *Educating Evangelicalism: The Origins, Development and Impact of London Bible College*. Carlisle: Paternoster Press, 2000.

Randall, I. M. *Evangelical Experiences: A Study of the Spirituality of English Evangelicalism, 1918–1939*. Carlisle: Paternoster Press, 1999.

Randall, I. M., 'Look To Jesus Christ': English Baptists and Evangelical Spirituality'; *American Baptist Quarterly*, Vol. 25, No. 1, Spring 2006. King of Prussia, PA: American Baptist Historical Society.

Randall, I. M. *Spirituality and Social Change: The Contribution of F. B. Meyer (1847–1929)*. Carlisle: Paternoster Press, 2003.

Randall, I. M. *The English Baptists of the Twentieth Century*. Didcot: The Baptist Historical Society, 2005.

Randall, I. *What a Friend We Have in Jesus: The Evangelical Tradition*. London: Dartman, Longman and Todd, 2005.

Randall, I., and Hilborn, D. *One Body in Christ: The History and significance of the Evangelical Alliance*. Carslisle: Paternoster Press, 2001.

Rees, J. *Stranger than Fiction*. Frinton-on-Sea: p.p., 1957.

Robbins, Keith, ed. *Protestant Evangelicalism: Britain, Ireland, Germany and America, c.1750–c.1950*. Oxford: Basil Blackwell, 1990.

Roberts, David Wyn, ed. *Revival, Renewal, and the Holy Spirit*. Milton Keynes: Paternoster Press, 2009.

Robinson, H. Wheeler. 'The Place of Baptism in Baptist Churches To-day.' *BQ*, Volume 1 (1922–1923).

Robinson, James. *Pentecostal Origins: Early Pentecostalism in Ireland in the context of the British Isles*. Milton Keynes: Paternoster, 2005.

Robinson, John. *Honest To God*. London: SCM, 1963.

Roxburgh, K. 'Eric Roberts and Orthodoxy among Scottish Baptists.' *BQ*, Vol. 34, No. 2 (2001).

Rushbrooke, J. H. et al. *The Faith of the Baptists*. London: The Kingsgate Press, 1926.

Russell, David. *Baptists and Some Contemporary Issues*. London: Baptist Union, 1968.

Bibliography

Samuel, Leith. *A Man Under Authority: Leith Samuel, The Autobiography*. Fearn: Christian Focus, 1993.

Schaeffer, Francis. *The Great Evangelical Disaster*. Eastbourne: Kingsway, 1984.

Schaeffer, Frank. *Crazy For God. How I Grew up as One of the Elect, Helped Found the Religious Right, and Lived to Take All (or Almost All) of it Back*. Cambridge, MA: Da Capo Press, 2008.

Schaeffer, Frank. *Patience With God: Faith for People who Don't Like Religion (or Atheism)*. Cambridge, MA: Da Capo Press, 2009.

Scotland, Nigel. *Evangelical Anglicans in a Revolutionary Age 1789–1901*. Carlisle: Paternoster, 2004.

Seat, Leroy. *Fed up With Fundamentalism: A Historical, Theological, and Personal Appraisal of Christian Fundamentalism*. Liberty, MI: 4-L Publications, 2007.

Sell, Alan P. F., *Nonconformist Theology in the Twentieth Century*, (Milton Keynes: Paternoster Press, 2006)

Sell, A. P. F., and Cross, A. R., eds. *Protestant Nonconformity in the Twentieth Century*, Carlisle: Paternoster Press, 2003.

Shakespeare, J. H. *The Churches at the Crossroads: A Study in Church Unity*. London: Williams and Norgate, 1918.

Shepherd, Peter. *The Making of a Modern Denomination: John Howard Shakespeare and the English Baptists 1898–1924*. Carlisle: Paternoster Press, 2001.

Shepherd, Peter. *The Making of a Northern Baptist College*. Manchester: Northern Baptist College, 2004.

Shuff, Roger. *Searching For The True Church: Brethren and Evangelicals in the Mid-Twentieth Century*. Milton Keynes: Paternoster Press, 2005.

Smith, Mark, ed. *British Evangelical Identities Past & Present Volume 1: Aspects of the History and Sociology of Evangelicalism in Britain and Ireland*. Milton Keynes: Paternoster, 2008.

Sparkes, D. C. *An Accredited Ministry*. Didcot: Baptist Historical Society, 1996.

Sparkes, D. C. *The Constitutions of the Baptist Union of Great Britain*. Didcot: Baptist Historical Society, 1996.

Spence, Alan. *Christology: A Guide For The Perplexed*. London: T&T Clark, 2008.

Spurgeon, Charles. *The Downgrade Controversy: Collected Materials from the Time*. Pasadena: Pilgrim Publications, n.d.

Stanley, Brian. '"The Old Religion and the New": India and the making of T. R. Glover's *The Jesus of History.*' Pages 295–315 in *The Gospel in the World.* Edited by D. W. Bebbington. Carlisle: Paternoster Press, 2002.

Stanley, Brian. *The History of the Baptist Missionary Society.* Edinburgh: T&T Clark, 1992.

Stonehouse, Ned B. *J. Gresham Machen: A Biographical Memoir.* 3rd Edition. Edinburgh, Banner of Truth, 1987.

Stott, John. *Evangelical Truth: A Personal Plea for Unity.* Leicester: IVP, 1999.

Tatlow, T. *The Story of the Student Christian Movement.* London: SCM Press, 1933.

Tidball, Derek. *Who Are The Evangelicals: Tracing the Roots of Today's Movements.* London: Marshall Pickering, 1994.

Torrey, Reuben, Dixon, A. C., eds. *The Fundamentals,* Reprint. Grand Rapids: Baker Book House, 2000.

Triton, A. N. *Whose World? The Christian's Attitude to The Material World, To Culture, Politics, Technology, Society.* London: IVP, 1970.

Trueman, Carl R. *The Wages of Spin.* Fearn: Mentor, 2004.

Underwood, A. C. *A History of the English Baptists.* London: Carey Kingsgate Press, 1947.

Valentine, T. *Concern for the Ministry.* Teddington: Particular Baptist Fund, 1967.

Vanauken, Sheldo. *A Severe Mercy.* London: Hodder & Stoughton, 1977.

Walker, A. *Restoring the Kingdom.* London: Hodder, 1985.

Wallis, Arthur. *The Radical Christian.* Eastbourne: Kingsway, 1981.

Walton, R. C. *The Gathered Community.* London: Carey Kingsgate Press, 1946.

Ward, K. and Stanley, B., eds. *The Church Mission Society and World Christianity 1799–1999.* Grand Rapids: Eerdmans, 2000.

Warner, Rob. *Reinventing English Evangelicalism 1966–2001.* Milton Keynes: Paternoster Press, 2007.

Wedel, Theodore. *The Coming Great Church.* New York: Macmillan, 1945.

Wellings, Martin, Evangelicals Embattled: Responses of Evangelicals in the Church of England to Ritualism, Darwinism and Theological Liberalism 1890–1930, (Milton Keynes: Paternoster Press, 2003)

Wellings, Martin. 'The Methodist Revival Fellowship 1952–1986.' *Proceedings of the Wesley Historical Society,* October 2009: 89–107.

Bibliography

Wells, David. *No Place For Truth: Whatever Happened To Evangelical Theology?* Leicester: IVP, 1993.

West, W. M. S. 'The Reverend Secretary Aubrey: Part I.' *BQ*, Vol. 34, No. 5, (1992).

West, W. M. S. 'The Reverend Secretary Aubrey: Part II,' *BQ*, Vol. 34, No. 6, (1992).

West, W. M. S. 'The Reverend Secretary Aubrey: Part III,' *BQ*, Vol. 34, No. 7, (1992).

West, W. M. S. *To be a Pilgrim: A Memoir of Ernest A. Payne.* Guildford: Lutterworth Press, 1983.

Whale, J. S. 'Jesus - Lord or Leader?' *Congregational Quarterly*, Vol. 8, No. 1, (1930).

Whittaker, Colin. *Seven Pentecostal Pioneers.* Basingstoke: Marshall Pickering, 1983.

Williams, C. *The Principles and Practices of the Baptists.* London: Baptist Tract Society, 1903.

Wood, H. G. *Terrot Reaveley Glover: A Biography.* Cambridge: Cambridge University Press, 1953.

Worrall, B. G. *The Making of The Modern Church: Christianity in England since 1800.* London: SPCK, 1988, 1993.

Wright, Nigel G. *Challenge to Change: A Radical Baptist Agenda for Baptists.* Eastbourne: Kingsway, 1991.

APPENDIX ONE

THE ORIGINAL DOCTRINAL BASIS OF THE INTER-VARSITY FELLOWSHIP (IVF)

(Source: Douglas Johnson, *Contending For The Faith: A History of the Evangelical Movement in the Universities and Colleges*, (Leicester: Inter-varsity Press, 1979), 359; The founding Constitution of the IVF, Clause Two)

That the object of the Conference shall be to stimulate personal faith, and to further evangelistic work among the students by upholding fundamental truths, including:

a. The divine inspiration and infallibility of Holy Scripture, as originally given, and its supreme authority in all matters of faith and conduct. (2 Tim. iii.15–16; 2 Peter i.21).
b. The unity of the Father, the Son and the Holy Spirit in the Godhead. (Matt. xxviii.19; John x.30; xiv.26 Romans viii.9; 2 Cor. xiii.14).
c. The universal sinfulness and guilt of human nature since the Fall, rendering man subject to God's wrath and condemnation. (Romans i.18; iii.19; v.12, 18).
d. Redemption from the guilt, penalty and power of sin *only* through the sacrificial death (as our Representative and Substitute) of Jesus Christ, the Incarnate Son of God. (Matt. xx.28; Rom. v.18,19; vi.10–12; vii.34; Gal. iii.13; Heb. x.10–12; 1 Pet. iii.18).
e. The Resurrection of Jesus Christ from the dead. (Acts xiii.30–37; 1 Cor. xv.3–4, 20).
f. The necessity of the work of the Holy Spirit to make the Death of Christ effective to the individual sinner, granting him repentance towards God and faith in Jesus Christ. (John xvi.7–11; Acts xl.18; xiv.27; xx.21; Rom. viii.9–11).
g. The indwelling and work of the Holy Spirit in the believer. (John xiv.26; Rom. viii.9–11,16; 2 Cor. i.22; 2 Thess. ii.13).
h. The expectation of the personal return of the Lord Jesus Christ. (Matt. xxiv.29–31,42–44; John xiv.2–3; Acts i.11; 1 Thess. iv.16–17; 2 Thess. iii.5; Titus ii.11 –14).

APPENDIX TWO

THE CONSTITUTION OF THE BAPTIST REVIVAL FELLOWSHIP ADOPTED AT THE BRF ANNUAL CONFERENCE, 1964

(source: copy held at the Angus Library, Regents Park College, Oxford)

I.   A brief history of the Baptist Revival Fellowship

The BRF emerged in the late 1930s out of the informal meetings of a group of London Baptist ministers who were burdened by the low level of spiritual life in the churches. As they prayed and studied the Scriptures together they saw clearly their own weakness and personal need of renewal by the Lord and also the need for Revival in the church. Later, other Baptist ministers, with a similar concern for Revival, joined them and some crowded, richly blessed meetings were held in central London churches.

During and after the war years the membership of the BRF grew rapidly and spread to all parts of the country. A quarterly bulletin and other literature was published; district fellowship groups arose, and Rallies were held in London and the provinces. Since 1954 Annual Conferences have been held, mainly, though not exclusively, for ministers.

In organisation the BRF was based on the close personal relationships of the original members, who, with a few other ministers chiefly residing in the London area, formed the committee. As the Fellowship grew and conditions changed, the need was felt for a more clearly defined constitution, and the following Doctrinal Basis, Statement of Objects and Rules were formally accepted by the Members' Business Meeting during the Annual Conference at High Leigh, November 23rd/26th, 1964.

II.   The Doctrinal Basis of the Baptist Revival Fellowship

We believe that true fellowship implies agreement on fundamental matters of faith, including:

1. The divine inspiration and infallibility of Holy Scripture as originally given and its supreme authority in all matters of faith and conduct. (II Timothy 3:15–17)
2. The unity of the Father, the Son and the Holy Spirit in the Godhead. (John 17:3 & 21)
3. The universal sinfulness and guilt of human nature since the Fall, rendering man subject to God's wrath and condemnation. (Isaiah 53:6; John 3:36)

4. Redemption from the guilt, penalty and power of sin only through the sacrificial death (as our representative and substitute) of Jesus Christ, the Incarnate Son of God. (II Corinthians 5:15–21)
5. The resurrection of Jesus Christ from the dead. (I Corinthians 15:3–8)
6. The necessity of the work of the Holy Spirit to make the death of Christ effective to the individual sinner, granting him repentance toward God and faith in Jesus Christ. (John 16:7–11)
7. The indwelling and work of the Holy Spirit in the believer. (Ephesians 1:13)
8. The expectation of the personal return of the Lord Jesus Christ. (Acts 1:6–11)
9. The sovereignty of God in redemption, Creation, Revelation and Final Judgement. ((Colossians 1:12–20)
10. The One Holy Universal Church, which is the Body of Christ, and to which all true believers belong. (Ephesians 4:4–6)

(The foregoing points are those accepted by many Evangelical Christians, as for instance in the Evangelical Missionary Alliance.)

We are also agreed in believing that:

11. Believers' Baptism by immersion is the only Baptism ordained by our Lord, practiced by the Apostles and taught in the New Testament.
12. Each "local church" is to be a "Gathered Community" of regenerate believers, living in fellowship with all other believers within the One Body of Christ, and having "liberty under the guidance of the Holy Spirit, to interpret and administer His laws," and is thus sufficient under Christ for the ordering of its life in obedience to His Will.

III. The Objects of the Baptist Revival Fellowship

1. To unite in a vital PRAYER FELLOWSHIP Baptists who are seriously concerned at our spiritual condition – so marked by powerlessness and ineffectiveness – and who long for a work of God's grace in their own hearts, in our Baptist Churches where God has set us and given us our first responsibilities, and in the whole Church of Christ throughout the world – and to this end:
2. To wait upon God in prayer for such a gracious, sovereign, mighty work of the Holy Spirit as has historically been called "Revival".
3. To pray for and, as the Holy Spirit shall lead, to work for a revival of belief in, and the Biblical expository teaching of, the Doctrines of Grace in all our churches.

Appendices

4. To pray for one another and to seek to encourage one another to holy living and to ever-deepening fellowship with the Lord Jesus that we may know in our lives an experience of personal revival.
And further as a Fellowship:
5. To arrange such conferences and meetings for members (and especially for ministerial members) as shall be desirable and shall provide opportunities for them to meet together for prayer, fellowship, exhortation and discussion.
6. To give testimony in the Baptist Denomination to the Biblical truths and emphases we hold dear and believe to be fundamental and essential to the enjoyment of God's blessing in all personal and corporate Christian living.
7. To seek fellowship with those of other Denominations who, while differing from us in some matters, are one with us in Evangelical conviction, and to seek, wherever possible, to work together with them.

[Author's Note: The following membership pledge was required on the accompanying Application Form]:

Having carefully read the terms of the Constitution of the Baptist Revival Fellowship and in particular its Doctrinal Basis, with which I am in general agreement, I declare myself in heart and spirit a true and sincere believer conscious that the urgent need of the people of God everywhere is a revival by the ministry of the Holy Spirit in individuals and in local fellowships. I shall count it a privilege every day to plead with God to grant us the heavenly blessing and to instruct me in the life and will of the Spirit in the reading of the Word.

APPENDIX THREE

LETTER FROM THEO BAMBER TO *BT*, FEBRUARY 29, 1940: 'A CLARION CALL.'

In this tragic hour one feels a great burden upon the spirit concerning the Church of God. We thank God for all the efforts made to evangelise the masses and the deep note of concern that is more audible now than a year or so back, but still it appears that the deepest issue has not yet been faced. The really desperate need is for the Christians of this country to come back to God in humble repentance for their sins as Christians. We need individuals and fellowships in public assembly to be bowed before God in confession of sin, to repent in humiliation, and to seek His forgiveness and pardon. Without that, I am persuaded we shall be definitely set aside by God; we shall be proved worthless branches by men, and the world will drift into the abyss.

There are several matters which must be definitely confessed, and some I would set forth: Our personal and secret vices with which, in spite of all our public profession, Christians continue to trifle. Our lack of love toward fellow-Christians and of redemptive love toward the world. Our sin in giving the world our own opinions instead of proclaiming what God has revealed in His Word. Our failure to declare to men their utter inability to save themselves either in this world or the next. Our failure to keep eternal things, which alone abide, before the hearts and consciences of men. Our failure to proclaim the end of the age in the personal return of the Lord Jesus Christ. Many other matters will be unveiled by the Holy Spirit to our consciences when once Christians get to their knees in confession and repentance.

A service of Repentance will be held at Rye Lane Chapel, Peckham, on Thursday March 14, at 7.30pm., and all who feel this burden are invited to make confession for themselves and for the Church, to press home the issue in private upon all who name the name of Christ, and to do all they can to arrange speedily for a public meeting of repentance in their own locality.

In thanking you for your kindness, sir, in inserting this letter, may I add the request that all who read it and share its conviction will write to me, telling me what they propose to do in this matter?

Yours Faithfully,

Theo M. Bamber, Rye Lane Chapel, Peckham, SE15[1]

---

[1] *BT* 29.2.40, 132.

APPENDIX FOUR

CHRISTIAN UNITY – A PAPER BY THEO BAMBER

Read to the Conference of the Baptist Revival Fellowship at High Leigh," on Tuesday, November 26, 1957. (Source: *www.theobamber.co.uk*)

It would be difficult within the reasonable scope of one paper to deal with all the important issues that are involved in the modern approach to Christian unity. I think the time is overdue, however, when we of the Baptist Revival Fellowship should state as plainly as may be the most serious and solemn thoughts that are in our minds. We are not unmindful, of course, that the Christian Church as a whole is indebted to those who have belonged to various denominations within the Church. As Baptists we make no claim that we are right, absolutely right and all other than ourselves are wrong. We resolutely disclaim the notion that Baptists and Baptists alone constitute the Church of our Lord Jesus Christ. Within the constitution of the Baptist Union every church is responsible directly to the Lord, the Head of the Church, for its resolutions, decisions, actions, practices and faith. In our view, therefore, no discussions should be taking place between representatives of the Baptist Union and the other churches without the prior consent of at least a majority of the constituent churches each having discussed the matter and decided accordingly. There is weakness, of course, in our system, and also strength, but it is only right that those other churches in the World Council of Churches and all other councils and committees should understand that nobody calling himself a Baptist has any credentials by resolution from the churches as such to discuss much less negotiate any measure of Christian unity.

UNITY URGENTLY NEEDED

Of course, any true believer in our Blessed Lord must regard true unity as essential. We believe, indeed, that were it attained according to the mind of the Holy Spirit it would produce a world-wide revolution, the effects of which no human being would escape, but having said this, we may be sure, that Satan, that *"angel of light,"* will be alert and alive not to oppose outright but to provide a substitute that looks like the real thing, and that is the peril of the critical hour in which we live. This brings us to what I feel to be a proper question: as to the reasons underlying the urge to unity manifested in the present century. The Pope so it is said prays daily for the unity of Christendom, but in his mind that unity is based upon the principle of absorption whereby all other so-called Christians are brought into the one and only fold of Rome. Our Anglican friends have the same kind of idea from their own angle. They see all the Christians in every parish gathered regularly within the parish church. They are agreeable to some kind of tolerance of Nonconformist ministers for a generation while they gradually drop into the grave, but from the moment the union comes into force every minister must be ordained by a bishop and such person alone shall have any valid powers to administer the sacraments.

So far as I know the Anglicans have made no concessions to the truths for which we, as Baptists, stand. Perhaps concessions have been made to Baptists in conference of which we are not yet to be told, but Rome is adamant, Canterbury is dominant and Baptists are quiescent, if not subservient. Lest therefore, Anglicans should be under the impression that within a few years Nonconformity will cease to exist, it ought to be placed on record that there are still a few Baptists, probably not many, but others not within the Baptist Union who will feel that any artificial scheme for unity which is absorption disguised will lead to a new Nonconformity which I am prepared to think will include not a few Anglicans who would prefer the religious wilderness with us to the delectable pastures chosen by Lot.

WHAT BAPTISTS REQUIRE

We declare that it is our solemn belief that within the Roman, Anglican, Greek Orthodox and Free Church denominations there are to be found true believers in our Lord. We are equally clear that in no one of these denominations are all the Church of Christ found to the exclusion of the possibility in the rest. That position must absolutely be accepted without equivocation by all interested parties before we sit down at the conference table, otherwise the Lord is dishonoured. Whatsoever is not of faith is sin (Romans 14, 23). Therefore, speaking in tender love, and with great respect for all who differ from us, we are bound before God to make this solemn declaration. In our understanding of the Word of God and in the sense of the truth given us we believe by the Holy Spirit we should be false to God, to those who differ from us and to ourselves if we did not say clearly and beyond the shadow of a doubt that the whole unscriptural system of consecrated buildings, apostolic succession of bishops, consecrated priests, vestments, reservation of the sacrament baptismal regeneration, godmothers and godfathers, secular interference of governments in the appointments of bishops is in essence superstition, doing incalculable damage to the Christian message and blinding millions to their need of salvation by faith through the blood of Jesus Christ.

Appendices

THE PRELIMINARIES

My fear is that Anglicans in particular have the notion that our little Chapels are gradually emptying, that our stock and prospects are so low that we shall soon be ready for a takeover bid on their own terms. One of the reasons Baptists are so weak at the moment is because we have no sure conviction of policy. We neither press forward to be absorbed into the Anglican Communion nor with any vigour press forward with our own testimony. We do not know whether to urge our young people to be all out for the building of the Church of Christ or dabbling about in local politics. Our young people are being denied the teaching of the fundamentals of our faith from the Word, and we are making them suitable subjects for the guile of the next 25 years. We believe that if all our Baptist ministers gave themselves to the preaching of Christ and Christ alone, making it clear to everybody that apart from Him there is absolutely no hope for mankind in any direction, we should be amazed at the upsurge of spiritual power in our churches and all the latent dynamic in our witness would be manifest.

In our view the essentials in discussions on unity are the common acknowledgement that all things necessary for our salvation, sanctification, translation and eternal glory are set forth and revealed in Holy Scripture. Nobody has any right before God to make demands or prescribe as a necessity for faith anything not clearly and unmistakably required within the terms of Scripture. In so considering the Scriptures all must be concerned to discern what the Scriptures teach and not what we may want them to teach. Finally, as we thus prayerfully and lovingly consider the Word, seeking continually the light of the Holy Spirit, let all is agreed that without waiting for concessions of others each will seek to be obedient to the Word. So we move in the light of the Eternal into all the good and perfect will of God. This may be the counsel of perfection but, unless I am mistaken, the goal in view is of the same character, and to reach it in the will of God will demand courage and great humility and obedience.

THAT THEY ALL MAY BE ONE

Our Lord's High Priestly prayer recorded in John 17, and in particular, verse 21, is the great text for Christian unity. If we start there we start with all who differ from us and at least we are on common ground at the commencement. This prayer is different from the Gethsemane prayer where our Lord prays for the passing of the cup and yet submits to the Father's will. It is usually thought that the prayer in John 17 may be regarded as a type of His prayer in resurrection and ascension where, invested in Omnipotence in heaven, He can say: "I will ". In this prayer He interceded not only for His then disciples, but for all also "that *shall believe in ME through their word."* The people, therefore, about whose unity our Lord is concerned, are believers! They are not believers in a system or a creed but believers in HIM and they come to that belief in Him through the apostles' word concerning Jesus. Personal belief in Jesus, in the revelation of truth through the apostles, is basic to Christian unity. Actually it has nothing whatsoever to do with the linking up of denominations. It has nothing to do with the alignment of churches in denominations; it has nothing whatever to do with churches as such, but is primarily the union of each and every believer in Jesus.

THE TRINITY

This is clearly our Lord's meaning because He speaks of a unity of persons, not of schemes or constitutions. And being persons it must be a union of life. Indeed, our Lord prays that believers may be one *"As Thou Father in Me, and I in Thee, that they also may be one in us."* Christian unity does not take us back to the headquarters of denominations, but to the profound mystery of the Trinity in the Godhead. The subject is beyond us in terms of theological definition, but it is not intended to be beyond us in the realm of experience. Because as is the union of the Father and the Son so is the union of each believer with the Father and the Son and so with all other believers. The Trinity is a Blessed Mystery which we may think to be the only possible manifestation of God in the light of redemption, creation, providence, consummation and the final revelation we have when God shall be all in all.

This union of the Father and the Son is in the Holy Spirit and this is the clue to our unity with them and with one another. The Trinity is a revelation of Divine accessibility. It is an indication that in this mysterious aspect of the Godhead there is the high, holy and almost unbelievable privilege of the child of God, even the humblest believer, to be one with the Father and the Son even as they are one. I cannot hope to understand all this, but it is my profound and earnest prayer that if in the mercy of God such an one as I may know the experience God will bring me to it. Even so I ask with trembling because inherent in this Trinitarian manifestation is that eternal redemption manifested in time in the blood of Christ and those who share the union must share in measure in it.

I am, nevertheless, profoundly convinced that if the people of God would consider Christian unity in this way, each true believer seeking to know the mysteries of God by the Holy Spirit, the Lord would do such a thing for us of which we have never dreamed and in sober truth the world would believe that Jesus was the sent of God. That is the goal of Christian unity and every true believer in our Blessed Lord will seek this deep and inexpressible unity in the Father and the Son in the ministry of the Holy Spirit. What love would be shed abroad in our hearts, what tender concern one for another, what anguish for a world perishing in its sin, what pleadings with God would be heard in all our churches, if every true believer were seeking this unity with the Father and the Son in life eternal and Divine!

SOME CONCLUSIONS

We believe that this approach to Christian unity would make it clear beyond doubt that the nature of the Church is Divine since it derives life from the Lord in heaven Himself. It would be clearly established that we are not in Christ because we are in a particular organisation, but that being in Christ we are by that fact members of the Body of the heavenly communion. Since in Christ we are all kings and priests unto God we could no longer sustain the unscriptural distinction between what is termed the clergy and the laity. If a believer is one with the Father and the Son in the life of the Spirit these other distinctions have no meaning. We should recognize that the Head of the Church separates who He will for the several ministries and that it is the duty of the Lord's people to recognize His sovereign acts in this respect but all of them are for ministry and not for domination. None of them promotes (if that is the right word) a person to an office of superiority, of exclusive rights, of a position with God closer than that of eternal union with the Father and the Son. Equally it would be utterly impossible to think of a Prime Minister advising the monarch as to the appointment of an archbishop or a bishop. The secular hand upon the eternal body of Christ is repugnant to every word of Scripture.

There is but One Head of the Church and His will is made known on earth by the Holy Spirit and by the Holy Spirit alone. One wonders how it is that any believer enlightened by the Holy Spirit can possibly tolerate the thought of the slightest association of political power with the Body of Christ. We do not say these things because we wish to be contentious, but because we feel we must be loyal to the truth so far as we see it. We believe that there are no priorities in the Christian Church and that every believer without exception before God is responsible for the life and witness first in his own walk, in the home of which he may be the head, in the local assembly of which he is a member, and of the whole body of Christ in heaven and on earth, with which in the Father and the Son he is in eternal communion. One is our Master and we are all brethren.

The responsibility of the pastor who is set apart for ministry is no greater and no less than that of any other member except in the ministry of service to which he has been called. He has no powers to make a sacrament valid by his presence and ministry. It is ever the Lord Himself Who offers the bread and the wine and from whose hands the bread and the wine are taken humbly and reverently by the believer. The Father and the Son are one so mysteriously that our Lord could say: "*I and My Father are One,*" and that is the mystery of Christian unity for which we are to pray, and towards which we must ardently long and work. I am bound to say that in my view ecclesiasticism is our peril. It may bewitch the world, which does not understand, but before the Lord returns, its evil will be apparent. Let us stand aside from all this and aim at simplicity, in dress, in the conduct of our services, in holiness of life, and in humble and sincere love for the wonderful people God has given us in our churches. Always reaching out whenever we can to brethren and sisters in other communions between whom as we know there is mutual recognition and love in the Lord. Ever praying that every believer may be in the blessed and mystical union of the Father and the Son as a redeeming, creating channel of blessing; through whom life, life eternal, life abundant, streams to those dead in sin for whom Christ has died and whom He longs should be in the Body of His glory in the transcendent unity of the Father and the Son.

My positive answer, therefore, to this most important matter is that first each of us who sees this deep truth of the unity of the Father and the Son shall recognize that it is the prayer of our Lord to the Father that each one of us may share it. How much of it, and in what way, each may know it as a present experience the Lord Himself will reveal as we hunger after the high and wonderful privilege. It may be beyond words to define, it may be beyond the bounds of theological concept, but it can still be an experience of the redeemed spirit after the manner of Paul's experience in the third heaven. As we long after it, believing that such a prayer by our Lord carries with it the certainty of answer and experience, we shall sense that we are longing after the supreme prize of time and eternity.

We shall be drawn to the Father and the Son by the Spirit in an inexpressible experience and drawn also very closely to others whose longing is identical. Let us therefore preach this positive unity, proclaiming it as that which is of God. Our people in the pews will begin to respond and there will be a unity in our churches that many churches need. We may be certain we shall be drawn outside of our own boundaries into touch with all others seeking as the supreme goal of life this union with the Father and the Son. The enrichment of life will be such that the unsaved will discover that in this company of the true union in Christ is all the plenitude of grace and abundant life and there will be responses plainly with the mark of the Holy Spirit in them. Thus shall we reach out finding ourselves in touch with men and women who are everywhere longing for fullness of life in this blessed and eternal union with the Father and the Son. It is my hope that this truth may be so communicated to us each one in the Spirit that henceforth with increasing longing this passionate desire may grip and occupy our hearts.

APPENDIX FIVE

STATEMENT APPROVED BY THE DENOMINATIONAL CONFERENCE HELD AT SWANWICK, MAY 23–26, 1961

(source: printed copy held at the Angus Library, Regents Park College, Oxford)

Those present at the Denominational Conference at Swanwick desire to express their gratitude at being able to meet in this fashion and to testify to their sense of the presence and guidance of the Holy Spirit.

In the considerable time spent in group discussion, in addition to matters connected with the current Ter–Jubilee Campaign, the following main topics emerged, and on them there was general agreement:

1. That the Independency which has characterized the outlook and practice of many, if not all, of our churches in the last 100 years, needs now to be supplemented by a much clearer realization of the necessity of their interdependency in fellowship, not only on practical grounds but in the light of the teaching of the New Testament and any true doctrine of the church based thereon. The meaning of this (implicit in Baptist principles and clearly expressed in the 17th Century Confession) for our denominational life, needs intimate study, that practical steps for manifesting our true unity in Christ may be agreed upon and put into effect.
2. There was unanimous agreement on the importance of the Associations for the healthy development of our denominational life on the grounds of both history and present experience. Some feeling was expressed that it might be wise to consider the redrawing of certain boundaries, the development of smaller district units and the importance of securing the truly representative character of Association Committees. The value was stressed of the Associations making careful surveys of the Baptist situation in their own neighbourhoods, bearing in mind present commitments and needs.
3. Various questions relating to the ministry of the church were raised and discussed. There was agreement that the total membership of the church is included and involved in its ministry, and that it is essential that all members realize their part in its total witness. In regard to those called to special forms of service, the following matters were raised:
   (a). Present methods of settlement and removal of ministers;

(b). The use and status of both Deaconesses and Probationer Ministers;

(c). The recognition and ordination of men over 40 years of age;

(d). The desirability of a clearer distinction between full and part-time ministries;

(e). The possibility of a system of increments to spends based on length of service;

(f). The need for training and refresher courses for Lay Preachers.

4. In the light of the general denominational situation, the spiritual and numerical weakness which is evident in certain areas, and the movement of population, the importance of "pilot schemes" was stressed. These might well include the development of larger church units or groupings, in towns as well as in the countryside, such units being served by a team of ministers.

A voluntary scheme of settlement was suggested through which ministers willing to be stationed and churches willing to have ministers appointed by a special committee, might be tried.

Considerable time was spent on discussing the needs of village churches. IN a number of places where such churches lack a settled ministry and trained leadership, they no longer meet the needs of children and young people whose education and family life take them more and more out into a larger setting, nor are they able to provide adults with the spiritual resources they need.

5. The urgent need for the sustained teaching of church members was emphasized, as well as their training in prayer and spiritual life. Such teaching should include Christian Doctrine, Christian Witness and Service in the 20th Century, as well as Christian History and our own denominational emphases and convictions. The possibility of a team of ministers able to give themselves to teaching missions was suggested, and also the importance of a booklet or booklets for new church members.

6. It was suggested that the Baptist Union appoint commissions to prepare reports on a number of the issues mentioned above, these reports to be sent for study to the Associations and through them to local church meetings.

7. The lack of knowledge on the part of many of our church members of the world situation was recognized. This lack of knowledge includes ignorance of the Baptist situation throughout the world and the general situation of the Christian Church, and contributes to frequent misunderstanding of the aims and activities of what is generally described as the "Ecumenical Movement".

APPENDIX SIX

OPEN LETTER OF 1964 FROM THEO BAMBER TO ERNEST PAYNE REGARDING RE-UNION AND ISSUES CONCERNING DENOMINATIONAL CENTRALIZATION, FOLLOWED BY PAYNE'S REPLY

(source: BRF Bulletin No.79 April/June 1964 And No.80, July/Sept 1964)

Dear Dr. Payne,

This letter is addressed to you, not as an individual but as the one occupying the most important office in the Baptist Union. You are not necessarily responsible for the matters to which reference will be made.

Some Baptists are genuinely troubled about re-union with the Church of England. The Anglicans and Methodists are making progress. At a meeting addressed by the Archbishop of Canterbury, Dr. Eric Baker, Secretary of the Methodist Conference, was reported in *The Times* as declaring: "Denominationalism is doomed. It is time to burst its bonds." He added that "The Methodist Church was representative of all the Free Churches. It was inevitable that the initial approach should have been made to the Methodists, but it was only one happening in a great ecumenical movement in which all the Churches sooner or later will play their part." Is this then the truth? Is some group of Baptists committed to this ultimate? Does the Secretary of the Methodist Conference know that Baptists are in the bag or was he presuming? Recent articles in the *Baptist Times* indicate a plan to adjust the supreme authority of the Lord over the local assembly. The larger company of the Association has greater wisdom than is possible to the local company of believers. The Associations and the Union in plan and purpose are one, and therefore once the direct and inescapable responsibility of the local Assembly to absolute obedience to the Lord is fretted away the episcopal halter will be round our necks. Do you think that in simple Christian fairness every Church should be asked to give its prayerful consideration to this matter of re-union? Will you see to it that the Assembly of 1965, instead of being overloaded with addresses so that the delegates are dumb, has all the time it needs to consider and determine the future of our Denomination? Or does Dr. Baker know more about Baptist policy than we do, so that in principle the issue is settled and one day the *Baptist Times* will announce that absorption is complete?

You are aware of the booklet issued by the British Medical Association on "Venereal Disease and Young People." It reveals a horrible state of affairs. The report is produced by a Committee which included "representatives of the churches." It may be, of course, that no Baptist was on this Committee, but one would like to know what views were put before such Committees by Baptists. Do we still believe that the blood of Christ indicates infallibly that the root trouble of man is his stubborn resistance to the will of God which is sin? Do we still believe that only as men are saved by faith in His atoning death can they be born again in newness of life, delivered from the power of sin and energized for holiness? Or do our representatives to these Committees remain silent about sin, silent about salvation, ashamed of the blood of Christ, looking at the problem humanistically and devising such human solutions as the decent people of the world may devise? Is Paul right when he declares the Christian minister is an ambassador for God pleading with men in Christ's stead, to be reconciled to God? Or is all this out of date, unnecessary, a fundamentalism happily doomed while we embrace a dead religion, wink at baptismal regeneration and with candle and liturgy press on into the darkness which could have been illuminated with Gospel light?

You must see that we are a dying denomination. We have lost our sense of direct responsibility for obedience to the Lord without which the Holy Spirit peremptorily refuses to aid His people. Is it not significant that a group of laymen are so disturbed about conditions in this country that, completely ignoring the hierarchy, they have turned away hopeless from every English, Scottish or Welsh religious leader and appealed to Dr. Billy Graham to come over and do something. Why have they ignored the British Council of Churches and the Federal Free Church Council? And why have they turned to a Fundamentalist? These are questions Baptists should be asking. These men are right; they can see the red light.

Do you not see that our immediate task is to seek the grace of God for a regenerate membership in our Churches? Could not the *Baptist Times* set forth for the edification of our people that every Baptist, beginning with the Deacons, or perhaps the ministers, should clearly know the way of salvation so that by the grace of God they can lead men and women into the joy of the new-born life. The joy of it all will mean a transformation of our Churches. The Holy Spirit will know where to send needy sinners that they may be found of the Saviour and thus giving ourselves completely and absolutely to this one matter, just as our Lord did, we shall begin to experience revival. Saved sinners will be joining us, their money may well solve our financial problems, which would disappear anyway, and the Baptist could be the spiritual light of our country in its desperate need.

But the time for words is ended: creative deed is essential.

Yours Sincerely,

T. M. BAMBER

Appendices

Reply from Payne, April 8, 1964.

Dear Mr. Bamber,

Since you choose the rather unusual and somewhat unsatisfactory method of using the Bulletin of the Baptist Revival Fellowship to address a letter to me as Secretary of the Baptist Union, you will, I hope, allow me to reply in the same manner, although the answers to most of your questions you raise (where not obvious) could have been obtained by less bizarre means.

One as experienced as yourself must be aware of the complexity of Church relations in this country and of the long story of conversations and discussions since 1920. In particular you must be aware of (1) the 1926 Reply of the Baptist Union to the Lambeth Appeal, (2) the Report adopted by the Baptist Union Council in 1937 on the question of possible union between Baptists, Congregationalists and Presbyterians, and (3) the comments of the Baptist Union Council in 1953 on the report "Church Relations in England" which followed the Archbishop of Canterbury's Cambridge Sermon. All these documents are readily available to all Baptists, the first and third being reprinted as appendices to my history of the Baptist Union. They set out the present official attitude to the issues with which they deal.

The third of these documents states explicitly:

"We have therefore to conclude that the report 'Church Relations in England' does not, as it stands, offer a plan of development which Baptists would consider it either right or practicable to try to implement."

The discussions between the Church of England and the Methodists, to which you allude, follow from the fact that the Methodist Church is the only Free Church to decide to investigate further the suggestions which were made in the report. Any remarks made by Dr. Eric Baker express his own views. If he is correctly reported as having said that "the Methodist Church was representative of all the Free Churches", he can obviously only have meant in this context that the Methodist Church is at the moment *a* Free Church wrestling with the problems involved in the kind of new relationship tentatively suggested by Lord Fisher when he was Archbishop of Canterbury. You cannot but be aware that there are a number of Anglicans as well as Methodists who are critical of the suggestions that have been made.

To insinuate that Dr. Baker has some authority to speak for others besides Methodists or "knows more about Baptist policy than we do, so that in principle the issue is settled and one day the Baptist Times will announce that absorption is complete" is as fantastic as it is false and unworthy of you and the official bulletin of the BRF. You must well know that it is nonsense.

Equally void of any truth is the suggestion that articles by individuals that appear in the *Baptist Times* on the many problems our churches face indicate that there are plans for putting "the Episcopal halter round our necks." My own personal views on episcopacy have not changed since I set them out in "The Free Churches and Episcopacy", which first appeared in "Theology" in June 1951, reprinted by the Carey Kingsgate Press in 1952.

The report of the British Medical Association on "Venereal Diseases and Young People" indicates that the Churches were represented on the committee by Dr. W. W. Kay, a medical man who is an Independent Methodist, Dr. Leslie Weatherhead, the Rev. Austen Williams, of St. Martin-in-the-Fields, and the Chairman of the Catholic Advisory Council. Answers to the questionnaire prepared by the BMA (and printed as Appendix II of the Report) were submitted by the Baptist Union, the YMCA, Major-General Wilson Hafendon and many other individuals and social and religious organizations. Your comment about "pressing on into the darkness with candle and liturgy" is another attempt to create alarm and suspicion in a manner which one with your record of pastoral and denominational service ought surely not to stoop to on so sad and grave a matter.

It would not be helpful, I think, in view of the fact that Dr. Billy Graham is likely to come again to this country, to comment on your paragraph about him, beyond pointing out that during his recent visit he had interviews with the Archbishops of Canterbury and York, and that he neither describes himself as a Fundamentalist nor is so recognized in the USA.

Only the future can show whether we are a dying denomination. Admittedly this is a difficult day for organized religions in this country. But the situation is not likely to be improved if Christians question one another's obedience to the Lord and snipe at one another. One of the booklets about the BRF states that it stands to emphasise "*Brotherly Love* as a distinctive manifestation of the indwelling Spirit".

I have written frankly, but you, as well as I, carry heavy responsibilities for our words, whether written or spoken.

Yours Sincerely,

ERNEST A. PAYNE

Bamber published the following addendum with Payne's letter: 'We thank Dr. Payne for his kindness in replying to the "Open Letter". The value of this correspondence will emerge as Members carefully note the precise questions put to Dr. Payne and the answers given above.'

APPENDIX SEVEN

STATEMENT OF THE BAPTIST REVIVAL FELLOWSHIP REGARDING THE ECUMENICAL MOVEMENT AGREED AT THE BRF CONFERENCE OF 1967

(source: BRF Archive held at Spurgeon's College, London)

Those members of the Baptist Revival Fellowship at Conference on November 22, 1967 approved the following statement regarding their attitude towards the ecumenical Movement as it finds expression in the World Council of Churches. We believe that there is a Unity which already exists in Jesus Christ amongst all true believers and regret that this Unity does not, at this moment, have a visible expression, but we cannot believe that the World Council of Churches is a vehicle for such visible expression.

(1). the fundamental premise for all our thinking on the complex issue is that we believe 'THE FAITH' has been "once for all delivered to the saints" (Jude 3) and that its essential elements have been clearly revealed in Scripture, the sole and final authority in all matters of faith and conduct. We hold, therefore, that this Faith can be clearly defined in words and doctrinal propositions. We believe further that there are certain doctrines which form the essential and irreducible heart of the Gospel, such as those dealing with the substitutionary nature of Our Lord's Atoning Death, Justification by Grace through faith alone, and the necessity for regeneration by the Holy Spirit to constitute anyone a child of God and so a "Christian". We hold that where these Doctrines of Salvation are not held, or denied, or are regarded merely as one of several equally legitimate facets of truth or ways of approach to God, or where they have some religious ceremony of "works" added to them as being necessary for salvation, then what remains, or results, is not "THE FAITH" but "another Gospel".

(2). We accept, therefore, that while the Doctrinal Basis of the WCC is orthodox as far as it goes, and could be a sufficient basis for *personal* relationships and discussions between individuals who subscribe to it, it is not, in these days of doctrinal uncertainty and confusion, a sufficient basis for involvement and co-operation in spiritual matters *at church level;* and further, that it is quite insufficient as a basis for a *constitutional association or union of churches* , since it does not include any statements on these essential doctrines. Conservative Evangelicals are often charged with unwillingness even to enter into dialogue with Christians of other traditions. But as far as we can see it is impossible to share in any real way in the life and work of the WCC except by joining it at the official denominational or church levels, which involves one morally in participating in issues and enterprises which may be unscriptural and unprofitable. We therefore deprecate and oppose the membership of the Baptist Union in the WCC by which all affiliated Baptist Churches and their members are formally involved in the Ecumenical Movement, although their attitudes and desires on this fundamental issue have hitherto never been directly sought by the Baptist Union Council.

(3). we wish to state our position courteously and with balance, but we must affirm that we have always been perturbed that the Churches in membership with the WCC, and their leaders as individuals, are so doctrinally mixed. In recent years we have noted with increasing concern the admission, and growing influence, of the largely unreformed, and non-Protestant, Orthodox Churches. Now we are deeply troubled by the attitudes and policies being adopted and advocated by many towards the Roman Catholic Church which, in spite of the apparent liberalizing of its approach and methods on some issues, has not altered a single basic doctrine, neither can nor will do so, for Rome's proud boast is that she is "always the same".

(4). as individuals many Ecumenical leaders openly avow that their ultimate objective is a single, united World Church, embracing all traditions and doctrinal positions. We recognize that British Baptist leaders have the much more restricted and moderate objectives of theological consultations with leaders of other member churches, the removal of denominational barriers and misunderstandings, and practical co-operation as possible. We respect this position, but, quite apart from the general reasons for our opposition to participation in the WCC, we believe that such a position will be finally untenable, and ultimately it will have to give way either to withdrawal from the Movement or acceptance of this all-embracing, one World-Church objective. Eventually, and that in the lifetime of many of us, we believe all Christians will be compelled to be either wholly committed to this Movement and World Church, or wholly outside it – at great cost. We believe this issue can and should be decided on the grounds of doctrinal principle, rather than forced later by the pressure of events. Further, contrary to much current opinion, we do not believe the Reformation was a mistake, but rather a mighty, liberating movement of the Holy Spirit changing the course of history. Nor are we convinced that the modern Ecumenical Movement as it finds expression in the Word Council of Churches in its overall, general trends is a movement of the Holy Spirit.

(5) We recognize the integrity and sincerity of those Evangelicals who are committed to the Ecumenical Movement and advocate approval of the WCC Some of these we know personally as brethren in Christ. But with all respect to them, we believe their judgement in this matter is grievously and dangerously mistaken. We must lovingly but firmly take our stand against their position and outside this Movement, and we shall do all in our power

Appendices

to awaken Christian believers to the serious dangers to the Gospel and to the well-being of their local churches involved in their participation in this Movement at local, as well as denominational, level.

APPENDIX EIGHT

'HOW MUCH OF A MAN WAS JESUS?'

(source: copy in the BRF Archive, held at Spurgeon's College, London)

An Address To The 1971 Baptist Assembly by the Revd. Michael Taylor, Principal of Northern Baptist College.

A little under 2000 years ago a young Palestinian Jew lived out most of his days in obscurity. During his last years he came into the public eye. Some were delighted by his activities, others were increasingly hostile. Eventually he was brought to the notice of the Roman authorities. Apparently tarred with the same brush as some of his politically left-wing friends he was found guilty on a somewhat dubious charge. He died at the hands of the Roman executioner at about 33 years of age. A few days later his close associates and admirers were convinced he was alive.

This sequence of events – the life, death and resurrection of Jesus of Nazareth – made an overwhelming impression first on a few and on millions ever since. From that day to this, men have tried to put its significance into words. That's what we're about tonight. It seems to me that there are two ways of setting about the task. I want to look at them both and tell you why I prefer the second to the first.

I.   A CONFESSION OF FAITH

The first way is to write down as clearly and concisely as we can what we believe about Jesus. It's a tough intellectual exercise. Words must be carefully weighed. The result is any one of the many creeds and confessions of faith to be found in the history of the church down to modern times. The most recent was the Declaration of Principle adopted by the Congregational Church in 1967.

These statements have been the children of fierce controversy, or displays of confidence in times of uncertainty. There are some who feel the time is ripe for our own denomination to attempt such a task.

When I am asked to speak to you about 'The Incarnate Presence – how much of a man was Jesus?' I'm probably being asked to attempt a draft paragraph for just such a confession. It would appear under the heading 'Jesus Christ.' This is one way of putting into words the significance of the overwhelming impact made by the Nazarene.

I personally have no great enthusiasm for it, but it has to be done and I had better not duck the issue.

Appendices

I will tell you what I would write. It must take account of those enormous mysteries referred to in traditional phrases like 'the true divinity and true humanity of Christ.' It must be a modern replacement for those splendid words in the Nicene Creed:

We believe ... in one Lord Jesus Christ, the only begotten Son of God, Begotten before all ages ... true God of true God ... of one substance with the Father ... who for us men and for our salvation came down from the heavens and was made flesh who and became man.

I have no wish to disown any of that, but those words were penned in very different circumstances, when men thought in different ways and moved about different intellectual maps. We have to re-write them without playing false to the reality which led them to speak as they did.

Here then is my draft paragraph: (I will comment afterwards)

'The story of Jesus makes such an overwhelming impression that I am not content to say he was extraordinary man. I believe that in the man Jesus we encounter God. I believe that God was active in Jesus, but it will not quite do to say categorically: Jesus is God. Jesus is unique, but his uniqueness does not make him different in kind from us. He is the same sort of animal. He is fully and unambiguously a man. The difference between him and ourselves is not in the manner of God's presence in Jesus. The difference is in what God did in and through this man and the degree to which this man responded and co-operated with God.'

... (original copy has some words missing at this point) ...? I had better explain myself. I will make four remarks. The first two underline the ways in which Jesus is the same as me and you. The second two underline ways in which he is different.

    a. First, Jesus is the same as me because like me he is a man. He is the same sort of animal. He belongs to the same human family.

It is difficult to know what to add to that. I ought to declare an interest. I want him to be a man or the rest of my theology doesn't work, just as others want him to be sinless or their understanding of the atonement doesn't work. If he isn't a man his life becomes irrelevant to all the questions about humanity. How can he be the clue to what it means to be human if he is not a man himself?

But having said that what else is there to say? The question 'how much of a man was Jesus?' doesn't appear to make sense unless you're talking about masculinity and not humanity. You're either a man or you're not.

I believe he is unambiguously man. Because of that I am not troubled or surprised to find that he doesn't know everything, or sometimes makes a mistake, or gets angry, or doesn't have all the gifts, or betrays himself as a child of his time. That's to be expected of a man.

But neither shall I have a closed mind about those aspects of his life which seem too extraordinary to be true of a man. I don't wish to say that because he's a man miracle can't happen, even the greatest miracle of bodily resurrection. There's no need for prejudice to explain away the miraculous. I must allow these extraordinary events to challenge my narrow views about what is possible for men when they co-operate with the activity of God. What is actual in Jesus may be potential in us – the divinely-intended truth about every man, which will not lie dead and wasted in some forgotten tomb.

But however remarkable this life, I think I must stop short of saying categorically: Jesus is God, and I understand the New Testament probably stops short of it as well. This is the most troubling aspect of some of the old creeds which keep insisting that Jesus is truly God and truly man, of one substance with the Father and one substance with us – as if the more you shout about it the more convincing it becomes. But it sounds like a contradiction to me. And can we evade the issue by calling it a paradox? Or is paradox another name for contradiction when we start talking about God?

Jesus is a man. I do not say that Jesus is God, but I do say with the New Testament that God was in Christ or that I encounter God in Jesus.

    b. Which brings me to my second remark. I do not believe the fact that God was in Jesus makes him different from me and you either. It is another way in which he is the same.

If I am honest with you – and presumably one is free to be honest in the Christian family – I am one of those who've experienced great difficulties in believing in God – or perhaps it's fairer to say in thinking about him. I felt the cold winds of the Honest To God debate and the Death of God controversy. This mattered to me and affected my existence. It was important. I never lost my admiration for Christ and my commitment to him, but at one point I found myself as a child of my time thinking more like a so-called Christian atheist who said either that Jesus is my God, or 'Love is God' rather than 'God is love,' or Jesus is a man without remainder.

Now that may have been mistaken, but the fact remains that it happened, and it happened to a lot of us – and I'm in two minds about it still. One part of me wonders if the controversy is over. Can we really dismiss it with light-hearted jokes about God being alive and well and pour scorn on the divine undertakers? Could it not represent more profound changes in man's understanding of his world which are not necessarily against Christianity? Could it be an early symptom of more far reaching mutations in human thought? I am not clever enough to say but we are still very young in history.

Appendices

The other part of me now agrees with those level-headed people who told us all along that it is not God who is dead but our way of thinking about him. I find it helpful to accept three of their now familiar suggestions.

The first is to think of God (and we can only talk in pictures) not up there or out there, or even down under, but in here – an all-pervading immanent God. He is transcendent. He is other than me and other than you – holy other – but he is transcendent because he is different not because he is distant. He is God with us.

The second suggestion is to think of God not as one who makes occasional sorties into the world, interrupting the ongoing sequence of events – who does his but 'in between' our normal affairs. He does not interrupt. He is active all the time, not here today and gone tomorrow, but always present and involved in the ongoing process of history.

The third suggestion is to think of God not as active in some places and not in others – in the religious but not in the secular, or the extraordinary but not in the mundane. Don't think of God as active here but not there; he is active everywhere. In any situation you can expect to find him at work – his presence is woven into the very fabric of life.

God is transcendent, he is different, but he is in this world, always active and active everywhere – and there is nothing special about this Jesus in that respect. God is present in that human life as he is present in all human life. God was there in Palestine 2000 years ago, and he is here in the Western word of the 20th century. God was active then and he is active now. If you like, there is always this Incarnate Presence. History is the story of God's unceasing involvement with his world, a story in which there is not only one occasion when he is present, but in which he is actively present on every occasion.

So first, Jesus is a man like me and you, and second God is present and active in Jesus as he is present and active in us all.

But haven't I thrown everything away? If Jesus is like us from both the human and divine point of view, what is so special about him? You've reduced this mountain to a plain. How is he different from us? How is he transcendent? How can you say he is unique and offer to him what you offer to no other man, your undivided loyalty and allegiance?

That brings me to my two other points. There are two ways in which Jesus is the same, and there are two ways in which he is different.

    c.   First he is different form us in the extent to which we actually see in him what life can become when lived in co-operation with God. You can give it various names. Call it his unique sonship expressed in the words 'Abba, Father.' Call it the quality of his life referred to rather misleadingly as 'sinlessness.' He was different – not different in kind but different in degree – and in this sense more of a man, more human, realizing more of what man can become than any other human being.

It is one of the mysteries of life that some people achieve so much more than others. One flowers and another does not. One man's life has great significance and another's is forgotten. It's a mystery but not a difficulty in that it's a commonplace of our experience which we accept.

We know more about these ups and downs than we used to; why one man's life is outstanding and others are simple mediocre. Some of the clues lie in biology, in DNA and hereditary, in our immediate social environment and our cultural heritage, in the way our conscious and subconscious minds are formed, in the relationships which happen to come our way and the opportunities which cross our path, in a thousand seeming accidents of history which pile up and may or may not come together at the right time.

In addition there is human freedom by which a man may unpredictably seize his chance and respond, or turn his back.

All of these combine to make many different men including that most exceptional man from Nazareth. He seizes his chances. He co-operates with God as no man before or since. He actualizes his potential, but he does so because of the reasons I have referred to – the reasons which make history not a level plain but a landscape of many ups and downs. He does so not because he is different in kind, not because he isn't really a man but something else, not because he's got what it takes – the magic ingredient – and we have not. If that is so, if the quality of his human life is different after all, then its whole integrity is destroyed and we are left with a charade.

Jesus is unique but that uniqueness is one of degree, not of kind. The reasons may be mysterious, but we are to look for them in the same places as we look for the reasons why others achieve so much more than their fellows – in all those factors which go to make us what we are and do what we do – and within which is woven the continuous activity of God.

    d. But, fourthly, is that all that we can say about the uniqueness of Jesus – a unique

fulfillment of the potential in man – different from us in degree but not in kind? Will that really take account of the insistent witness of all Christian history that there is more to be said? No. I don't think it will. We haven't yet fully reckoned with God.

Appendices

God indwells in Jesus in the same way as he indwells in his greatest saints and in all of us. God is in Christ as God is in all men. Jesus is not of a different kind of stuff or substance. But Jesus is unique because God did something quite unique in Jesus. That uniqueness is not in the presence – 'God was in Christ.' It is in the activity 'reconciling the world to himself.' God is always active in the world, and his actions are never out of character, but he does not need to do it again: he showed with unrivalled clarity that he loves this world, is involved in its struggles, is suffering to death for its salvation. He acted in a decisive way for the reconciliation of man to himself and for the healing of the whole creation. He raised the Nazarene to life, the first fruits of the harvest of the dead. Of no other can it be said that God did in him what God did in Christ.

These then are my four remarks:
   a. Jesus is a man like us (and there are no half measures here).
   b. God is present in Jesus in the same way that he is present everywhere and all the time.
   c. In Jesus I discover a unique example of what human life becomes when lived in co-operation with God. It is different in degree but not in kind from all other lives.
   d. In Jesus God acted in a unique and decisive way for our salvation.

That kind of reasoning leads me to make the confession I do.

II.   RESERVATIONS

So much then for the first way of trying to put into words the significance of Jesus of Nazareth. I have e no great enthusiasm for this way of doing things. I can see it has positive value and must be done somewhere in the life of the church. We must subject ourselves to the discipline of trying to say what we believe. We must make sure that we're talking sense and not nonsense. We must explain ourselves to other people. We must examine the intellectual roots of our faith.

So the attempt to write these confessions has to be made, but I am not enthusiastic. I'm not convinced it's the most important task to be about, and I'm not at all keen to express my own faith in this way. There are a number of reasons. I will mention four.
   a. First, I'm not happy about confessions of faith and statements of belief if its implied

we must all agree with them. I do not believe that Christian fellowship and common action is based on this kind of agreement. Even if it were possible it would be undesirable and very uninteresting. I do not see the need for us all to believe the same things.

For example, I do not claim too much for what I have said to you this evening. I do not say this is the truth and you must believe it. I do not say I am right and anyone who disagrees with me is wrong. I am bound to be wrong in some respects – but we are wrong within the circle of the church where the checks and balances exist.

That is my opinion. This is the conclusion I have come to at this stage of my own intellectual pilgrimage. This is the result when I try to listen to the tradition of the church, to the contemporary mind and to my own inner voices. I may well learn better as I grow older. One day I may see it differently. This is how I see it now. How do you see it? By sharing opinions we may nourish one another's faith.

This is all I can claim – and such modest claims can be just as serious about truth as dogmatic ones.

Christian fellowship is not based on doctrinal agreement. If you disagree I shall invite you to an argument but I shall not ask you to leave. How many of us have shared together in the task of the Gospel where our theological formulations have been firmly put in their place and seen in perspective.

    b.   Second, I'm not happy about stating our beliefs in this way if we mistake them for

adequate expressions of the truth. I am not committed to a confession of faith, I am committed to a Person, and the truth about that Person is not carried for me by a number of intellectual propositions. The truth about Him is carried by a story.

When I have weighed my words and polished my theological phrases as part of an important intellectual discipline, there is a sense in which I have not got hold of Jesus but he has slipped through my fingers. I have not found his significance, I have lost it.

This enormous personality is not contained in a few sentences or a number of abstract ideas. The truth is conveyed in a much more elusive way in a story told by 4 writers in the New Testament, with is particular incidents and pictures and parables and narrative material and historical setting – a story which is open to more than one interpretation, whose meaning is never wholly exhausted. It cannot be tied down as easily as that. The story is constantly capable of challenging what has been said about it before and of surprising and impressing me in a new way.

I would rather sign my name on a dotted line under the Gospel story and declare that here for me is the bearer of the truth about God and man, than give my assent to a statement of faith and suggest that here is the truth about Jesus.

It's a story not a creed, which represents the permanent, bedrock, unchanging deposit for the Christian church. It's a story, not a creed, which represents the essential unalterable gospel which she must carry as she carries her life.

    c. Third, I'm not happy about confessions of faith if they lead us to being over-pre-occupied with arguments between ourselves. Of course we could argue – and argue a good deal more rigorously and merrily than we do. Of course I'm interested in sharpening my mind against those of my fellow Christians. This is part of the intellectual discipline for which I have the greatest respect.

But we must keep it in perspective. We may wish to argue in our circles as to whether Jesus was sinless or performed miracles and rose bodily from the grave and was born of a virgin and was really and truly a man. But we must not spend too much energy on this kind of debate. We may wake up one morning to find that what looms large to us in here is of little consequence to those outside. They are not interested in how much of a man was Jesus – but they are wondering what it means to be a man at all. They will not assume that he's the only person to be referred to as a criterion of humanity. 'What's so special about Jesus?' asks one shop steward, 'when there are so many admirable characters?' Once we start talking to the world we may find we've been answering the wrong questions and when we join in the ordinary conversations of men and try to explain to them what Jesus is all about we are de-skilled, unable to communicate, in a strange land where our cosy maps no longer chart the way.

You may reply, if the world isn't interested in the things that seem important to the church, so much the worse for the world, but I wonder if that can ever be the answer of the Christian missionary.

    d. Finally, I'm unhappy about stating the significance of Jesus only in the form of a

confession of faith because at the end of the day I fear a number of people, Christians among them, are going to say, 'So what?' It's an interesting, and no doubt necessary exercise, but it rings very few bells with e, and what difference does all this really make to my life and all the other lives of men. It's a little like the highly abstract and cerebral game of mathematical logic that the very clever can play endlessly in complete detachment from empirical realities and which need never be applied or touched down on the face of the earth.

It is an ironic state of affairs if the significance of the Incarnate Presence can be left suspended in the realm of abstract ideas, seemingly removed from the incarnate realities of our human lives.

III. STARTING FROM THE OTHER END

These and other considerations make me far more interested in a second way of trying to up the significance of Jesus into words. I can only mention it briefly. It is sometimes referred to as 'starting from the other end.' It is really a greater concern with other things – not with the abstract but with the concrete, not with the church but with the secular world, not with a creed or confession but with the story about Jesus, not with general statements but particular insights, not with finalizing the matter in doctrinal agreement but by open-ended contributions to be taken and used for what they are worth.

I prefer to begin, and of course, I am not alone by taking very seriously indeed the concrete situations of life – any situation you may care to mention, where men and women actually wait for their salvation.

It may be the person you are dealing with at the moment, yourself included, with his hopes, grief's, strengths and weaknesses. It may be a small community like the family, or the life of the neighbourhood where you live. It could be the situation that presents itself at work, or the life of the city. It may be a question about sex, or technology, or industrial relations, or one of the dominant issues of our day like Race, War and Poverty. It can range from the smallest human groups to the great international communities of mankind, from what appears to be straight-forward to the most complicated situations that confront us when we look at man in his social and natural environment.

Any situation, but whatever it is, it is a recognizable part of this world and t us in that situation – incarnate – that we must ask the Jesus questions. They do not turn out to be questions like 'How much of a man was Jesus?' but questions like 'What is the significance of Jesus for us in here?'; 'How does Jesus illuminate this situation?; 'What is the God who was active in Jesus doing now, and how do we co-operate with him?'; 'Where is this concrete set of circumstances can we celebrate and say 'Yes' and where must we say "No", and how are we called to respond?'

The main tool we shall bring to this task of exploring our experience is not a confession or a creed or abstract ideas or a set of propositions – important as they may be. The too we shall bring is a story – the story of Jesus of Nazareth as told in the New Testament Gospels. It is this story we must 'tell' as it were, over and over again inside all the situations of life.

And as this world and the story are allowed to confront one another, the result will be not a formal statement of faith but increasing insight – a revelation of significance – that will lead to words of hope and judgement, of gift and demand as this part of life is transformed and transfigured by the light and glory of the Christ and us seen to be full of his gracious influence.

Appendices

The words that come will be particular, incarnate words. They will be for this particular situation. They may or may not do for any other. They are not generalities. They speak the language that rises from this area of experience and they are expressed in its own idiosyncratic terms.

It is these words, words about Jesus but also words about the world which matters to men, these words are the most important for us to speak.

But why would we hope that any such words can ever come – that it is possible to answer the questions about Jesus in the terms of our world now and the questions of our world now in terms of Jesus? For the same two reasons as I suggested in my earlier remarks. I can hope to draw lines and relationships between the Jesus story and any human situation because he is not different from us in kind. We are talking about the same humanity. He is fully and unambiguously a man. I can also hope to draw lines between the Jesus story and any situation in the world today because the same God is present and active still. He is doing different things. What he did in Jesus was unique, but he behaves in the same way, always in character, he is about the same business and working for the same ends. The God Incarnate and Present in Jesus is the God Incarnate and Present in our world.

It is sometimes suggested that there is too much talk today about the renewal of the forms for the church and too little about the renewal of faith. There is truth in that. But it is also true that until the church takes new forms and itself becomes more incarnate and present within the concrete situations of the world as it is now; until it tells the story from the inside of this strange territory and stops inviting people outside to an abstract religion, we shall not be in a position to discover what has to be said about Jesus, nor find the most important words we need to speak for the healing of men and to the glory of God.

APPENDIX NINE

THE RESOLUTION AND ADDENDUM AS AGREED BY THE BAPTIST UNION COUNCIL OF NOVEMBER 1971 FOR PRESENTATION TO THE BAPTIST ASSEMBLY OF 1972

(source: BU Minutes, held at the Angus Library, Regents Park College, Oxford)

With deep concern for the truth of the Gospel and the unity of the Churches and in the knowledge that the recent Assembly address of the Rev. Michael Taylor has caused serious concern to some among us who have judged it to fail to do justice to the teaching of the New Testament as to the Deity of Christ:

1. This Council recognizes that, Jesus Christ being the same yesterday, today and forever, in every age the task of theological restatement has been accepted by His Church in order that she may be equipped to speak the Word with power.
    It believes that it is of critical importance for the life and health and witness of the churches that this task should not be renounced in our day.
    It recognizes that it is the special responsibility of Christian thinkers and scholars to venture in humility and in reliance on the Holy Spirit.
    It believes that it rests upon the churches, in obedient listening to the Scriptures, to discern what is good in such restatements, to accept or reject.
2. This Council recognizes that the address given on the humanity of Jesus given at its invitation by the Rev Michael Taylor was an individual attempt made, with integrity, by a member of the Baptist community expressing faith in the living Christ as a contribution to the ongoing theological task.
    It is as such it must be received and assessed. It is not to be considered as a statement on the Person of Christ made on behalf of, or expressing the mind of, the Council or the Union or to be judged as something to which these bodies are in any way committed. This council itself is unequivocal in its profession of the Deity of Our Lord as also of His humanity.
3. This council gladly and explicitly re-affirms that the Basis of the Baptist Union is the declaration of Principle set out in the constitution.

Appendices

In this it asserts its belief in God the Father, Son and Holy Spirit into whose Name are baptized those who have professed repentance toward God and faith in our Lord Jesus Christ, who "died for our sins according to the Scriptures, was buried and was raised the third day".

It acknowledges this Jesus Christ as both "Lord and Saviour" and "God manifest in the flesh", recognizes Him as the sole and absolute authority in all matters pertaining to faith and practice as revealed in Holy Scriptures and acknowledges the liberty of each church under the guidance of the Holy Spirit to administer and interpret His laws.

ADDENDUM

This Council declares that whilst asserting and cherishing its special affinities with those of the Evangelical tradition, our denomination has always claimed a place in the one holy universal church and desires the closest possible fellowship with all who love and trust our Lord Jesus Christ. Not only is it characterized by evangelistic and missionary zeal; it possesses a treasured heritage of liberty of opinion and utterance and since the 17th century has shared in the struggle for religious toleration and the freeing of men's minds and consciences from intellectual and civil fetters. Accordingly, the Union has always contained within its fellowship those of different theological opinions and emphases, believing that its claim for toleration involves tolerance and mutual respect in its own ranks.

APPENDIX TEN

THE RESOLUTION OF THE BRF CONFERENCE OF NOVEMBER 1971 CONCERNING WITHDRAWAL FROM THE BAPTIST UNION

(source: The Minutes of the Baptist Union GP&F Executive Committee, December 7,1971)

We believe the address of the Rev. Michael Taylor given at the BU Council's invitation at the 1971 BU Assembly was a denial of the essential Biblical truth concerning the Deity of our Lord Jesus Christ.

We believe this truth is fundamental to Christianity and without it there is no gospel. We believe the BU Council's resolution of November 10th, 1971 failed to discern and declare all this. We note that at one and the same time the resolution affirms the Declaration of Principle concerning the Deity of Christ and yet allows a view which denies His Deity. We believe this indicates a radical change from the Union's original position.

We cannot in conscience remain associated with the life of a union which has decided to tolerate the denial of the Deity of our Lord Jesus Christ among its accredited ministers.

The details of the way in which we translate this conviction into action will be a matter of individual judgement. We understand that some of our members will resign in the immediate future from the BU accredited list and that some will do so later.

We wish it to be known that we are not acting precipitately. Many of us have been deeply concerned and burdened for years and have sought be every means in our power to witness within the BU to influence it to a more Biblical position; we sadly believe these endeavours have been largely in vain.

APPENDIX ELEVEN

BRF LETTER TO DAVID RUSSELL: THE FINAL PLAN FOR A NEW BAPTIST BODY

(source: Baptist Union GP&F Minutes, December 7, 1971)

Dear Dr. Russell,

At our meeting with you and your colleagues last week I promised to summarize in writing the points I made on behalf of the BRF. I apologize for the delay in doing this, but you will appreciate that the present situation is making me very busy, especially in the realm of correspondence.

On behalf of the ministers and churches who resign from the Union because of their consciences, we made the following points:

1. We promise to do all in our power to act in love, to avoid recrimination and any kind of animosity. We ask the officers of the Union to use their influence to make sure that the same spirit be shown towards us in the actions we take.
2. We feel special concern for older men, who, if they resign, will suffer badly in their ultimate superannuation. Even under the new arrangement we still feel it is a pity if men and their wives are caused grievous loss and suffering because they act in conscience. We plead with the Union to do all in their power to make as full provision for such cases as is possible.
3. There will be churches desiring to withdraw, yet bound by their Trust Deeds. We realize that legally they are in a difficult position, but again we urge that their actions be looked at from the Christian viewpoint, and every effort made to allow them to follow their sense of the leading of God with as little penalty as possible.
4. We who are leaving the Union are still convinced Baptists. We have no desire to go into isolation, but have a real concern for fellowship with others in the same position. Some of these will need practical help. We do not want to form another denomination, but feel we must form some kind of association or fellowship to keep our links in the Gospel.
5. In response to your question, we would only return to the Union if the Union, on its own initiative, not only dealt firmly with heresy, but also made its doctrinal position clear, and acted towards those who could not accept that position.

The Baptist Revival Fellowship

May I again thank you and the other brethren who met us so graciously. We appreciated the spirit of the meeting. We see little point in further discussions in the immediate future, but if at any time you wish to meet us, we should be happy to come to Church House at your request.

Yours on behalf of the Committee,

H. G. Owen, Chairman, Baptist Revival Fellowship

APPENDIX TWELVE

'THE CHRISTOLOGICAL CONTROVERSY IN THE BAPTIST UNION'

An article by G. R. Beasley-Murray, first offered for publication in the Baptist Times and when refused, circulated as a booklet to every Baptist minister and Church Secretary in January 1972

[Author's note: the pagination of the booklet has been indicated below for ease of comparison with the published version].

/p.2.

Impassioned pleas were made in the *Baptist Times* at the close of 1971 that a halt be made to the endless disputing that has been going on in the denomination of late. "Let's end the argument, and let's get on with the job!" was the demand. The Editor of the *Baptist Times* agreed with the sentiment. We've had enough!

I understand the reaction. I, too, hate controversy, especially with my own people. But may I in turn plead that we take time to think again? What are we wanting to "get on" with? Preaching the Gospel? But it is precisely the gospel which is at stake in the present discussion. My great fear is that we may be so anxious to secure peace within the denomination that we may find ourselves paying the price of – *Christ*.

If that appears a mere rhetorical exaggeration, I don't intend it as such. It is my conviction that the vast majority of our denomination does not realise what has taken place in our midst. The issues are of such importance we must make time to look at them, steadily and objectively, insofar as we are able.

Well what has happened that is so important? Briefly it is this. An interpretation of Christ has been set forth among us which maintains that the belief that Jesus is truly God and truly man is a contradiction. Jesus, it is said, was a man in whom God was present just as He is in the rest of us. The uniqueness of Jesus lay in the completeness of his response to God and in the way God worked through him.

The Council of the Union was asked to consider its attitude to this exposition. It declined to pass judgement on it, beyond recognising it as a contribution to the knowledge of Christ made sincerely on the basis of faith in the living Christ. It further reaffirmed its own faith in the Deity of Christ. Beyond all doubt however most members of the Council assumed that the new exposition is compatible with its faith. Others have been more forthcoming:

for them the new approach was a breath of fresh air, and the Baptist Renewal Group has asked for more like it at our assemblies.

/p.3

Well, why not? What's wrong with it? Permit me to answer by unfolding some notes which I prepared for the Baptist Union Council, but which I scarcely used through the confusion of the occasion.

The view outlined above appears to me to set aside the New Testament teaching that God *was* in fact uniquely present in Jesus. Hebrews 1:1 is typical of this teaching: God spoke in former times through prophets, but now He has spoken to us "by His Son". That is, Jesus was different from all other men by virtue of his being the Son of God. (The passage goes on to speak of him as "the heir of all things", and affirms that God created the world through him, and that he sustains the universe).

But here comes objection number one: this teaching is not acceptable on the new view. Norman Pittenger, who has expounded it over a number of years, had laid it down that however understandable or however scriptural it may be, thought on Christ has been confused ever since the term "Son" has been used to denote the second hypostasis of the Godhead.

Objection number two is more fundamental still, and the reader is asked to be quite clear about it: according to the new Christology *the concept of the incarnation of God in Christ is no longer to be received. The idea of incarnation is regarded as based on early religious thinking about the relation of God to the world which we can no longer accept.*

According to this outlook therefore the interpretation of Christ in the Gospel and letters of John, the Letter to the Hebrews and Book of Revelation etc., wherein the Christ is set forth as the pre-existent Son of God made flesh for our redemption, must be recognised as belonging to an outmoded world view. It was the early Church's way of trying to state the importance of Jesus, but we can no more accept it than as can accept the early church's view of the universe.

Now this is why the creeds of the early Church are deemed to be inadequate. Let it be clearly recognised that it is not their *language* that's primarily at fault. The Fathers who shaped the creeds accepted the *ideas* about God and Christ that are found in the New Testament, and they tried to work them out with the aid of concepts of their day. But the new approach can build neither on the New Testament nor on the Fathers.

If it be asked, "On what then can we build?" attention is drawn to the philosophy of A. N. Whitehead. Undoubtedly Whitehead's thought is very stimulating, but it does not easily combine with incarnational theology. If that be so, then on the view we are considering, the idea of incarnation must go. And go it does!

Once this has been adopted, a whole range of Biblical

/p.4

thought requires change. The New Testament writers' ascriptions of the attributes of God to the Son of God have to be dropped. This theology therefore can never allow Jesus to be described as Alpha and Omega, the first and the last, the beginning and the end (cf. Revelation 1.8 with 22.13). The belief that the Son of God was Mediator of creation (1 Corinthians 8.6, Colossians 1.55ff) must go, as also the idea that he is the goal of creation (Colossians 1.16). The Book of Revelation has to be recognized as one long appalling mistake, and can have no place in the new Christian teaching: its Christology is far too "advanced"!

The doctrine of the Trinity naturally becomes impossible of acceptance in this scheme of things. There is no question of an eternal Son in eternal relation with the Father in the Holy Spirit, for there's no such thing as an Eternal Son. New Testament Trinitarian statements are to be regarded as the product of Christological enthusiasm.

What about the doctrine of salvation? Happily this theology does attempt to make room for a doctrine of reconciliation through Christ, but on its basis the concept has to be used with care. John Knox (not the Reformer!), the only New Testament scholar known to me to have embraced this theology, explicitly includes among the "unessentials" of Christian faith "Christ's effectual vicarious sacrifice on the cross for man's guilt" (his language). The "once for all" note of the New Testament lies uneasily with process theology.

Inevitably therefore this doctrine of salvation has a different accent from the apostolic teaching. Paul teaches that we share in Christ's redeeming acts through union with him by the Holy Spirit. We are reconciled to God *in Christ* (2 Corinthians 5.21). We died and rose in him, and we know the power of his redemption in union with him (Romans 6.1ff). The life of the new creation is ours now in fellowship with him (2 Corinthians 5.17). For us therefore life is quite simply, Christ. But candidly all such talk is impossible if Jesus is not the God-man. However great the superlatives we may use to describe the uniqueness of Jesus in his life for God and man, how can you and I live "in Christ", i.e. in living fellowship with him, if he be no more than man? And how can we hear him say to us today, as Paul declared he said to him, "My grace is sufficient for you?" This language shows that "in Christ" represents much more than an impersonal new humanity; the spiritual reality has to be expressed in what is virtually God-language.

And to look for the coming of Christ in the glory of God to complete God's purpose for creation, judge the world and reveal the new creation is inconceivable on the new view. Strauss thought this element of Christian eschatology was sheer fanaticism, because he views Jesus

/p. 5

as a man, and no more than a man. But if that's all Jesus was, I would be compelled to agree with Strauss against the Bible and the Church.

What room is there for traditional Christian worship on the basis of this theology? What of our praying "through Jesus Christ our Lord"? Can that remain? Surely not. This would put us in a similar position to those (undoubtedly sincere) Christians who pray to saints, or seek the good offices of Mary or Joseph as they look to God. If the risen Christ is not Lord in the sense that the New Testament declares, we can neither address prayers *through* him nor *to* him.

As for our Christian hymns, what are we to do with them? "All hail the power of Jesus' name, let angels prostrate fall." But why? How can we possibly worship a man? The primitive church, as reflected in the Book of Revelation, addressed their adoration to "God and the Lamb, but only because they saw the Christ as one with God. On the basis of this theology a new hymn book is demanded, from which all ideas of dependence on Christ, life in Christ, trusting in Christ, glorifying Christ are eliminated.

Finally, what about the Church? Can we still view it as the Body of Christ, the Bride of Christ, the Temple of the Holy Spirit? I do not see how we can. The notion of believers united by the Holy Spirit to the glorified Christ is rationally excluded on this basis.

Nor can I see sufficient justification for retaining baptism and the Lord's Supper. All that apostolic teaching about fellowship with the crucified and risen Redeemer and renewal by the Holy Spirit, to which baptism points, is logically excluded. So is the interpretation of the Supper as the fellowship of the Body of Christ and the Blood of Christ (1 Corinthians 10.16ff). On the view we are considering, the sacraments have to be so reduced in significance, it is best to regard them as survivals of primitive religious belief and abandoned. In that case what possible justification exists for the continuance of the Baptist denomination? Our day was long since done.

These observations may sound outrageous, and I don't know any Christian theologian prepared to go along with them to their bitter end, but in my judgement, they follow from the teaching we are considering as surely as night follows day. It is my settled conviction that the logical end of this theology is the reduction of Christianity to a Reformed Judaism. That would not be a new thing in the history

/p.6

of Christianity of course. There were such phenomena as Ebionism in the early Church. I observe that in our day John Knox has declared that he looks forward to the union of Judaism and Christianity in the not distant future, and on his view of Christ that would be quite natural.

The lesson of this story is one every preacher knows. Christ and the Gospel are inseparable. A Christ who is a man but not God entails a different religion from that of the New Testament. Admittedly the New Testament presents us with diverse elements with which to construct a Christology rather than a finished product. The great issue is whether in its pages there is a reality corresponding to the declarations about the Paraclete in the Fourth Gospel (John 14–16). *Have we or have we not testimony to Christ from the Spirit of Truth which conveys an understanding of who He really was and who He is?* The Church through the ages has answered that question with an affirmative. Baptists can claim a place in that Church only in so far as they join in that affirmation. If otherwise, they become a "sect" in the worst sense of the term, as their adversaries have so often regarded them. What then should we do at this juncture? The answer is plain: we must recognise that this interpretation we have considered is not one we can embrace, and preach that Gospel of Christ to which we are committed. But in view of the confusion that exists, we must declare where we stand. If we fail to do so we call in question our existence as a Christian denomination today

And maybe forever.

APPENDIX THIRTEEN

THE 1972 ASSEMBLY RESOLUTION ON 'THE ASSEMBLY ADDRESS'

(source: Baptist Union Minutes, held at the Angus Library, Regent's Park College, Oxford)

A. The Draft Proposal Agreed By The GP&F Committee On January 11, 1972

In view of certain serious misunderstandings which have arisen concerning its statement in November 1971, and more especially concerning the addendum to it, the Council now wishes to make the following comments by way of clarification.

1. The addendum is to be read within the context of the whole statement and not in separation from it.
2. This applies in particular to the remark that "the Union has always contained within its fellowship those of differing theological opinions and emphases, believing that its claim for toleration involves tolerance and mutual respect within its own ranks". Two things should be made clear:
   a. This was intended to be a factual historical observation and in no way an attempt to justify any or every doctrinal expression or to make room for such within the Union.
   b. The "tolerance and mutual respect" here mentioned refers specifically to those "within its own ranks". That is, it refers to those who are prepared, as the preceding statement explicitly says, to associate together on the basis of the Union's Declaration of Principle which professes Jesus Christ as "God manifest in the flesh".
3. The statement unhesitatingly and unequivocally declared its profession of the Deity, as well as the humanity of Our Lord. The Council reaffirms its profession now and cannot identify itself with any position which would deny the fundamental tenet of our faith which, by general consent and usage, is the intention of the Declaration of Principle.

[Author's note: this resolution was abandoned after discussions with Sir Cyril Black at the BU Officers' Meeting of February 4. In its place, it was agreed that Sir Cyril's own resolution would not be contested, but that it would nevertheless be presented by him as a private motion.]

Appendices

B. The Final Resolution Proposed By Sir Cyril Black And Seconded By George Beasley-Murray

This assembly of the Baptist Union of Great Britain & Ireland places on record its deep sadness that during the past year divisions and misunderstandings have arisen among us that have disturbed our fellowship, caused the withdrawal from us of certain Ministers and Churches, and may possibly cause the withdrawal of others. We earnestly seek at this critical time for the removal, by God's help, of these divisions and misunderstandings, so that unitedly we may labour more effectively together for the extension of the Redeemer's Kingdom.

Following the example of the Council, we gladly and explicitly reaffirm our wholehearted acceptance of and belief in the Declaration of Principle set out in the Constitution. We thereby unreservedly assert our belief in God the Father, Son and Holy Spirit, into whose name are baptized those who have professed repentance towards God and Faith in Our Lord Jesus Christ, who "died for our sins according to the Scriptures, was buried and rose again the third day". We acknowledge this Jesus Christ as both "Lord and Saviour" and "God manifest in the flesh" (understanding these words as expressing unqualified faith in His full Deity and real humanity). We recognize Him as the sole and absolute authority in all matters pertaining to faith and practice as revealed in the Holy Scriptures, and acknowledge the liberty of each Church under the guidance of the Holy Spirit to administer and interpret His laws.

We firmly and unhesitatingly place on record our conviction that the Declaration of Principle represents the basic requirement for fellowship in the Baptist denomination and that we attach high importance to the loyal and wholehearted acceptance of it. In particular we assert the unacceptability of any interpretation of the person and work of Jesus Christ our Lord which would obscure or deny the fundamental tenet of the Christian faith that Jesus Christ is Lord and Saviour, truly God and truly Man.

We recall that a rule of Ministerial Recognition stipulates that "all persons who become or remain Ministers or Probationers accredited by the Union are required to accept the Declaration of Principle as contained in the Constitution of the Union".

We earnestly desire that these emphatic reassurances may be effective in removing all misapprehensions, and may make it possible for Ministers and Churches contemplating secession to remain in the Union, and for Ministers and Churches of the Baptist Faith and Order who have departed from, or never belonged to, the

The Baptist Revival Fellowship

Union, to enter into discussion with us with a view to entry or re-entry into our Fellowship.

We are profoundly convinced that the unity together of all who can sincerely and wholeheartedly subscribe to the Declaration of Principle will enable us to witness and work more effectively in these challenging days, so that God may be glorified and His Kingdom extended.

C. The Amendments Proposed At The Assembly

1. That following the end of the sentence (in Paragraph 4) "as contained in the constitution of the Union", there be inserted a new paragraph:

"We affirm that it is the duty of the Ministerial Recognition Committee to ensure that this rule is observed by taking action with respect to any Minister or Probationer who clearly and openly denies that our Lord Jesus Christ is truly God and truly Man, or contradicts by statement or action any other teaching of the Declaration of Principle" (Proposed by Rev. George Stirrup, seconded by Rev. Derek Moon).

2. That in the first paragraph, after the words "This Assembly of the Baptist Union of Great Britain and Ireland places on record its deep sadness that" there be inserted these words:

"the full Deity of our Lord and Saviour Jesus Christ was denied by one of the addresses at the 1971 Assembly, as a result of which" and continue as published "during the past year," (Proposed by Rev. J. T. Pretlove)

3. That the last paragraph of Sir Cyril Black's motion be deleted and that the following paragraph be substituted therefor:

"we confess that the controversy which has taken place within our ranks during the past year has not assisted the extension of God's kingdom and we therefore call upon all who have the cause of Christ at heart to declare that we will have done with this argument and so free ourselves to face the demand of these challenging days" (proposed by Mr. P. J. Cooke).

4. That paragraphs 3 and 4 be deleted, commencing with the words, "We firmly and unhesitatingly place on record." And ending with the words "as contained in the constitution of the Union". (Proposed by Dr. Leonard Champion).

[Author's note: All the amendments were defeated by large majorities and the resolution was carried with 46 voting against, and with 72 abstentions.]

APPENDIX FOURTEEN

MARTYN LLOYD-JONES' PREACHING ENGAGEMENTS IN BAPTIST CHURCHES BETWEEN 1950 AND 1973

(source: The Private Papers and Diaries of David Martyn Lloyd-Jones: Preaching Diaries, [held at the National Library of Wales, Aberystwyth: Manuscripts and Papers Collection])

[Author's Introductory Note

This record of Lloyd-Jones's preaching engagements provides a clear indication that his primary circle of contacts was ministers of BU churches, and that his links with them and their churches remained over many years. Lloyd-Jones's diaries are somewhat cryptic and only the churches that are clearly identifiable as Baptist causes are shown as such, either because 'B' was sometimes suffixed to the church's name as an indication and the church can be identified from the BU Handbook, or because the minister is stated and can similarly be traced. In some instances relating to South Wales, when diary entries were written obscurely, sometimes giving only the town and sometimes only the church, it was often possible to supply the missing information, either because it is mentioned elsewhere in the diary more clearly, or because a minister from a particular town was known to me as a member of the Westminster Fellowship or the BRF.

Where the name of a contact is stated, it appears in normal brackets. Square brackets indicate where I have expanded the entry for clarification. The symbol ?" within a bracket indicates that the entry is not sufficiently legible to admit of certainty. Outside a bracket it indicates that although a conservative evangelical BU church may be referred to, it has not been possible definitely to identify that as the intended reference.

It should also be noted that the diaries are not entirely dependable as a comprehensive record. For example no entry was made for the BRF Conference of 1956 at which Lloyd-Jones spoke and there may have been occasions when he withdrew from a commitment. I recall such an example while I was a student in Bristol. Lloyd-Jones was due to speak at Widcombe Baptist Church in Bath (also not mentioned in the diaries) but withdrew at the last moment so that in his place Arthur Wallis spoke.]

The Diary Entries

1950

11.2.50   Barking [Baptist] Tabernacle

The Baptist Revival Fellowship

25.2.50   Muswell Park Baptist Church

15.3.50   Tunbridge Wells (Revd. Nash?)

22.3.50   Norwich (E. T. D. Jones?)

19.4.50   Abertillery [Baptist Church]

17.5.50   Richmond [Baptist Church] (A. Redpath)

23.5.50   Park [Baptist Church], Merthyr [Tydfil]

4.10.50   Shirley Baptist Church, Southampton

11.10.50 Mt Pleasant [Baptist Church], Swansea

23.11.50 Kensington [Baptist] Tabernacle, Bristol (Rowland)

1951

10.1.51   Torquay

3.3.51   Muswell Park [Baptist Church] (Rev. Blackmore)

13.3.51   Dudley Baptist Church (Hugh Butt)

1.5.51   Shrewsbury [probably Claremont Baptist Church] (Ridge)

22.5.51   [probably the Welsh Baptist Church], Aberdare (S. P. Jones?)

6.6.51   Avenue B[aptist Church], Southend

13.6.51   Gunnersbury B[aptist Church]

20.6.51   [Bethesda Strict Baptist Church, Ipswich] for Revd. J. Bird

27.6.51   [Baptist Church] Abertillery

3.10.51   Dorking Baptist

9.10.51   Griffithstown [Baptist Church]

10.10.51 Philip Street [Baptist Church] Bedminster

27.11.51 Pontypool [could be Baptist or Presbyterian Church] (Rev. E. C. Phillips?)

1952

19.3.52   Old Meeting, Norwich (E. T. D. Jones?)

26.3.52   Winton [Baptist Church], Bournemouth

21.4.52   Station Rd [Baptist Church], New Barnet

4.6.52   Gunnersbury [Baptist Church]

Appendices

1953

3.2.53   Kingston (on Thames?) Baptist

1954

9.2.54   Philip St [Baptist Church], Bedminister

23.3.54 Barry [Baptist Church?] (Paul Tucker)

15.6.54 Park [Baptist Church] Merthyr [Tydfil]

16.6.54 Rev. Ben Davies?

1955

6.1.55   [indecipherable] Bap[tist] (H. D. Reynolds?) [Brinkley?]

16.2.55 Purley Baptist

2.3.55   Bap[tist] Tab[ernacle] Blackpool (W. H. Davies)

29.3.55 Church St(?) Baptist [Church] Finchley (Rev. H. C. Shadick?)

26.4.55 Bap[tist] Tab[ernacle] Derby Road Walford(?) Watford(?)

1.6.55   Tabor [Baptist Church] Brynmawr (Rev. T. Richards?)

9.6.55   East Cliff [Congregational Church?] (Porter)

21.6.55 Gillingham [Baptist Church?] (Rev. A. E. Bickle?)

2.7.55   East London Tab[ernacle]

27.9.55 Bristol Rd Baptist Church, Weston-Super-Mare (Lawrence)

5.10.55 West Croydon [Baptist] Tabernacle (King)

18.10.55 Christchurch Rd [Baptist Church], Worthing (H. W. Janisch)

1.11.55 Slough(?) (A. J. Tugwell)

22.11.55 South Street [Baptist Church], Exeter (L. P. Jones)

23.11.55 Truro [Baptist Church?] (Lever)

29.11.55 London Rd. [Baptist Church], Mitcham

1956

15.2.56 Compton Rd. [Baptist Church?], Winchmore Hill (Rev. Monkcombe?)

20.3.56 Tenby Baptist [Church] (Lumley-Williams)

11.4.56 Aberystwyth E[nglish] Baptist [Church] (Rev. Francis)

9.5.56   College Rd. [Baptist Church], Harrow (T. Read)

The Baptist Revival Fellowship

23.5.56 Holland Rd. [Baptist Church], Hove (Rudman)

30.5.56 Bethesda [Strict Baptist Church] Felixstowe

11.7.56 Woolwich [Baptist] Tabernacle

12-14.11.56.1 Charlotte Chapel [Baptist]. Edinburgh

5.12.56 East Cliff [Baptist Church] Bournemouth (N. G. Porter?)

1957

27.2 57 Kingsbridge [could be Baptist or Independent Evangelical] Devon (W. F. Lock?)

12.3.57 Bedford (T. H. Aldridge?)

20.9.57 Corsham (Matthews?)

8.10.57 Bristol Rd. [Baptist Church], Weston-Super-Mare

23.10.57 Honor Oak Baptist [Church]

6.11.57 Spurgeon's College, London

1958

[Author's note: The frequency of Lloyd-Jones' engagements in Baptist Union churches is indicated in this fairly representative year. He had 30 church engagements, of which 12 were identifiably in Baptist Union churches, more than any other denomination. The others were Congregational 5, Presbyterian 2, Evangelical Mission Hall 1, Methodist 1, Anglican 1, unidentifiable 7. He also noted meetings with BCC leaders four times and, either just before or after that, also with John Stott].

8.1.58 East Finchley (Rev. Ward?)

21.1.58 Devon Rd., Bow?

19.2.58 London Rd. [Baptist Church], Portsmouth

18.3.58 Bedford (Aldridge?)

13.4.58 Charlotte Chapel Edinburgh

29.4.58 Shrewsbury [Baptist Church] (Rev. D. Butler? Jones?)

11.6.58 Gunnersbury B[aptist Church]

12.6.58 Cherry Hinton B[aptist Church]

9.7.58 Grove Rd. [Baptist Church?], S[outh] Woodford (White)

1.10.58 Corsham [Baptist Church?]

7.10.58 Totteridge Rd. Bap[tist Church], Enfield

Appendices

8.10.58 Bristol Road Baptist Church, Weston-Super-Mare

21.10.58 Park Baptist [Church], Merthyr

4.11.58 Gunnersbury [Baptist Church]

5.11.58 Bethesda [Strict Baptist Church]. Ipswich

1959

4.2.59 Lansdowne [Baptist Church]. Bournemouth

17.2.59 New Rd. B[aptist Church], Camberwell (McKie)

14.4.59 Surbiton (Arthur Coffey?)

5.5.59 Buckhurst Hill B[aptist Church] (H. S. Tylor)

4.6.59 Northampton (Rev. H. T. Wigley?)

11.6.59 Brackley (Charles Lawrence?)

6.9.59 Rhyl (Booth?)

7.9.59 Toxteth [Baptist Tabernacle] Liverpool (R. Rowland)

14.10.59 Christchurch Rd [Baptist Church], Worthing (Janisch)

20.10.59 Tenby [Baptist Church]

21.10.59 Broadmead [Baptist Church], Bristol (Penry Davies the contact!)

9.12.59 Bexleyheath (Gibbon Smith? – contact)

1960

10.5.60 Shrewsbury [Baptist Church]

18.5.60 Calvary Baptist [Church], Liverpool(?)

8.6.60 R...d Rd. Parkstone (Rev. Gordon?)

14.6.60 Corsham [Baptist Church?]

20.9.60 [Bristol Rd. Baptist Church] W[eston]-S[upper]-M[are]

21.6.60 Moriah [Baptist Church], Risca (Russell Jones)

18.10.60 Park [Baptist Church], Merthyr [Tydfil]

1.11.60 S...e (P. C. Goodlad/land?)

2.11.60 Bethesda [Strict Baptist Church], Ipswich

16.11.60 Tabernacle [Baptist Church], Blackpool

23.11.60 BRF [Annual Conference] High Leigh, (Alec Steen)

7.12.60 Worcester (Gordon Jackson?)

The Baptist Revival Fellowship

1961

7.3.61 Bedford – Aldridge

9.3.61 East London Tab[ernacle] (Tucker)

14.3.61 Upton Vale [Baptist Church, Torquay]

23.3.61 Met[ropolitan Tab[ernacle, London] (Hayden)

26.4.61 Plymouth (D. Ford n…h?)

1.6.61 Gunnersbury [Baptist Church]

15.6.61 Newtown Baptist [Church], Chesham, Bucks (Rev Sh…?)

22.9.61 Corsham c/o J. Bird (Matthews?)

3.10.61 W[estern]-S[uper]-M[are] (Rev R. A. Lawrence)

11.10.61 Toxteth [Baptist] Tab[ernacle] (Rowland)

18.10.61 Worthing B[aptist Church] (Janisch)

25.10.61 West Croydon [Baptist] Tab[ernacle] (King)

22.11.61 Haverfordwest (Rev. Cerwyn Davies?)

1962

30.1.62 Leigh on Sea [Baptist Church], (Rev. Marshall?)

31.1.62 Brompton Lane, Strood (Rev Walker?)

14.2.62 Redhill (Rev C. S .M…?)

20.2.62 Woodside B[aptist] C[hurch] South Norwood

21.2.62 London Rd. Portsmouth (Tugwell)

6.3.62   Drummond Rd. B[aptist Church], Bermondsey (J. D. Parker)

13.3.62 Carmel [Baptist Church], Aberdare

27.3.62 Cheltenham (C. B. Harris?)

11.4.62 met Geoffrey King at Baptist Church House

1.5.62   Shrewsbury (Rev. E. L. Evans?)

29.5.62 Harlow Baptist (Rev. Barker)

30.5.62 Central B[aptist Church], Walthamstow (Rev. B. Snelling)

14.9.62 Corsham [Baptist Church?]

18.9.62 Hereford (Rev Wigley?)

3.9.62   [Bristol Rd., Baptist Church, W[eston-S[upper-M[are]

Appendices

17.10.62 [Baptist] Tab[ernacle] Blackpool

13.11.62 Park [Baptist Church], Merthyr [Tydfil]

11.12.62 Tab[ernacle Baptist Church] Swindon (A. J. Wheeler)

1963

23.1.63 Shepshed [Baptist Church] (D. A. Bugden)

30.1.63 Bexleyheath (N. G. Jennings?)

12.2.63 Redhill [Baptist Church] (C. S. Medhurst?)

26.2.63 Bedford – Aldridge?

5.3.62 Hull (Eric Gurr?)

12.3.62 Derby? (Rev. A. E. Anderson)

8.5.63 Calgary/Calvary Bap Knotty Ash, Liverpool (Rev A. E. Phillingtone?)

15.5.63 Southcourt Bapt[ist Church], Aylesbury (Rev. G. C. Illinges?)

21/22.5.63 Plymouth (D. Forb Nash?)

24.9.63 English Association Abergavenny (D. P. Thomas?)

2.10.63 Toxteth Tab[ernacle Baptist Church, Liverpool]

8.10.63 W[eston]-S[upper]-M[are]

16.10.63 Worthing [Baptist Tabernacle] (Janisch)

23.11.63 Broadmead [Baptist Church] Bristol

6.11.63 Beth[esda Strict Baptist Church] Ipswich (Bird)

1964

28.1.63 Leigh on Sea [Baptist Church] (Marshall?)

5.2.64 Godalming Bap[tist Church] (Frost)

11.3.64 Shepshed [Baptist Church] (Bugden?)

17.3.64 Hull – Aldridge?

7.4.64 Gorsley [Baptist Church?] (Rev. S. G. M. Evans)

21.5.64 Shrewsbury [Baptist Church] (Rev. C. O. D…?)

26.5.64 Gunnersbury [Baptist Church]

27.5.64 Muswell Hill Bap[tist Church] (Ronald Parks)

29.9.64 Park [Baptist Church] Merthyr [Tydfil]

The Baptist Revival Fellowship

7.10.64 Alma Street Bap[tist Church], Newport (Graham H)

14.10.64 Blackpool Tab[ernacle]

20.10.64 Charlotte Chapel [Baptist, Edinburgh]

1965

3.2.65 Lansdowne [Baptist Church], Bournemouth

18.5.63 Kingston [Baptist Church] (H. E. Ward)

17.9.65 Corsham [Baptist Church]

29.9.65 Porthcawl [Baptist Church] (Stanley Jebb)

5.10.65 [Bristol Baptist Church, W[eston-S[uper]-M[are] (Ray Lawrence)

13.10.65 Toxteth Tab[ernacle Baptist Church] (Rowland)

3.11.65 Beth[esda Strict Baptist Church] Ipswich (Bird)

17.11.65 Kensington [Baptist Church], Bristol (Abernethie)

1.12.65 Godalming Bap[tist Church] (Frost)

1966

16.2.66 Chester (A. G. Banford?)

24.5.66 Trinity Rd. Bap[tist Church], Gloucester (Douglas Jones)

6.6.66 Silver St. Bap[tist] Church, Norwich (D. Bugden)

20–22.6.66 Maesycwmmer [Baptist Church] (Malcolm Jones)

29.8.66 Maidstone (Rev Don Davies?)

5.10.66 [Bristol Road Baptist Church], W[eston]-S[uper]-M[are]

11.10.66 Park [Baptist Church] Merthyr [Tydfil]

26.10.66 Kensington [Baptist Church], Bristol

1967

[author's note: note the changes of venue in 1967 following Lloyd-Jones' call to leave mainline denominations. Most of the following churches were either secessions from a denomination or in membership of the Fellowship of Independent Evangelical Churches. This indicates that Lloyd-Jones was putting into practice his policy of secession, although there was at least one Baptist Union Church that remained in the BU (Park, Merthyr Tydfil).

21.2.67 Stowmarket (Rev. P. A. Day?)

21.3.67 Paul Bassett?

Appendices

18.4.67 Rev A. Coffey

2.5.67 Abertillery [Baptist Church] (Rev. W. Heath)

3.5.67 Plymouth (Forb Nash?)

17.5.67 Old? Baptist, Devizes ((Rev Mr. D. J...?)

23.5.67 [Tabernacle Baptist Church], Porth (Rev. D. J. Morgan)

7.6.67 Gunnersbury [Baptist Church]

15.9.67 Corsham

20.9.67 [Bristol Road Baptist Church], W[eston]-S[upper]-M[are]

8.11.67 Beth[esda Strict Bap=st Church], Ips[wich]

1968

[author's note: The diaries this year become even more badly written and several were used and abandoned during the year].

31.1.68 Lansdowne [Baptist Church], B[ournemouth]

7.2.68 Leigh on Sea [probably Leigh Rd. Baptist Church]

19.3.68 Welsh Bap[tist], Aberdare

1.5.68 Grosvenor Rd. [Baptist Church], Dublin

22.5.68 Long Crendon [Baptist Church] – (R. Copping/Coffing/Coffey?)

8.5.68 [Bethesda Baptist Church], Felixstowe (Rev Alford)

23.4.68 [probably Claremont Baptist Church], Shrewsbury (Tylor?)

8.10.68 Park B[aptist Church], Merthyr [Tydfil]

9.10.68 [Horeb Baptist Church], Blaenavon (Brian Harries)

16.10.68 [probably Baptist Tabernacle]. Blackpool

13.9.68 Corsham

8.10.68 Park [Baptist Church], Merthyr [Tydfil]

9.10.68 [Horeb Baptist Church], Blaenavon (Harries)

16.10.68 Tab[ernacle Baptist Church], Blackp[oo]l

20.10.68 Colchester (H. Clark)

23.10.68 Tunbridge Wells (Nunn)

27.11.68 Thornbury Bap[tist Church], Bristol

1969

The Baptist Revival Fellowship

29.1.69 Bexleyheath [probably Trinity Baptist Church]

11.3.69 Trinity [Baptist Church], Gloucester

22.3.69 Borough Green Bap[tist Church], Sevenoaks

26.3.69 Abertillery [Baptist Church], (Heath)

19.10.69 Corsham

18/19.10.69 Queensbury St, Old Basford [Baptist Church], Nott[ingham] (Steen's church)

23.11.69 [probably Upton Vale Baptist Church], Torquay (J. W. Hon…?)

26.11.69 Stanmore Bap[tist Church]

1970

4.1.70 Lansd[o]wne [Baptist Church], B[our]n[e]m[ou]th

11.1.70 West Woolwich Baptist (W. J. Bidston?)

8.2.70 West Street [Baptist Church], Dunstable

14/15.2.70 Selly Park Bap[tist Church, Birmingham], (Mawdsley)

18.2.70 Barking Tab[ernacle Baptist Church] (W. R. Foster)

4.3.70 Bethel Baptist [Church] Hanley, (Rev P. E. Brown)

10.3.70 Beulah Baptist [Church], Rhymney (Irfon Hughes)

14/15.3.70 Coventry (Ifor Owen)

14.4.70 Shrewsbury [probably Claremont Baptist Church]

15.4.70 Calvary Baptist (rest indecipherable)

23.4.70 East London Tab[ernacle Baptist Church]

26.4.70 Dereham Baptist [Church], Norfolk (A. S. Stangler?)

27.4.70 Stoke on Trent (Rev. D? Howe?)

3.5.70 Hatchland Rd Redhill (Fletcher?)

4.6.70 Philip St. [Baptist Church], Bedminister

14.6.70 Leyton Baptist [Church, north-east London]

12.7.70 Ventnor Baptist [Church] (Rev. B. R. Birches)

26.9.70 Aberfan Baptist [Church]

4.10.70 Cheam Baptist [Church]

8.10.70 Alfred Place Baptist [Church] (Rev Geoff Thomas)

Appendices

11.10.70 Crossley? Green Baptist [Church] near Watford (S. A. Bugg)

17/18.10.70 [Leigh Road] Leigh on Sea Baptist (E. L. Walling)

20.10.70 Park Baptist [Church, Merthyr Tydfil]

25.10.70 Hainault Rd Baptist Church, Leyton

30.10.70 Sheffield [Baptist Church] (Rev. Pretlove)

16–18.11.70 BRF Conference

28/29.11.70 Brent...d (W/Rev/Mr B. G. Welch)

1971

13.1.71 Golden Valley (Basil Howlett)

16/17.1.71 Dudley Baptist Church

3.2.71 Long Crendon [Baptist Church]

20/21.2.71 Brighton (W. S. Semmons?)

20/21.3.71 Brixham Baptist (Arthur Neil)

1.4.71 Clementswood Baptist Church, Ilford (Rev Tylor)

3.4.71 Day to...? (c/o George Stirrup)

14.4.71 Soham (Ely) (Harris)

22/23.5.71 Trinity Rd Bap[tist Church], Gloucester (Douglas Jones)

4–7.6.71 Evangelical Fellowship of Cong[regational] Churches

27.6.71 Weymouth Baptist [Church] (Williams)

3.10.71 Redhill (Medhurst)

9/10.10.71 Toxteth Tab[ernacle Baptist Church]

20.10.71 Blackpool Tab[ernacle]

31.10.71 Queens Rd Bap[tist Church], Wallington, Surrey

6/7 11.71 Bristol Rd. Baptist Church W[eston]-S[uper]-M[are]

23.11.71 Ebenezer Baptist [Church], Chester? (Rev Macey)

1972

9.2.72 Milford on Sea and Lymington (Wyre?)

12.4.72 Selly Park Bap[tist Church]

14.5.72 Horley Baptist [Church]

30.4.72 E[ast] L[ondon] T[abernacle Baptist Church]

The Baptist Revival Fellowship

21/22.4.72 Gorsley Bap[tist Church]

11.6.72 Maulden Baptist [Church] (Benn)

1.10.72 B.... Rd. Bap[tist Church], South Croydon (Rev. J? W. Borky?)

22.10.72 Dudley Bap[tist Church] (Peter Collinson)

29.10.72 Wallingford Bap[tist Church] (Rev Elliott)

5.11.72 Hainault Rd. Bap[tist Church] Leyton (Dawson)

12.11.72 Buckingham Bap[tist Church] Clifton, Bristol

3.12.72 Park Hill Bap[tist Church, Haverfordwest?] (Rev. Bock)

1973

11.2.73 Sudbury Bap[tist Church]

4.3.73 Carey [Baptist Church], Reading

11.4.73 Little Stoke Bap[tist Church] (Neil Mobbs)

1.4.73 Fryerns Baptist [Church], near Basildon (Rev Day)

8.4.73 Bap Tab[ernacle] (– not decipherable)

10.6.73 Priory St. Bap[tist Church]. York

1.7.73 Surbiton Bapt[ist Church], (Gordon Sayer)

9.9.73 West Street [Baptist Church], Dunstable

30.9.73 South Lee Baptist [Church], London

7.10.73 Charlotte Chapel [Baptist, Edinburgh]

14.10.73 Toxteth Tab[ernacle Baptist Church, Liverpool]

21.10.73 Philip Street [Baptist Church], Bedminster

4.11.73 Kingfield Baptist [Church], Woking

2.12.73 Ealing Rd Bap[tist Church], Brentford

APPENDIX FIFTEEN

BRF BOOKLETS AND PAMPHLETS

(source of information: copies held in the BRF archive or mentioned in BRF minutes therein)

[Author's note: There is no complete record of BRF publications, and therefore this is a list only of those publications I have been able to find, or which were clearly referred to in the BRF Archive, the BRF Bulletin or the BRF Minutes. Further, BRF publications were usually undated. Definite dates drawn from the Minutes or the Bulletin are given without qualification, otherwise dates are indicated as approximate or unknown. Approximate dates can sometimes be identified by which Secretary or Treasurer is mentioned, and until the modernization of the BRF after Bamber's retirement, publications always included an early BRF pictorial motif of a military figure blowing a trumpet from which hangs a banner inscribed with 'BRF]'

BRF Booklets

Geoffrey King: *By All Means Save Some* (Booklet Number 1, 1938 or 1939)

A. Morgan Derham: *Winning Through in the Christian Life* (Booklet Number 6, pre-1961 when a new range of booklets was issued with a more modern design)

Ralph Martin: Preparing the Way of the Lord (1961)

David Kingdon: Baptists at the Crossroads (1968)

Stanley Voke, What is a Christian Believer? (1961).

BRF advertising pamphlets:

Baptists Awake! (pre-1950)

Opening of The Door to Mid-Century Revival (1949/50)

Introducing the Baptist Revival Fellowship (1960/61, revised and reprinted in 1966)

Other BRF published material:

BRF Constitution, 1964

Ecumenism: Statement of The Baptist Revival Fellowship Regarding the Ecumenical Movement (1967)

Is Jesus God? (1971)

APPENDIX SIXTEEN

BRF CONFERENCE THEMES AND SPEAKERS

(Source: BRF Archives and the *BRF Bulletin*)

[Author's note: Themes were not usually publicized because revival was assumed to be the theme].

1954: Duncan Campbell, Stanley Voke

1955: Robert Rowland

1956 D. Martyn Lloyd-Jones

1957: Godfrey Robinson, Ernest Kevan, Robert Rowland

[Author's note: I have not found any record of the conferences in 1958 and 1959]

1960: Gerald Griffiths, Paul Tucker, H. Dermot McDonald, D. Martyn Lloyd-Jones, Ernest Payne.

1961: Duncan Campbell, Stanley Voke, John L. Bird, (Richmond).

1962: A. Skevington Wood, F. S. Fitzsimmonds, Dr. Stern (Late of S. Africa), Geoffrey King, Leonard Moules (WEC).

1963: Alan Redpath, J. I. Packer, Ronald Park, A. J. Matthews, Ronald Park, Ernest Rudman [Author's note: King gave a closing message because Redpath had to leave early (BRF Bulletin No. 78, Jan/Mar 1964, p. 1)].

1964: David Pawson, Leith Samuel, Canon W. H. A Butler.

1965: *[Author's note: themes are first stated this year]*: 'The Person and Work of the Holy Spirit.' Speakers: Theo Bamber, Geoffrey King, James Packer (speaking on 'The Quest For Fullness'), Arthur Wallis.

1966: 'The Doctrine and life of the Church': Speakers: David Pawson, Stanley Voke, Glyn Morris, Harold Owen.

1967: 'Revival and Reformation': Kingdon on 'How Baptists have faced the cross-roads in the past'; Graham Harrison on 'The Present Ecumenical Challenge – an appraisal for Baptists;' Ron Luland and Leslie Larwood gave two presentations, one being a BU loyalist and the other a secessionist, entitled, 'A call to face the challenge.'

1968: 'The Glory of Christ': Leith Samuel, Sam Nash (Leigh-on-Sea) Henry Tyler (Ilford), David Shepherd *[Author's note: a well-known Welsh evangelist]*.

Appendices

1969: J. Elwyn Davies (General Secretary of the Evangelical Movement of Wales), T. Omri Jenkins, (General Secretary of the European Missionary Fellowship), Dr. W. Lees (North Borneo Evangelical Mission).

1970: D. M. Lloyd-Jones and Campbell McAlpine [Author's note: McAlpine had become well-known as a charismatic renewal leader. Peter Collinson also spoke, indicating that the advertised speakers were only the 'outsiders.' A thanksgiving service for Bamber was also held this year, at which Geoffrey King preached] (Bulletin 106, Jan/March 1971, p. 8, which also reported an attendance of 260).

1971: Sydney Lawrence, (Leicester), Vernon Higham (Cardiff). [Author's note: Lawrence had recently founded Knighton Evangelical Church, Leicester having seceded from Methodism and Vernon Higham was then involved in a protracted legal battle to re-form Heath Presbyterian Church as Heath Evangelical Church, Cardiff, without losing its buildings to the Presbyterian Church of Wales].

APPENDIX SEVENTEEN

BRF OFFICERS AND COMMITTEE MEMBERS FROM 1938–1972

[Author's Introductory Note:

The Officers remained remarkably constant over many years, as listed in the BRF Bulletin. The first record of a committee appears on early BRF publications, then from time to time in the BRF Bulletin. The BRF Committee minutes do not always list the committee members present. What follows is therefore tentative but an important indication of who comprised the key leaders. Theo Bamber remained chairman from the beginning until his death in 1970 and was then replaced by Harold Owen. Alec Steen was the only person mentioned as secretary. Geoffrey King remained the stated Prayer Secretary even after he resigned from the Committee. R. H. Thorn became the treasurer early in the life of the BRF and was replaced in 1965 by John Pretlove. Leslie Larwood, a denominational loyalist, served on the committee for many years before briefly replacing Bamber as the editor of the BRF Bulletin, as did Alec Steen, a secessionist who served throughout his time on the committee as its secretary. A number of well-known Baptist ministers appear in the list, notably Ernest Rudman and Stanley Voke, while High Butt was on the committee during the mid-sixties when he was appointed an Area Superintendent, the only BRF member to achieve senior office in the BU.

There were also Area Representatives at various times, but they were locally chosen and no complete record of them was kept].

THE COMMITTEE IN THE 1950s

[Source: Introductory leaflet *Baptists Awake!* (probably published in the early 1950s)]

T. M. Bamber, H. Butt, A. J. G. Hipperson (Treasurer), G. R. King, L. Larwood, A. McMillan, MA, R. J. Park, B. W. Peake (Secretary), S. P. Plunkett, MA, J. Pritchard, E. G. Rudman.

THE COMMITTEE IN THE 1960s

[Source: 1965 Committee as listed in the *BRF Bulletin* No.82, Jan/March 1965]

Hugh Butt, Michael Frost, Geoffrey King, Douglas Jones, Leslie Larwood, Ron Luland, Glyn Morris, E. G. Rudman, H. Tyler, Stanley Voke, and ex officio Theo Bamber (Chairman), Alec Steen, (Secretary) and R. H. Thorn (Treasurer).

Appendices

1967 COMMITTEE

[Source: Minutes of the BRF Committee, January 30, 1967]

Theo Bamber (Chairman), Hugh Butt, Michael Frost, Douglas Jones, Geoffrey King, Edward Kirk, Leslie Larwood, Ron Luland, Glyn Morris, Harold Owen, Ernest Rudman, Alec Steen (Secretary), Henry Tyler, Stanley Voke, John Waterman (John Pretlove was Treasurer at this time but is not listed for some reason).

1971 COMMITTEE

[Source: Letter to Ernest Payne, dated May 25, 1971]

Harold Owen (Woking), C. P. Collinson (Dudley), R. M. Horn (Horley), E. M. Kirk (Cheam), R. S. Luland (Bedford), P. Nuttall (Liverpool), J. L. Pretlove (Sheffield), G. Stirrup (Sidcup), H. C. Tyler, [*Author's note: no placement was stated for some reason, but he had been since 1966 at Clementswood, Ilford*], A. J. Waterman (Barnet), J. Wood (Crewe).

CHAIRMEN:

Theo Bamber (1938–1970)

Harold Owen (1970–1972)

EDITORS OF THE *BRF BULLETIN*:

Theo Bamber (1945–1965)

Leslie Larwood (1965–1967)

George Stirrup (1967–1971)

Henry Tyler (1971–)

www.ingramcontent.com/pod-product-compliance
Lightning Source LLC
Chambersburg PA
CBHW051640230426
43669CB00013B/2382